ENDORSEMENTS

"A magical juxtaposition of the Mexican heritage, alongside mourning practices in the Jewish tradition, from a unique storyteller. Matilde Konigsberg goes beyond merely sharing reality and facts, and delivers a heartfelt perspective on unresolved family matters, complete with ghostly visitations seeking forgiveness. A must-read mystical memoir!"

–June Gottlieb, psychotherapist, writer, actress.

"*The Seven Jewish Samurai* is a captivating story of spirits mingling with the living, and a rich blending of the Latin and Jewish cultures. This intriguing tale of family secrets is filled with nostalgia, childhood memories, and grief over the loss of both parents. It's a daring and honest exploration of family dynamics that will captivate you from beginning to end."

–David Rosell, wealth manager, speaker, author of *Failure Is Not an Option*, and *Keep Climbing*.

"*The Seven Jewish Samurai* is reminiscent of Isabel Allende's surrealism: ghostly apparitions, fast-moving scenes, and the dwelling of psychic presences both humorous and morose. The story grows into the captivating tapestry as the colors and theatrics of Mexico intermingle with stories from the author's childhood.

The bilingual narrative—Spanish and English dancing together—soars with the integrity of the author's journey into heroic and impressive individuality. This book will have a long-lasting impact over time for many readers."

–Katya Williamson, author, *Awakening in Avebury: A Woman's Call to Pilgrimage,* and *Bringing the Soul Back Home: Writing in the New Consciousness.*

The Seven Jewish Samurai of Guadalajara

A MEMOIR

Matilde A. Konigsberg

Bend, OR

Copyright © 2019 by Matilde A. Konigsberg

All rights reserved. This book or any portion thereof may not be reproduced or used in any manner whatsoever without the express written permission of the author except for the use of brief quotations in a book review.

Matilde A. Konigsberg
SevenJewishSamurai.com

ISBN 978-1-7332676-0-1 print
ISBN 978-1-7332676-1-8 ebook

Library of Congress Control Number: 2019913244

Publisher's Cataloging-In-Publication Data
(Prepared by The Donohue Group, Inc.)

Names: Konigsberg, Matilde A., author.
Title: The seven Jewish samurai of Guadalajara: a memoir / Matilde A. Konigsberg.
Description: Bend, OR: Matilde A. Konigsberg, [2019]
Identifiers: ISBN 9781733267601 | ISBN 9781733267618 (ebook)
Subjects: LCSH: Konigsberg, Matilde A. | Jewish families--Mexico--Mexico City--20th century. | Family therapists--Biography. | Jewish women--Mexico--Biography. | Mexican-American women--California--Biography.
Classification: LCC F1392.J4 K66 2019 | DDC 972.004924--dc23

Printed in the United States of America

DEDICATION

To my beloved husband,
and to my beautiful daughter.

And to my brothers, my guardian angels.

TABLE OF CONTENTS

Dedication — v

Prologue — ix

Author's Note — 13

Chapter 1: Dancing Candles — 15

Chapter 2: White Feathers — 25

Chapter 3: Family Secrets — 43

Chapter 4: Sand from Jerusalem — 53

Chapter 5: Día de los Muertos — 72

Chapter 6: Defying Gravity — 93

Chapter 7: Rites of Passage — 113

Chapter 8: Los Abuelos — 133

Chapter 9: Acapulco Tropical — 155

Chapter 10: Las Amantes — 173

Chapter 11: One Last Tear — 193

Chapter 12: Twisted Lies — 215

Chapter 13: Raven's Dream — 239

Epilogue — 257

Acknowledgments — 262

PROLOGUE

In the summer of 2008, I attended a women's writing workshop in Idyllwild, California, at Spirit Mountain Retreat. The workshop was lead by Katya Williamson, a talented and inspirational writer and teacher. The participants were witty, open-minded, and highly supportive of each other. The beautiful San Jacinto Mountains with their granite peaks and magnificent redwood trees were our inspiration.

I really did not want to write anything related to my personal life. I was more interested in writing something about my work at that time: counseling cancer patients and their families. Nevertheless, as the weekend unfolded, some bits and pieces of stories and poems related to my family—specifically to my father's death—began to permeate my notebook pages.

Katya suggested that perhaps these stories needed more space to expand.

Knowing myself, I probably rolled my eyes and thought: I am *done* with my family issues. Why do I need to write about *that*? But Katya—who, in a very loving way, does not take no for an answer—continued to encourage me to write more about this topic. I also received similar support and encouragement from the women in our group, who were eager to hear more of my writings.

I went home, and as much as I wanted to dismiss the whole weekend experience and move on with my busy life, my father's story began to emerge. *It* wanted to be written, and would not leave me alone. It followed me around! The words in English and Spanish began to intermingle and dance with each other.

PROLOGUE

I had never written a book, so I was not really attached to the outcome. I just kept listening to Katya's advice, and continued to write without stopping to judge what I had written.

I was daring enough to share the first few chapters with my husband, who made suggestions and helped my first draft sound more coherent. To my surprise, he liked it. I heard him laugh at times, which was important to me. I was writing about serious matters, yet I saw the humor in it all. I wanted readers to laugh and have a good time, while also finding something meaningful.

My husband encouraged me to keep writing. After making some changes in the first draft, I sent a few chapters to Katya. She was pleased with the work, and encouraged me again to continue to write. She was convinced that there was something of great value in the story I was telling, and in the way I was weaving both languages together.

A couple of my dear friends were intrigued with my writing as well. They wanted to be a part of the *trial troupe*. I sent them both a chapter at a time to see if it would resonate. They liked it, and asked me to please keep sending more chapters.

That was when this experience became quite fun for me.

A few other friends heard bits and pieces of the manuscript, and urged me to finish the book because they wanted to *buy* it. Imagine that!

Armed with all the support and encouragement from loving friends, I continued to write. I had to take a few pauses though. I was recovering from a car accident that did not allow me to spend too much time at the computer. I sold my home in San Diego, moved to a smaller place, and soon after I underwent a major surgery. It took me several months to recover. Then, a few months later my husband and I moved to Oregon.

Yet the story needed to be told. While life continued to move on, my past kept seeping through, and the memories of my past

PROLOGUE

continued to *demand* I write them down. And so, without any experience in the art of book writing, in a language still foreign to me, I continued.

At some point I participated in a storytelling performance in Bend, Oregon, and I embarked on creating a 20-minute show on the Seven Jewish Samurai of Guadalajara. It made the audience cry and laugh. The experience kept me engaged in the process of completing the memoir.

At the end, the memoir was healing for me. It brought back dreams and memories forgotten long ago, as well as nostalgic feelings for my family, my country, and the magic of a city I was so fortunate to have been born in.

I hope that this memoir inspires you to understand the mysteries of life and death, to appreciate the complexities of leaving home and family behind when people migrate to another country, and to consider the textures of experiencing multiple cultural realities at once—in my case, Mexican and Jewish, both of which dance together forever in my heart.

As a memoir, this book is based on a cascade of memories. In the process of conjuring them, I chose to combine certain incidents, and create a few composite characters to help capture the story. All of the names used in the book are pseudonyms.

AUTHOR'S NOTE

This book is not a complete guide to Judaism, or the rituals of death and dying. It is a personal note about how I experienced these rituals, and the complexities of the religion, from my unique perspective. I consider this book to be a mystical memoir, meaning that the narrative crosses religious, cultural, psychological, and spiritual realms. I leave you with ample space to explore and contemplate the possibilities of a reality that is not always tangible. I invite you simply to keep an open mind.

CHAPTER ONE
Dancing Candles

*"Death is not the greatest loss in life.
The greatest loss is what dies within us while we live."*

–Norman Cousins

Abraham Beraja said to me in a sharp, authoritative voice, *"No te vayas, tu papá quiere hablar contigo."*

"What do you mean my father wants to speak to me?"

At that instant, the candles that sat above and below the coffin where my father lay exploded. The force of gushing wax paralyzed me.

"Siéntate," Abraham said urgently.

"If I have to sit for something important perhaps I ought to call my brothers."

"No." He was adamant. *"Sola. Quiere hablar contigo sola."*

I was afraid but curious. Why would my father want to talk to me alone?

Any good Capricorn would be in total disbelief. My rational mind said I needed proof. Maybe this guy Abraham was crazy and pulling my leg. But the goose bumps that came over me were hard to ignore.

CHAPTER ONE

I thought I was imagining this conversation with Abraham, because it had been a long day. It had taken us most of the day to retrieve my father's body from the hospital's morgue. My father's side of the family arrived at his home around 9 p.m. My two brothers and I sat in his living room, exhausted, sharing fleeting glances with his relatives. It all felt distant and contrived. My father's nurses and the house help hid in the kitchen whispering the Rosary. My skin felt raw under my dark suit. I was shivering.

Rabbi Norman came to visit an hour later. He talked to all of us about what to expect the next day during the burial ceremony. His words broke the awkward, monotonous silence.

One by one, our relatives left. The rabbi was last to leave. When I accompanied him to the door he suggested that I get some sleep. I must have looked awfully tired.

I was dreading the next day: burying my father at the Sephardic cemetery and beginning the Jewish shiva, a *full* seven days of mourning with nothing to do but to sit low, eat, and endure endless hugs, kisses, and small talk from aunties, cousins, distant relatives, and friends I hadn't seen for years. We would remove the sofa cushions so my father's immediate relatives could sit low, closer to the ground than to the world of the living. *Más cerca de la tumba que del mundo de los vivos.* We would also cover all the mirrors in the house so we wouldn't be tempted by vanity. It would be a time of introspection, not about whether we looked good or had food stuck in our teeth (even if some of us would take furtive glances in the mirror behind closed doors).

I was mostly dreading the familiar scrutiny, shallow comments, and the gossip I would hear:

"Oh dear, you gained some weight. *Estás mas gordita, no?*"

"Do you know that your *ex* got married again? *Ya supiste que se casó tu ex?*"

DANCING CANDLES

"Would you like *flor the calabaza*—squash blossom soup—for lunch?"

"*Nos hace falta una sábana para cubrir los espejos.*"

"Do you know where the sheets are to cover the mirrors? This one has a hole in it."

"Do you mind if we bring more help to serve the meals? *No te importa si traemos mas muchachas para servir la comida?*"

Catching up with the community gossip might work as a diversion from grief, but I was sure it wouldn't work for me. Anticipating it agitated my poor little *espíritu*. I was a mess!

I also knew the parade of rich Mexican and Jewish dishes would be endless during my father's shiva: *tapadas*—pastries filled with spinach and feta cheese or eggplant, hard-boiled eggs, potato dishes, *kugel*—a sweet egg noodle dish, sweet rolls, honey cakes, *rosquitas de anis*, anise donuts, and Turkish coffee. Everything would be passed around all day long. I loved all of the food, but I didn't need more pounds on me. There would be early prayers at the synagogue too, and at sunset at my father's home. Attending these prayers would be considered a *mitzvah*, a good deed. And every minute would be accompanied with more food.

I was already dizzy with anticipation in the pit of my stomach when I said goodbye to Rabbi Norman. My brothers had gone upstairs to sleep, while the help, worried about my father's soul, continued to pray in the kitchen. They didn't feel comfortable praying by my father's casket. I reassured them that Abraham would be praying for my father's *Jewish* soul, and that we couldn't mix Jewish and Catholic prayers together.

I returned to the living room after the rabbi left, needing a moment alone with my father. Abraham was concentrating deeply, reading from a worn-out prayer book. I didn't pay attention to him. I just stood quietly behind the simple wooden casket and placed my hands on it. It was covered in black velvet fabric embroidered

CHAPTER ONE

with a Star of David on top. I was mentally saying goodbye to my father when Abraham brusquely interrupted and demanded that I sit down.

I was suspicious of Abraham even if the rabbi had explained to us that Abraham's presence in the house was to function as a *shomer*—a guardian of my father's body. He would sit throughout the night reading passages from the Book of Psalms to honor my father and comfort his departed soul. When my mother died several years earlier, she hadn't had the services of a *shomer*. I couldn't understand why she didn't have one, or why she spent her last night alone at home. The only thing she had were four colorful plastic buckets placed under each corner of her coffin. They collected water that melted from the ice cubes that were helping to preserve her body. Thinking about it, I shivered—why hadn't I accompanied her through that lonely night, remove the ice from around her body, and infuse warmth from my heart into her skin?

Abraham interrupted my thoughts again.

"*Siéntate.*"

I sat obediently and looked hard into his round face. I scanned his eyes behind his glasses, trying to figure him out. Was he a pious man, or a charlatan? Before the rabbi left, Abraham seemed timid. He had spoken softly to my brothers and me, suggesting that we needed to be good children and show kindness and respect towards our father. His words annoyed my oldest brother, who told Abraham to just do his job and stop lecturing us.

"You don't know anything about our father or his relationship with us," my brother had added, to which Abraham nodded.

But now that I was alone with Abraham, his tone shifted. He spoke with composed authority.

As soon as I sat, the candles around my father's coffin gushed wax. Explosively!

Abraham leaned toward my father's body and whispered in Hebrew. Then he listened, waited, and began translating my father's words in Spanish. I was baffled.

"*Tu papá quiere que lo perdones.*"

"Forgive him for what?" I asked. I didn't wait for his response. "I have already forgiven him," I said dismissively.

"*No es cierto,*" Abraham said. "It's not true." Then he became more urgent. "*Tu papá está muy ansioso. Se arrepiente profundamente de sus errores y quiere que lo perdones.*"

"I told you already, even if you don't believe me. *I have* already forgiven him. I'm sorry if he's feeling anxious about his faults and *now* he wants to repent."

Abraham whispered to my father again in Hebrew. Then he repeated in Spanish.

"*Esto es un asunto muy serio. No se va a ir hasta que lo perdones.*"

His words were beginning to sound like a mantra. This must be the Jewish way, I thought. To his mantra, I offered my own mantra again.

"Tell him that I have truly forgiven him," I said. "Tell him that he can go now, rest in peace next to my sweet mother, or do whatever he wants to do. Tell him that the best way of showing him that I have actually forgiven him is through the fact that I am getting on with my life, and that *I am happy.*" I stressed the importance of this last statement. "You can also say that I am not dwelling on the past. I'm a busy person and have lots to do. The past is the past."

Abraham was translating my words to my father. I couldn't help but wonder what the point of all of this was. I felt that I had released my father, perhaps not with the greatest love and admiration, maybe with a little coldness, but nevertheless, I had forgiven him as well as any daughter whose father had been indifferent to her could.

The candles flickered wildly, as if my father was in my head and didn't approve of my thoughts. I began shaking at the serious-

CHAPTER ONE

ness of the situation. Then Abraham said my father wouldn't leave until I *truly* forgave him. Otherwise, if I were to believe what was happening in front of my eyes, my father's ghost would be following me around for the rest of my life.

"You are scaring me, Dad, *me estás asustando,*" I muttered under my breath. But now I could feel his agitation in my gut.

"Abraham," I said. "Tell him to go now. It really is okay. Tell him not to worry. Just move on. We will all be okay. I can take care of his house and my brothers too."

As I said the words, I couldn't help the thoughts that ran wild through my mind. What was the point of this wacky conversation? Why should I even try to talk to my father? I had given up so long ago. Yet now, after he was dead, he wanted to talk with me? *Que se vaya al demonio.* Why couldn't he say something when he was alive?

The candles flickered even more violently. Wax gushed forcefully. I was still shaking. Could my father hear my thoughts? Did he hear me thinking, *go to hell*? Or was I simply exhausted to the point of hallucinating? I just wanted to go to sleep, wake up, and bury him. Why did I have to forgive him on top of everything else?

Now the candles began to move differently—elongating, bending, literally distorting their form until one took on the shape of a tear. I had never seen anything like it. And I felt my father's spirit grow more agitated. Goose bumps consumed every inch of my skin.

"*Tu papá se arrepiente profundamente por sus acciones sobre la tierra,*" Abraham said. "*Especialmente por haber no haber sido un buen padre y no haberse preocupado por sus hijos. Su pena es muy grande. Esta desesperado por que lo perdones. Anhela tanto el perdón que no se va a ir hasta que lo perdones.*" Abraham paused. "*Además,*" he continued, "*ahora también es un buen momento para que tú le pidas perdón a él.*"

DANCING CANDLES

"Excuse me?" I asked, snapping out of my trance, like a light suddenly being thrown on. "I didn't do anything to hurt my father. Why do I have to ask *his* forgiveness? What did I do wrong? How dare you tell me I need to apologize to him. This is his deal. If he feels terrible for the kind of father he was, why didn't he ask for forgiveness when he was alive? And if he doesn't want to leave until I forgive him and is so desperate, it's not my problem. He can stay if he wants to."

Abraham started to speak again. His voice was shaky.

"*Tu papá tiene una lágrima que le está rodando en su mejilla,*" he said. "*Está llorando dentro de su ataúd…llorando con una tristeza muy profunda. Le ruega a tus hermanos recitar Kaddish para él y te pide a tí que le prendas una vela para tranquilizar su alma.*"

"Yes, of course," I said. "I can light a memorial candle to quiet his soul if that's what he wants. I can also ask my brothers to say the Kaddish for him. That's not a problem. But what do you mean he is crying inside his coffin, and he has a tear coming down his cheek? You are teasing me, right? He is dead, Abraham. Dead people don't cry!"

Wow, I thought. Not only do the dead talk, but apparently, they also cry. I wanted to open the coffin and look, just to see which part of me would be most appeased—the curious self, or the cynic.

Again, the flames bent and bowed, moving sadly from side to side in a slow-motion dance. I fell into a trance.

"*Perdónalo,*" Abraham interrupted.

"Forgive him for what?"

Abraham rolled his eyes.

"*Ya te lo dije,*" he uttered. Even he was getting tired of this. "*Por el daño que ha hecho.*"

"I told *you* already," I shot back. "All the harm he has done is not a big deal anymore."

I was lying.

CHAPTER ONE

The night grew dense, the air thick and cold. My head was heavy. I felt sick. Despite my outward bravado, I was petrified, especially as the candles continued their furious dancing, and wax gushed down like rivers of blood.

Forgiving my father was not an easy task. I tried hard and searched for answers in my soul. I dug deep. I found nothing but a void.

I wondered if I would be haunted for the rest of my life with these words coming from my father: "Forgive me, forgive me, forgive me…!" How can one forgive so many years of solid indifference? I had to be honest with myself. I couldn't possibly find forgiveness in my heart, at least for now. I asked myself if I could live with my inability to forgive, if it was morally or ethically right to *not* forgive him. Was it allowed from a religious perspective to hold on to my pain and hurt?

I was frustrated because I didn't have any answers. After all, my father wasn't such a bad person. He hadn't been an alcoholic or an abusive father, or anything like that. But I could never understand his rejection, or his lack of interest in his children. The deep ache in my gut was palpable. There was a bitter taste in my mouth. Why couldn't I find a soft place in my heart for him? Perhaps because he didn't ask for it when he was alive.

Abraham must have been reading my mind. I could tell he was getting more impatient with me, but that he also knew I wasn't budging.

When I looked at the clock it was 3:30 in the morning! I was stunned. How had three hours gone by? The exhausted Jewish psychic took his glasses off and rubbed his eyes. He mumbled something about needing the seven Jewish Samurai to come help my father. I didn't know what he was talking about. I didn't dare to ask him either, but I was happy to know that someone might have my father's back, even if it sounded ridiculous. Jewish Samurai? What was that about?

Frustrated, he said, "*Ya véte a dormir.*"

The room became still—the air, the candles, even the wax stopped moving.

I dragged myself upstairs to follow Abraham's command and go to sleep. My room was just above where my father's coffin lay. I was too shaken and wired to fall asleep right away. I stared at the ceiling awhile, then fell into something sleeplike.

A half hour later, the sound of my own heartbeat startled me awake. It was abnormally fast, and much deeper than I'd ever felt.

Now it was my heart that began to speak:

"*A spirit who is fully repentant of his earthly actions deserves our forgiveness.*"

I knew this thought did not come from my mind. I felt my heart vibrate and begin to open. There was an emotion at the back of it I had never known, something that felt heavenly, as if a spirit had found its way into me.

From this place of divine compassion, I suddenly knew I could forgive my father. Yet, I was left with a dilemma. From a place of this higher vibration—from spirit to spirit—forgiveness could be effortless. But the challenge remained to forgive from my ego self towards his spirit.

It felt like a monumental task. I pulled the covers over my head.

CHAPTER TWO
White Feathers

"Los pájaros se comen la noche."
–Pablo Neruda

I cannot remember exactly when my father got ill. The line was blurry between his progressive dementia and his personality traits. I believe he was having small strokes that went unnoticed over a period of several years as he grew more and more estranged from people. His eyes were more vacant than usual, and he seemed disconnected from the world. His angry outbursts grew more acute. Were these the effects of old age, dementia, or an imploded personality?

When I was six, sitting at the old Formica dining room table, my father seemed stern. He sat at the head of the table. I sat to his right, and my mother sat to mine. I liked being between my parents. My two brothers sat across the table from me.

I knew that if my father had had a good day at work, which was not very often, he could be sweet, and smile innocently. But he'd never ask how our days were. I always prayed that he'd be in a good mood, and at times even crossed my fingers under the table.

I hid my hands under the table for another reason too—I was biting my nails. My father would ask to see if I'd been biting them. He'd threatened to rub *serrano* pepper on my fingernails to stop

CHAPTER TWO

my habit. My mother wouldn't say a thing, and my brothers would hold their breaths as I sweated, petrified. I had failed my father again. I certainly didn't want to accidentally rub my eyes or mouth with chili on my nails, then suffer the consequences.

But then I'd be saved by some miracle of my father's own self-distraction. The napkins would get stuck, for instance, and he'd begin swearing vehemently.

"*Malditas servilletas,* damn napkins!" He was the only one in the family that pulled two or three napkins at a time from the napkin holder. What a guy!

My father's most common phrase, "*maldita sea,* goddamn it," was something he used extensively—about anything that didn't go his way. He would clench his jaw tightly as the words hissed between closed teeth. At times when he directed his *maldita sea* towards my little brother, it sounded harsher. Maybe he didn't want to have three kids. A third child was probably out of his carefully crafted family plan, but his scientific calculations of a two-child family had failed.

Once, he tried to force my sweet little brother to eat string beans—and I don't believe it was because he thought vegetables were all that healthy for children. He did it because Jonatán defied him by refusing to eat the green beans. My father actually seemed to want to choke him with them. His wrath was palpable. I shrank in my seat, even if I was thankful for the fact that he was focusing on my brother, and not my chewed-up nails. Soon he forgot about all of us, because his tortillas were not warm enough. He snapped and directed his exasperation at Luz María, one of our help.

Without fail, the moment he sat down at a family meal, he would start complaining, often about things no one understood.

"*Ya estoy harto de la fábrica. No estamos ganando dinero y todo se va en impuestos. Vamos a quebrar. Nuestros provedores no nos entregan los productos a tiempo y nuestro clientes no nos pagan.*"

WHITE FEATHERS

I had no idea what he was talking about. Why was he so fed up with his own chemical manufacturing plant? Why wasn't he making money? What did taxes mean, and why was he paying too many? Why were his suppliers not delivering products on time, and the clients not paying? He sounded so bitter. He kept talking about his business being on the verge of bankruptcy. Then his face grew red, and he began to curse the Mexican politicians, whom he said were thieves.

"*Los políticos estúpidos son unos ladrones.*"

My head spun trying to figure him out. My mother nodded quietly, and we chewed our meals in silence.

Little by little, his nightly outburst would subside if we left him alone, or after he drank two glasses of Coca-Cola from a family-sized bottle he reluctantly shared with us. A Coke had a soothing effect on him.

Following our afternoon meal, he would go upstairs to take a nap. He would carefully place an open newspaper sheet on his bedspread, then lie down for an hour with his shoes on. I thought that was weird. Was he so lazy that he didn't want to take his shoes off?

Once when I was eight, he tripped on my little vacuum cleaner toy that I hadn't put away. When I heard him angrily looking for me, I ran and hid in my closet. One of our maids conspired to help me hide. From the depths of my closet I heard his boisterous voice.

"*Adónde está esa mosca muerta?* Where is that mud rat?"

I held my breath in the closet, and stayed very quiet for a long time, sitting still and alert among smelly shoes until he gave up the search. I didn't like him calling me a dead fly, a *mosca muerta*. I wasn't a mud rat! I was just clever to hide from him. When it was safe to come out of hiding, I chewed my nails again and eventually went to sleep. But he was all show and no go—he was not the kind of father to hit his children, for instance. Still, he was a frightening guy.

CHAPTER TWO

One lovely afternoon we were all playing outside. When my father woke up from his nap, he got ready to go back to work. As he pulled his car out of the garage he somehow picked a fight with a neighbor. I saw my father chasing him down the street, threatening him with an ice pick! I had no idea what this guy had done to aggravate him so much, but my father was ready to chop him into *cubitos de hielo*—little ice cubes. I was horrified and filled with so much shame that I didn't play with my friends for the rest of the week. I was afraid they would think my father was crazy.

Later that evening, he came home like nothing had happened. But I was still feeling scared. I searched in his car to see if he still had the ice pick. I was going to hide it, but I couldn't find it. After dinner, he went to his bedroom and began spraying DDT in his quest to eliminate mosquitoes. I dared to confront him.

"Dad, I hate the smell of DDT. I feel sick to my stomach and can't breathe."

"*Ay mi'hija, no exageres.*"

"I'm not exaggerating. *Pleeease*, don't spray that smelly stuff in my bedroom."

I followed him to make sure he didn't. He pulled the pump out of his bathroom closet, and sprayed a thick cloud of DDT in his bedroom. I ran for my life like a mosquito out of hell. Behind his bedroom door I yelled, "Dad, that's disgusting. Really! Don't bring that to my bedroom, okay?"

"*Okay. Bueno ya no me fastidies!*"

"I'm not bugging you. I truly get sick. Why do you spray that awful stuff?"

"*Odio los mosquitos. Los voy a matar a todos.*"

"Even if you hate mosquitoes, I don't think you can kill them all. They keep coming back! And besides, couldn't you find something less smelly?"

He didn't respond. Thankfully, he desisted from coming out and spraying DDT in *my* territory.

Besides the oily DDT pump, his bathroom closet was filled with intriguing items and remedies he concocted in his chemical manufacturing plant and brought home for us to sample. I liked the scent of the shampoo and conditioner he gave me for my long wavy hair, the pure glycerin for my chapped hands, the special coconut lip balm, and ointments that actually worked well if I had skin rashes. Once, when I had an eye infection, he tenderly held my eyelids open and put stingy drops in my eyes, and even if I didn't like the burning sensation I trusted him and let him do it. Sometimes my father was my hero. Why couldn't he consistently be my hero instead of frightening me with his yelling and bad moods at the dinner table, or chasing a neighbor with an ice pick? I thought maybe the DDT made him irritable because it smelled so awful and got me dizzy.

My father mystified me. At times he was charming, especially with our extended family, and his friends. Always in good spirits with others, for them he was like a lamppost out in the street, while at home he was all darkness—*farol de la calle, obscuridad de su casa*. His personality shifts stunned me. What an actor! People actually loved him, and considered him a good friend.

He indeed had a talent for giving sound advice. One Sunday afternoon, his cousin Mario came to see him. Mario didn't visit often. He seemed unusually quiet and preoccupied. He hardly said hello to me, which was odd. He was always chirpy. I thought something was going on, but I just went to my room to finish my homework.

My father and Mario sat in the den close to my room. I overheard Mario saying he was having problems with his wife, and was

CHAPTER TWO

considering a divorce. This would be his second divorce, something that was uncommon in our Jewish community. This was a big deal. Mario spent a couple of hours chatting with my father, and when he was on his way out he seemed cheerful and happy. The last words I heard him say to my father were "*gracias por tus consejos, Salomón.*" He thanked my father for his counsel and left to go fix his situation.

I was flabbergasted. I didn't know my father had it in him to turn a situation around based on his advice. Sometimes I would see him spending lots of time on weekend afternoons visiting friends from our street. He went to his sister's home and chatted for hours with his brother-in-law. He also went to see Dr. Gomez, who lived just a few houses down from ours, and to visit Joe Arditi, a close friend who had lost his wife to cancer. Because I was outside playing, I watched my father come and go from house to house, finally returning home whistling and in good spirits. Did they give him a special potion? What was *their* secret that kept my father so happy?

There were a few times when my father was actually sweet to me, too. He would say "*si mi reinita*" in a soft voice, calling me his little queen, reminding me that somewhere inside him he loved me. Knowing there was a little *reinita* spot in his heart gave me some kind of status, and a few ounces of hope—*unas cuantos gramos de esperanza*. I gladly took the title rather than nothing. The problem was that even if he called me *reinita*, he didn't treat me like his little queen when money was involved. He kept a tight leash on it, and our conversations about money always ended on the same note.

"Dad, I need a new dress for a party. Can I have some money? I also need some money for a painting class I want to take."

"*El próximo mes cuando tenga dinero de los intereses del banco.*"

"Why do you have to wait for a month to get money? What are interests from the bank?"

Then he'd snap and tell me to leave him alone.

"*Ya déjame en paz.*"

That was the end of the conversation about money.

The next month would come around. He might have even gotten some extra money from the interest on his bank CDs. But he didn't have the initiative to offer it to me graciously. It was confusing—every year he bought himself the Ford motor company car of the year, and his closet was filled with elegant Florsheim shoes, and expensive, custom-tailored suits. Fuming inside, I didn't know whom to blame—the banker, or my father for always being a month behind in fulfilling *my* needs and desires.

Around the time I was turning 15, he actually fulfilled my desire without me nagging. This was a special gift because it required an excursion to downtown Mexico City. *El Centro*!

On a Friday evening, my father announced he was taking me to *el Centro* the next day to buy me a typewriter, something I wanted for my birthday. I was so excited because *he* offered it!

I woke up early the next morning and quickly got ready. After breakfast, we hopped in his flaming new car and took off. Sitting in the passenger seat, I felt like the *reinita* I deserved to be. We drove over half an hour to downtown Mexico City, which was always busy on Saturdays. We had trouble finding parking, and he dared to leave his car in a garage, letting the attendant know he would give him a big tip to wash his car and keep it from being scratched.

We started walking, holding hands along the way. I didn't know where we were going, but I was fascinated with what was happening around me. Everything seemed like a Hollywood set, lit up with multicolor items. Something was for sale in every direction—Mexican folk costumes, colorful shawls, shoes, fancy clothing, furniture, and electronics. There were small restaurants and bars, and retailers that sold fake jewelry—*joyería de fantasía*—like the earrings and necklaces my grandparents sold from their homes.

CHAPTER TWO

We proceeded to the street where they sold *piñatas*, party favors, and candy of all shapes to stuff inside the *piñatas*.

Finally, we reached the store that sold office supplies. My dad was in good spirits. So was I, especially to be walking around the streets of *el Centro* with my handsome father. And I was thrilled he was going to fulfill his old promise: buy me an Olivetti typewriter for my 15th birthday!

I knew exactly what I wanted: a sparkling Olivetti Lettera 22, with a light blue cover with a black strip in the middle. Puffed up like a *pavoreal*, my father said to the shopkeeper, "*Esta es m'hija. Está cumpliendo quince años, y le voy a regalar su primera máquina de escribir.*"

The shopkeeper smiled broadly.

"Good for you," he said to me. "Fifteen is the perfect age to receive your first typewriter."

My father seemed so proud of me. But at the same time, I got a funny suspicion about something I couldn't quite put my finger on. A strange sensation landed in the pit of my stomach.

"Why is he so happily getting me a typewriter?" I wondered. I had learned to type in middle school, and I was very fast at it. Why was he so eager to get me what I wanted, especially since he had never been so eager about my desires before? Was there an ulterior motive? Did he think I should have a career as an executive secretary? Was that the obscure reason behind his master plan?

I brushed off my suspicion—I was too excited—and put those thoughts on the back burner. My father paid without bargaining or complaining. As we left the store, his good spirits continued. He offered to take me out to lunch to the *Sanborns de los Azulejos*. I was elated. This was my favorite family style restaurant. Located in a pretty building, the inside was adorned with white and blue tiles. Plus, there was a glorious patio in the atrium, colorful murals inside, and a lovely fountain. And all the waitresses dressed in a typical Mexican costume.

I ordered my favorite dish, *enchiladas Suizas*—Swiss enchiladas. We shared my favorite dessert, *rollo de helado*, a delicious ice cream cake, and I felt like the queen of Mexico. After our sumptuous lunch, we walked to the parking garage to pick up his car. I was relieved that his car was there in one piece. That meant my father wouldn't end up ruining a perfect day with an outburst.

When we got home, I ran upstairs to my bedroom, blissful with my new acquisition. Pulling the typewriter from its case, I began typing my homework, feeling on top of the world. I treasured that typewriter throughout my high school years, not only using it to type my homework, but also for writing poetry. It became my most trusted friend.

Unfortunately, my suspicion about my father's plans for my future proved true. Perhaps he was encouraged because I continued to excel at typing. One day, he simply proposed that I lead a technical executive secretary career, instead of going to college. My mouth dropped.

"No," I said adamantly. "Being an executive secretary is not my plan. I want to go to college, and I will. I will never be a secretary. I'll be my own boss."

"*Bueno, pues si así quieres está bien pero estás cometiendo un error.*"

"Yeah, that's what I want, and I don't think I'm making a mistake."

He just shrugged his shoulders. He knew I was stubborn, and wasn't going to budge. I left our conversation infuriated because he truly didn't know anything about my academic aspirations or my talents. Plus, his views of women were skewed. I was also pissed off because he never noticed an independent trait of mine. And, to add insult to injury, the school he wanted to send me to

CHAPTER TWO

was an all-girls school. *La escuela para señoritas ejecutivas.* Yeah right! Flirtatious as I was by 18, I wasn't going to stride into an all-girls school for an executive secretary career. A world without boys was unthinkable. Having a boss was unthinkable. Typing for the rest of my life to make a living was unthinkable. My father was definitely *out to lunch!*

I couldn't understand why my father didn't see any other qualities in me other than typing. Meanwhile, even my first-grade teacher, Ms. Carmelita, had noticed different talents right away. I was fortunate to have a shining light at school when I was six years old. I used to follow her around like a little duckling. She was thin and delicate, with dark, smooth skin, and sparkling eyes. She wore long, navy-blue skirts and long-sleeved, impeccably pressed white shirts.

One of my favorite projects she gave us was tracing big cursive letters onto a large piece of paper with colored pencils. Every letter I traced became a beautiful rainbow.

"*Qué lindos tus colores,*" she said as she stood watching from behind my chair. "*Lo estás haciendo muy bien.*"

I was startled. I had never heard those words at home. "What beautiful colors, you are doing it very well." And then she took my letter 'A' and posted it in front of the classroom as an example. I swelled with pride.

I was lucky to get Ms. Carmelita again in third grade. She noticed that Dalia and I were friends, and liked to do projects together as well. Dalia and I had been best friends since kindergarten. We played every day after school, did our homework, danced, sang, colored, created stories and spent every afternoon together, either at my house, hers, or out in the streets with other kids. We always made sure we were on the same team. By third grade, we were inseparable. We even told our classmates that our birthdays were on the same day, which was a lie.

We were studying the Aztec culture, and Ms. Carmelita chose us to work on a project at home. We felt special. She gave us a large wooden board, an assortment of colorful ribbons, wooden sticks, a big bottle of glue, and a large bag of white feathers. She wanted us to build a *penacho*, an elaborate headdress that the Aztecs wore in their religious ceremonies and dances. She showed us pictures of the Aztecs during a *Danza del Venado*, the Deer Dance. Each wore a *penacho*, and small bells on ankle bracelets. They shook rattles in their hands as they danced and mimicked the movements of a deer.

Like two chosen golden girls, we were excited to be challenged with such complex homework. On our way home, we talked endlessly about how we were going to make the *penacho*. We went to my house, settled on the den floor, and got our supplies together. We set the wooden board on the carpet, placed the glue on the side, and began gathering sticks and ribbons with great enthusiasm. We thought it was going to be a piece of cake to put it all together. We were wrong. We tried several times, took turns holding the sticks in one place and weaving the ribbons across them. It didn't work as easily as we thought. The ribbons got tangled up, and when we tried to glue things together, everything turned into a mess—sticks were scattered all over. We needed more hands to hold it all in place.

After many trials and errors, we got anxious and frustrated—we were used to doing things easily. On top of our failure, we accidentally spilled glue all over the carpet. Now we'd be in trouble, and had to hide the stain after we desperately tried to clean it up with soapy water. I was beginning to bite my nails in desperation.

CHAPTER TWO

Suddenly, Dalia and I started giggling nervously. We went looking for our older brothers, but they weren't around to help us. At some point, we gave up and quit the project altogether. We decided to relax, and went to Dalia's house to play—straight to the patio where she had swings. Soon we were doing a swing competition to see who could get higher. Afterwards, we played for a bit in her backyard, and did our own version of the *Danza del Venado*. Then we went to the store to buy our favorite candies, *dulces enchilados*, which were covered in chili powder. But nothing inspired us to try our assignment again. Already an exercise in futility, now it was getting late. We decided to play in the street with the feathers.

First, we pulled one feather out of the big plastic bag and threw it in the air. Then another. And another. We were fascinated by the patterns the feathers drew in midair as they fell to the ground. We loved how they floated like snowflakes down to the dark pavement. Then, we ran and twirled around pretending we were Aztec warriors. We grabbed and tossed more and more feathers until the feathers covered a good part of the street. We were being creative in our own way, but I doubted Ms. Carmelita would have appreciated our free-spirited efforts.

This feather extravaganza was far better than blowing soap bubbles, or watching the dancing bear that would come to our street occasionally, or the bicycle guy who sold yo-yos and other toys. We had transformed the cul-de-sac into a white feathery stage for our dance. In total rapture from being *c-r-e-a-t-i-v-e*, we felt we'd reached the pinnacle of an Aztec dance ceremony.

After a long afternoon and evening of events, we grew tired and hungry. We went to our respective homes, and forgot all about the problems we had to face the next day when Ms. Carmelita would ask to see the *penacho*.

WHITE FEATHERS

Soon after, my father arrived home from work. He honked several times in his usual neurotic way, expecting the maids to quickly run downstairs to open the gate for him, *el Señor*. He stomped upstairs, making me suddenly anxious.

He asked sternly, "*Quién tiró esas plumas en la calle?* Who dumped all those feathers outside on the street?" He looked straight at me. Of course, he *knew* it was me! Who else would do such a thing? The boys were definitely not into feathers.

Before I opened my mouth, and not even needing to confess my crime, he handed me a broom and a dustpan and sent me outside to sweep the street. *Me dió una escoba y un recogedor y me mandó afuera a barrer la calle.*

By now it was raining. Trying to sweep wet feathers was an impossible task. I was crying, and went inside to call Dalia. I asked her to come out and help me. She just laughed.

"*Oye, tu papá esta loco, yo no voy a bajar a barrer las plumas,*" she said. "*Además, a mi papá no le importa eso.*"

"Yeah, I know my dad is crazy, but why are you not going to help me sweep the street? We both did it! Even if your dad doesn't care about the mess, you should come down and help me."

"Nope," she said. "I'm going to sleep." She hung up on me.

I was furious. So, this was my best friend talking? Maybe her father was right not to care. But my father did. Sadly, I realized I was on my own, except for our kindhearted maid who tried to sneak behind my father to come help me sweep. But she was no better equipped to remove the wet feathers than I was.

I thought my father was an alchemist of the wrong kind, one who turned gold into lead. Why would he want to destroy our masterpiece? The feathers looked so beautiful. Why couldn't he let them be? Why did he need to spoil everything? My heart was crushed. I did my best to clean up what he called a mess, but didn't have much success. Exhausted, I finally quit and went to sleep.

CHAPTER TWO

The next morning on my way to school I was awestruck to see the birds completing the job I'd abandoned the night before. They collected the feathers one by one, for their nests.

Since that day, I deeply love birds…and hate sweeping.

After the feather incident, I made up my mind not to trust my father. If he didn't understand my spirit, how could I trust him? Besides, he was totally unpredictable. Over time, I moved on with my life to the best of my abilities. I played with my friends and cousins, and hung out at other people's homes. Even if I desperately needed a father, I knew better than to ask for advice.

Nevertheless, much later in adult life, I needed his blessing and advice—I was about to file for a second divorce, which was like a double murder in our traditional Jewish community. None of my cousins had done it. None of my friends had done it either. One divorce was kind of okay. But two? That was too much to handle alone. I recalled the way my father had helped Mario when he needed a divorce, so I dared to call him.

"I need to talk to you," I said. "Things are not going well in my marriage. As a matter of fact, they're really bad. I'm very unhappy. I've tried so many times to make it work."

He was quiet for a moment. I took a deep breath, fearing his judgment. Instead he asked, "*Qué piensas hacer?*"

"I've been thinking that I need a divorce," I said. I felt terrible about even thinking it, let alone saying it. "I can't see my way out of this situation. There is no other solution."

To my surprise, my father listened carefully, even if he wasn't aware of the things that had gone badly in my marriage. He must have sensed my desperation and unhappiness, especially when I mentioned that my husband was so mean that he threw my type-

WHITE FEATHERS

writer out the window—the same typewriter my father had given me for my 15th birthday. Now the frame was broken, and it was ruined for good.

After he listened to my litany of complaints about my marriage, my father took a long breath. Then he began speaking in metaphor.

"*Este asunto es como una hojita de otoño que va cayendo poco a poco,*" he said. "*Simplemente, déjala caer y ya se irá acomodando.*"

I was shocked by my father's poetic words. He said that the resolution about divorce was like an autumn leaf that needed to fall on its own, little by little. My dad, *the poet*, had shown up for a change, and was actually helping. I was impressed with his phrasing. I'd never heard him speak like that. I felt he had given me his blessing. Why this sort of gem had been absent in my younger years was a puzzle to me. It still is. At the time, it made me question if he resented having a family.

Aren't men supposed to be providers, and guiding lights for their children? From the outside, it seemed like my girlfriends' fathers loved and supported their families. I always thought that we were nice Jewish people. (We were all nice Jewish people!) We happily shared big meals among extended family. We went to temple, the Jewish sports center, and the Jewish school together. In my little world—my Mexican *shtetl*—the fathers worked, loved, and cared for their children. Why, then, was my father always complaining?

Whenever I'd begin to think that maybe things were fine and normal at our home growing up, I'd witness something that reminded me that the opposite was true. I remember Becky Bialostovsky's high school graduation party. She was one of my classmates. The party was also a farewell celebration—Becky was going to Israel to

CHAPTER TWO

study abroad for a year. My whole family was invited to the party. While we were there, the thin veil of denial about my father's kindness disintegrated before my eyes.

At some point, Becky's father gathered everybody together. He wanted to share a speech about Becky.

"I love my daughter dearly," he started. "I feel so proud of her and her new life choice. Here is a little something special for you so you remember this day and all of your accomplishments. Brava!"

To celebrate her achievements, he gave her a case that held a fabulous pair of gold earrings inside. Becky was beaming. I had a knot in my throat.

Her father wasn't done.

"To my lovely wife, Miriam, I know you feel you have lost a diamond as Becky is going away for a year. But here is a new one for you so you don't feel so sad."

I gasped for air as I stared at the huge diamond he gave to his wife. I was frozen—I'd never heard words like that from my father...had never even conceived that a father could speak like that to his daughter or his wife. A diamond ring? I felt like I was having a panic attack. I bit my lip hard, trying to slow down my heartbeat, and keep myself from crying in public. It was an unfortunate wake-up call for me. I went home devastated.

Were moments like these some of the reasons my father's soul was asking for forgiveness? Was he repenting his greedy ways, his sudden outburst, or his lack of love and attention? Was it about trying to choke sweet little Jonatán with string beans? Or was it because he never helped me with my chemistry homework? Was he crying in his coffin because he didn't know how to love his own flesh and blood? Did he finally realize that he'd ignored our talents? That trying to mold us in his image, wishes, and desires was the wrong decision? Was he sorry for all the grief he dished out at the dinner table? Did the afterlife make him aware of his indifference, his self-indulgence, and his inability to give from his heart? And what about all of the business about forgiveness that Abraham was talking about? Did it include all these incidents I couldn't get off my mind as the candles flickered wildly, and his poor soul dwelt in despair?

Was there more to the story of his life than what I already knew?

CHAPTER THREE
Family Secrets

"If you reveal your secrets to the wind you should not blame the wind for revealing them to the trees."

–Kahlil Gibran

Jonatán bolted out of bed at 6 a.m. the day of our father's funeral. He intuitively sensed something was wrong. He got dressed and rushed downstairs, *como un trueno*, like a lightning bolt. His expressive eyes were wide open as he sat and listened to Abraham mumble in Hebrew. He watched the candles quizzically.

I went downstairs soon after Jonatán. He looked at me, then at Abraham, and did a double take.

"*Qué onda hermanita, que pasó?*" he asked. "Did something happen last night?"

At that moment, the candles went wild again, flickering and belly dancing in the same distorted way as the night before. Abraham continued to pray with his eyes closed. I couldn't believe it! I didn't blink either, and thought perhaps I was sleep deprived and not seeing straight. That was not the case.

Weary to start the whole ordeal again, I watched Jonatán raise his eyebrows while his eyes grew as big as plates. He held his breath as I told him what transpired the night before.

CHAPTER THREE

I coughed slightly to see if Abraham could be shaken from his meditative trance. Nothing. He was out of it. *Estaba fuera de servicio.* I coughed again much harder, which caused him to open his eyes so suddenly, he scared me out of my wits.

Looking tired and pale, even a bit discombobulated, he seemed so much older than the night before. His eyes were red and teary, and he shook his head incessantly.

"Are you okay, Abraham?" I asked. He didn't answer me. *No me contestó.* Now I was getting more freaked out as I offered him a glass of water, which he refused.

"What else happened after I went to sleep?" I asked him. He looked up with glossy eyes and tried to speak, but no words came out. For a moment, I thought the situation was going to get much worse. Was it possible that Abraham was now possessed by my father's spirit?

The Jewish story of the *Dibbuk* came to mind. In Jewish folklore, stories about the *Dibbuk* were common from around the time of the Second Temple of Jerusalem. Back then, people thought that if a dead person's spirit was not laid to rest, it could become a demon, and seek refuge in the body of a living person. *Un espíritu maligno podría entrar en una persona viva y adherirse a su alma.* An evil spirit could enter into a person, cleave to his soul, cause mental illness, talk through his mouth, and create a completely separate, alien personality.

I was contemplating this possibility and trying to figure out our next step. Did we need to contact a rabbi versed in exorcism to try to extricate my father's soul from poor Abraham?

To my great relief, Abraham became more animated.

"*Qué pasó?*" I asked. "What happened?" He muttered something so quietly that I couldn't understand. Then with a clearer voice he said, "I've never heard such horrible stories in my entire life as a guardian of the soul in this community. *Funda-*

mentalmente tu papá me dijo tres cosas de las que se arrepiente profundamente."

Basically, our father told Abraham three things he felt deeply remorseful about: the kind of father and husband he was, the fact that he forgot all about being a good Jew, and the many fatal mistakes he made in his life.

We pressed for details, but Abraham wouldn't mention specifics.

"I can't say another word to you guys," he said. "May God forgive your father...may he find peace...may his soul rest in peace even if I don't know how this may be possible to achieve. Please don't ask me any more questions. I can't answer them, nor can I help your father. What kind of a man was he to have abandoned his faith, his children, and his wife the way he did? I can't believe it. I have to leave now."

"What about the Jewish Samurai you mentioned last night?" I asked. "Can *they* help him?"

Without another word, Abraham stood up, grabbed his worn-out, black leather jacket, and left in a hurry. Great! There goes Mystery Man with all of my father's secrets.

A dense silence, and a chill in the air, followed Abraham's departure. Bewildered and speechless, Jonatán and I looked at each other. A tingle ran down our backs as we sat in a stupor on the sofa, next to the coffin where our father rested. Or not! I had a metallic taste in my mouth.

"So, what do you think *he* did?" I asked, thinking about the ice pick.

"*Yo no sé,*" Jonatán said. He didn't know either.

We couldn't move. We felt heavy as lead as we breathlessly watched the candles flicker right and left, our heads swiveling as if viewing a slow-motion ping-pong match.

CHAPTER THREE

Shortly after 6:30, the swinging door to the kitchen creaked open. We both jumped off the sofa. We were sure the *Dibbuk* was in the kitchen creating havoc. But it was just a procession of maids and nurses who appeared tentatively one by one with rosaries in their hands. They asked our permission to come and pay their Christian respects to my father before his body went to the cemetery.

They had not expected us to be there so early in the morning, and were hesitant to come in. Even if my father was Jewish, they had seen enough of his antics to know his soul needed extra help from their faith. They were not sure if my brother and I would approve, but after that rocky night, we welcomed their prayers and rosary beads with gratitude.

My father's cadre of helpers—Luz María, Esperanza, Silvia, and Angélica—stood around his coffin and began whispering prayers. We stayed for a moment, but soon left so they could perform their rituals more comfortably. Also, I didn't feel like being my father's watchdog. Hey, if they wanted to convert him to Catholicism, or absolve him from his sins, I wouldn't stand in the way. He needed all the help he could get to transition to the other world. Obviously, Abraham and his Jewish prayers hadn't been enough. So what if Jesus, the Virgin Mary, or Saint Francis of Assisi—and not the mighty Jewish *Elohim* or the Seven Jewish Samurai—could help him cross to the other side? At this point, I could care less. He was on his own. I wouldn't interfere. *Yo no iba a interferir.*

These women were true angels. They'd taken care of our father in his final years. They were kind and dedicated, and cared for him no matter what. By the end of his life, as his dementia progressed, his outbursts subsided radically. He was docile like a little lamb.

It was easy for me to recall times when the help at my parents' house was not so kind. Rosa, our maid from when we were in elementary school, had a terrible mean streak, for instance. When I was only seven years old, I remember sitting on the bathroom stool while she brushed my long thick hair with harsh strokes. Tears fell from my eyes. I wanted to run to my mother, but she wasn't home. I had to stay put, and because Rosa was so intimidating, I was afraid to say anything to my parents.

She was in charge of us when my parents were not home. In the afternoon, she mostly sat in front of the TV and watched Mexican *telenovelas*, soap operas we weren't allowed to watch. I just wanted to watch *Mister Ed* or *Viruta y Capulina*, my favorite shows. But Rosa wouldn't let us change the channel. I wanted to punch her in the stomach, but she was way bigger than me.

Sometimes, my older brother and our mean neighbor Roberto would gang up and pester little Jonatán. Rosa would just look the other way. I wanted to kill her. Whenever I needed clean clothes that were downstairs, she would laugh at me and take her time laying them out. Then one day, after many years of working at my house, she simply left. I didn't know why, but was I glad to see her go.

This morning, with the gloomy burial approaching, I was relieved to have the help and nurses around. They were kind, and had good intentions. I thought their prayers helped, because the candles finally settled down from their frenzied dances.

A bit more relaxed, Jonatán and I sat at the dining room table, ready to have strong coffee and breakfast. Our older brother, Yosef, joined us soon after. We never told him what happened during the night. We didn't think he'd believe us.

Luz María prepared a meal while we sat quietly at the table. She was a big woman with dark, curly hair, and a fabulous belly covered by a tiny apron. Scents of onion and garlic followed her everywhere she went. She loved to stand with her feet apart, arms crossed as if to say, "Don't mess with me... *ni se te ocurra chingarme.*"

She watched us like a hawk, squinting and making sure we ate enough. It was like she was becoming a new version of the *Yiddishe*

CHAPTER THREE

mamma, an iconic Jewish mother. She'd definitely been the guardian of the house in the years after our mother died. Luz María had promised her that she'd come back to work for my father, and to take care of us. I wasn't aware of this promise until much later.

Truth be told, Luz María despised my father. She had witnessed his neurotic behaviors for more than a decade.

When we finished breakfast, my brothers went upstairs to get ready for the memorial service. I stayed a bit longer and chatted with Luz María. That's when she began confessing things to me that I was unaware of.

"I have some things I need to say to you," she said out of the blue. "You may not like what I have to say, but I have to say them anyway now that your father is dead."

She took a deep breath, then went on.

"*Si señora, su papá era muy malo y le quería pegar a su mamá cuando estaba enferma, se lo juro por Diosito santo.*"

Luz María swore to God that when my mother was alive and weakened by her heart condition, she had to physically get between my parents several times, as my father threatened to hit my mother. She said that my father was mean and cruel to my mother.

I swallowed hard. I was never aware of this situation. My mother never told me. I lowered my eyes into my empty plate where Luz María had served *huevos rancheros*. Sad tears of shame and pain streamed down my cheeks. I felt angry and betrayed. The idea that my father could hit my mother when she was ill was hard to handle. How could he be capable of such cruelty? My Jewish notion of right and wrong was shattered. Was this one of the situations that Abraham heard while deep in meditation that he didn't dare speak of? I wanted to open the casket right there and confront my father.

Luz María didn't notice my anguish. She went on.

FAMILY SECRETS

"*Después que falleció su mamá, una mujer y su hijo de la misma edad de Jonatán y muy parecido a su papá cuando era joven, vinieron a visitarlo.*"

"What do you mean by that?" I asked. "A woman came to see my father soon after my mother died? And she had a son about the same age as Jonatán, who looked exactly like a younger version of my father? What are you saying, Luz María?" I was so confused.

"*Si, se lo juro,*" she said, swearing it was the truth.

My hands were shaking. She explained that she had been leaving for her day off, but returned to grab something she forgot. That was when she met this pair of strangers. My father was so aggravated that he fired her on the spot.

"*Empaqué mis cosas y me fuí sin decir otra palabra,*" she said. "*Estaba muy sorprendida y asustada de ver una copia exacta the su hermano y su papá que no les pude decir nada.*"

She explained how she'd packed her things and left without saying another word. She was so stunned and upset to see a carbon copy of my father and my brother that she couldn't mention a word to us.

I began coughing uncontrollably. Luz María patted me hard on the back until my throat cleared.

"*Me estás cotorreando verdad?*" I said. "You are kidding me, right?"

"*No, se lo juro por mi mamá que lo que le dije es verdad.*" She swore on her mother's grave that what she said was the truth.

More tears rolled down my cheeks. I could barely compose myself. I didn't want to have a meltdown! For so many years she had kept these secrets, I didn't know what to say. But now I knew why she quietly disappeared soon after my mother died. After my father's stroke, my brothers and I tried desperately to track her down. When we did, she reluctantly agreed to take care of him.

CHAPTER THREE

After she came back, she never said a word about what she witnessed, but she took it upon herself to cook us the dishes that only our mother knew whenever we visited. Our mother had passed on her traditions and gastronomic secrets to Luz María. Slowly, she became like a second mother to us. She knew how to make *chiles rellenos* filled with ground meat and pine nuts, seafood paella, *tapada de berenjena*—eggplant pie—and *enchiladas de mole y arroz rojo*—rice with tomato sauce—just like our mother did. Everything tasted exactly the same.

Now I could see why Luz María, despite my father's questionable actions, felt obligated to come back: a culinary promise is a culinary promise. But she got a bit of revenge on my father too. She stole some of his clothes and adult diapers, settling a few scores in the process. She needed them for her ailing father. A few other objects went missing in the days after our father's illness. Yet, as a token of appreciation, I gave Luz María one of my mother's handwritten recipe books. It belonged to her more than anyone—even me.

Luz María was like a good auntie in my adult life. In the moment, however, I felt sick with her stories. Before I left the dining room to get ready for the memorial, she had one last thing to share.

"*Pero ya no se preocupe tanto*," she said. "*Su mami está aquí, qué no la ve? Allí está, vestida de blanco y viene a cuidar a su papá.*"

Okay, this Luz María *of all saints* claimed that she could actually see my dead mother. This was too much. First Abraham was talking to my father, now Luz María was seeing my mother. In fact, she claimed that my mother was standing right next to me, dressed up in a beautiful white gown, and looking very peaceful. She was ready to take care of my father, and help him move on.

"Don't worry so much…can't you see your mama?" she asked.

"Yeah, right Luz María," I laughed—my first laugh in a while. "I can see *three* mamas!"

FAMILY SECRETS

My mother floating around in a white gown was a curious idea. I imagined she probably looked good in it. She'd been an elegant, sweet, and kind woman, so this image was not out of character.

I concentrated on this sweet vision of my mother, and even tried hard to spot her in the dining room. But then Yosef came downstairs and pulled me away from Luz María's revelations. He reminded me that I needed to get ready for the pallbearers.

As I stood up I felt as if my feet were pushing through molasses. I knew it was time to clean up and be as presentable as possible for the Jewish congregation and the memorial service, but I felt nauseated.

When we were all ready for the pallbearers, and had a moment to spare, Jonatán and I gave Yosef the light version of our psychic session with Abraham. He would have been totally freaked out if I mentioned that our mother was floating around in a white gown, or that our father was speaking to me all night via Abraham.

I decided to keep Luz María's confessions secret for now. How could I bear sharing this information with them? *Como iba a compartir estas noticias con ellos?* I would carry this secret pain like a thorn in my heart. Perhaps at another time I would share it. These were suffocating realities, and I didn't know what to do with them. Were they connected to the stories Abraham had heard? What other secrets had Abraham heard? *Qué otros secretos escuchó?*

Once we got ready, we sat quietly on the green velvet sofa. The candles stopped flickering, and gave off a faint, somewhat spooky light. Our hands idled on our thighs as we waited for the pallbearers to arrive. They were late. I was trying to gain strength and composure, anticipating with trepidation the journey to the temple, the cemetery, the burial ceremony, and the beginning of the seven days of sitting shiva.

CHAPTER FOUR
Sand from Jerusalem

*"Cuando ya se fueron los huesos,
quién vive en el polvo final?"*

–Pablo Neruda

Time was strange during the morning of my father's burial. At first it was sluggish, as if moving through mud. Waiting for the pallbearers was tortuous. My mind danced between trying to make sense of everything that had happened the night before, to worrying about what the next week would be like. My head was spinning, and my heart galloped like a wild horse. I had seven days of shiva ahead of me, and was already at the end of my wits—almost to the point of a nervous breakdown. Luz María's words were a lingering dagger in my chest. I tried desperately to collect myself. *Estaba tratando despesperadamente de tranquilizarme.*

I looked around to distract myself, which only added to my apprehension. Everything was run-down at my father's home, like something out of the Gabriel García Marquez novel, *One Hundred Years of Solitude*. In the book, spirits mingled with the living, and things took on lives of their own.

Was that happening here?

I imagined vines growing inside the house like Remedios Varo's paintings, where she portrays the furniture and people's legs

CHAPTER FOUR

merging and growing intermingled roots. I envisioned people riding on transparent bicycles in states of stupor, or the moon locked up in a bird's cage in the living room, the walls revealing the presence of bizarre faces. I was in a daze, and kept checking my hands to make sure I wasn't growing roots or fabric patterns.

Why had my father let his home run down like this? He had lived here eight years after my mother died. He didn't take pride in keeping his home in one piece the way my mother did. He let things go, and procrastinated when something broke. If a window cracked, he would let it be. If one bathroom had a leak, he would just use the other bathroom instead of fixing the problem. If the carpet had stains, he would just stop looking down. He simply didn't care.

His house deteriorated the way his body did, a little at a time, without warning or redemption. We kept his home going on a shoestring during the years that followed his major stroke, which were wrapped up in his mental deterioration. Money went mainly for his care. And now, right before the shiva, I couldn't help feeling embarrassed when I thought of all the people from the community who would come to pay their respects. What would they think of my family? Of this house? What would they think of my father's children as we sat low to the ground? Would they silently accuse us of neglecting his home?

Since they were the part of what I call the *Prosperous and Mighty Jewish Community of Mexico City*, I was convinced the congregation would have a long list of items to gossip about. Not fun! Why didn't my father take responsibility for keeping his own house together before he got ill? Why did *we* have to fix his home? Besides being almost unable to care for the house, we could barely keep up with my father's care.

Jonatán took it upon himself to do this since he was the only one of us still living in Mexico City. He deserved a medal for the most distinguished son. He was in charge of our father's medical appointments, along with paying and overseeing the help and the nurses. I was merely the long-distance supervisor. I talked to the cooks, maids, and nurses by phone. I had to make sure the house personnel didn't kill each other, or leave out of the blue.

"Hi Luz María, how is everything?" I would ask by phone from my house in San Francisco.

"*Ay señora, no le quería decir pero Esperanza se esta emborrachando con las botellas de vino que tiene su papá en la despensa.*"

"Oh God, really? Since when is Esperanza getting drunk with the wine my father keeps in the pantry?"

"*Uuuuy señora, pa'que le digo.*"

"Well, at least you are telling me *now*, Luz María. I'll talk to Esperanza later. Can you put Angélica on the phone?"

"*Ay señora, le tengo que decir que los pañales de su papá se están acabando otra vez. Yo creo que Luz María se los está llevando.*"

"Angélica, we just bought a bunch of adult diapers for my dad. How do you know Luz María is taking them?"

"*Bueno, eso pienso yo.*"

"Okay. Thanks for letting me know what you think."

Then she would hand the phone to Silvia.

"*Ay señora, no tengo las notas de su papá de Angélica del turno de la mañana. No creo que tomó notas.*"

"Are you sure? Did you ask Angélica if she took notes on the day shift? Are you sure she was not taking notes on my father's status during her shift?"

"*Si señora.*"

"Okay, I'll talk to her about it."

I didn't want to confront Esperanza about the bottles of wine. I thought I'd let my brother know what was going on behind his back, so I just asked Esperanza casually.

"Hi Esperanza, how are things?"

CHAPTER FOUR

"*Ay señora, no hay suficiente dinero para la comida.*"

"Esperanza, my brother just left a lot of money for food. How come there is not enough?"

"*No sé, pero no hay.*"

Clearly, we were feeding a lot of families, because the money went like water. To top it off, Luz María, the greater gossiper, got on the phone again.

"*Ay señora, estoy preocupada porque su hermano esta muy fastidiado porque Esperanza está coqueteando con el todo el tiempo. Yo no sé que hacer. Hablo con ella pero no me hace caso que lo deje en paz.*"

"Luz María, I'm sorry, but I have to go now."

This last news made me want to scream. Esperanza flirting with my brother and annoying him every time he went to see my father was more than I could take. There was nothing to do. We needed them desperately, but the help for my father didn't come without causing chaos and gossip—like in a small Mexican *mercado*.

Our extended family was no support at all. With our mother dead, her side of the family vanished as soon as my father got ill. Her brother and sister grew to dislike my father immensely over the years, and my brothers and I were also on the receiving end of their scorn. Maybe they also knew things we didn't know about our father, just like Luz María did. As for my father's side, whenever they bothered to visit him, they spent most of their time criticizing and bossing the maids and nurses around. And nobody ever asked my brothers or me if we needed help. We were on our own.

"Dad, please," we begged him when he was still coherent. "Perhaps it would be best for you to move to the Jewish assisted living home in Cuernavaca. It's a wonderful place. They'll take care of you beautifully. You'll have new friends, and they have lots of activities. They will take you to visit nice places. Plus, the weather is warmer than in Mexico City. It will suit you well. We can get you physical therapy too."

SAND FROM JERUSALEM

"No," was his only reply. "*Yo no me voy de mi casa.* I'm not leaving my home!"

His adamant decision caused us a serious dilemma. We had to keep him in his four-bedroom, three-bathroom house, all 3,500 square feet of it! And he'd need help 24 hours a day, plus in-home physical therapy twice a week. So, we decided to keep going with this colossal task until we ran out of money, even though we were in no financial position to pay these expenses. We just prayed that his money would last, since it had dwindled away with his escapades before his stroke.

By the time he died, we were relieved that we were able to honor his final wish—keeping him in the home. I thought it was *un milagro*, a miracle that the money lasted for almost seven years. It was like the story of Hanukkah, when the oil that was meant to last a day or two in the temple lasted eight days. I believe in the possibility of divine intervention. Otherwise, I can't explain how it was possible that my father's money stretched so long.

Besides being the second in command via phone, I also had to visit Mexico City often to check things out in person, and take care of what my brother was unable to do. Small house repairs, for instance, fell to me. The to-do list included changing the flooring in my father's bedroom, replacing the old blinds that fell apart every time someone tried to open or close them, fixing the leaking bathrooms, and attending to gas leaks. I also had to get a wheel chair, a new mattress, and a hospital bed, along with new clothes for my father. And I needed to consult with my brother on treatment plans, medications, and doctors.

While in Mexico City, I often got into a frenzy of cleaning closets, rearranging things, and throwing away broken items. I'd take our father to the *Parque México* to watch the ducks trail slowly on the old pond, *ver a los patos en el estanque viejo*. Or we'd go out for Chinese food when he was well enough.

CHAPTER FOUR

My brothers and I treated him with all the respect an ill person deserves. At the same time, I kept my distance to protect my heart. I knew I wasn't going to get a *thank you* from him, for instance. And after each marathon trip to Mexico City, I would come home to the Bay Area exhausted. Taking care of a run-down home, and a run-down father, was quite challenging.

Looking at the clock, I snapped out of my ruminations. The pallbearers were so late! Well, maybe they were on typical *Mexican* time.

"*Adónde diablos están?* Where the hell are these guys?"

Didn't the dead earn the right to have people show up on time?

"What's the hurry?" I heard a small voice say. "*Cuál es la prisa?*"

I was biting my nails! I tried to breathe. Still waiting, and with nothing else to do, I pointed out to my brothers the leakage in the corner of the living room wall, where the wallpaper was peeling off. The dark stain from the humidity had crawled up the wall and moved to part of the dining room ceiling as well. They didn't care much, and just shrugged their shoulders.

"And the sliding doors to the backyard don't open easily, not since the ironwork rusted," I went on. "We have two options. We either put up a fight to open them, or we suffocate in the afternoon heat."

Yosef got up and tried to open the glass door, which he did with great effort. I was relieved. I stepped outside for a moment, but was quickly dismayed to see that the backyard had turned into a small jungle.

Back inside, my eyes continued to run over problems. The curtains in the living room were too short. At some point, the maid had washed them in the tub instead of taking them to the cleaners. Several windowpanes had large cracks, and the glass looked

SAND FROM JERUSALEM

ready to come crashing down! The living room's green carpet was so worn that holes showed up in parts, especially where someone had watered plants and let the water run down. Where would one even start to put this place in order, and have it ready for people as they paraded through for an entire week?

Was I the only one asphyxiating with shame?

I needed to pull a disappearing act quickly. But my brothers and I were the main actors, and there was no bailing out from the scene.

"Could the pallbearers arrive now . . . please?"

Imagine being saved by the pallbearers!

Nothing could soothe my anxiety. My mind was like a pinball machine. Why had both my parents died on Friday evenings, the beginning of the Sabbath? In the Jewish tradition, people cannot be buried on the Sabbath. The night before, the rabbi mentioned that when someone dies on the Sabbath, it is a sign that he or she had been a good person. He'd even said "saint-like," which made my jaw drop when I heard it.

I could believe this about my mother. But my father? He'd probably tricked the guys up above with his big smile. That would have been the only way he could have earned dying on the Sabbath.

"Stop!" I said to myself. I begged for the pallbearers to arrive, just to help put an end to my crazy, fleeting thoughts.

Why hadn't my mother gotten a night guardian, either a messenger like Abraham, or a Sabbath navigator? Why didn't she have the same chance to talk to me through the candles the way my father had? I didn't even see her in the hospital before she died. I could have at least touched her warm hand and said goodbye, even if she couldn't respond because she was in a coma.

CHAPTER FOUR

The night my mother died, the phone woke me at 3 a.m. It was my father. He said my mother was very ill. In reality, she had already died. *Mi mamá ya se había muerto.*

No one in my family had the nerve or courage—*o los cojones*—to call me days earlier when she'd gone into a coma. Why? The only word that comes to mind is *cobardes* . . . cowards!

When I got to my parents' home, my relatives were waiting for me at the top of the stairs. They seemed solemn and worried. Then, from the corner of my eye, I caught sight of the coffin in the middle of the living room. I was in complete disbelief. How could this be? My mother could never die!

Unhinged, I pushed my father, aunts and uncles out of the way and rushed upstairs, straight into my mother's bedroom. I can still see their blank eyes and looks of pity. I slammed the door shut. In the shelter of her bedroom, I held my breath as a silent, animal-like scream welled up from my insides. My whole body trembled.

I stumbled into her bathroom, where she kept a fishbowl. In a stupor, I gazed at her little goldfish and started talking to it.

"Come on little fish, talk to me, please! *Andale pecesitos, háblenme, porfavor!*"

I could hear the song my mother used to sing to me:

"*Lindos pescaditos, no quieren venir a jugar conmigo vamos al jardín.* Sweet little fish, don't you want to come play with me in the garden?"

Sobbing, I begged the fish to talk or sing, and desperately waited in vain. I finally had to acknowledge that fish don't talk, sing, or come out and play.

I stayed in her bathroom for a long time. When I was calm enough to walk out, everyone was gone. I was gone too, but in a much different way. My spirit was floating, motherless, into the unknown. My umbilical cord was crushed. My roots disintegrated under my feet.

The next day, I learned that Ashkenazi and Sephardic Jews have different burial traditions. My mother, born Ashkenazi, was not veiled with a guardian of the body, like in the Sephardic custom. Then why was she headed to a Sephardic cemetery instead of an Ashkenazi one, where she could be near her parents? We never discussed these issues while she was alive, and I didn't get to ask her about any last wishes. Instead I asked my father.

"*Porqué no la entierras en el cementerio Ashkenazi?* Wouldn't she be happier in the Ashkenazi cemetery, close to her parents?"

My father was unmoved.

"I've already purchased her a burial plot next to mine at the Sephardic cemetery," he said. "She didn't object while she was alive."

Sadly, I bit my tongue. There was no asking her anyway. As far as their final resting places went, death would not split my parents apart. *Ni siquiera la muerte los iba a separar.* But unlike my father, my mother did not receive the gift of someone like Abraham, a traveling navigator, watching over her during her passage.

Where were the stupid pallbearers? I continued to sink deeper into the caverns of my mind, and couldn't take the waiting much longer. I was dreading the *sand in the eyes* Jewish ritual that undoubtedly would be a part of my father's burial ceremony. I had done this with my mother years ago, and the image haunted me forever.

According to the Jewish tradition, we were instructed to put sand from Jerusalem on my mother's eyelids. It was one of the most visceral experiences of my life. Everything happened in slow motion. First, the sand fell slowly from the palm of my hand and landed right on my mother's painfully still eyelids. The

CHAPTER FOUR

sand stayed right where it fell. I stood there, mouth wide open, shocked by the effect.

This ritual was important in that it kept the living from questioning whether or not the dead were truly gone, or wondering if they'd suddenly open their eyes. I was so shaken by the ritual that I almost fainted. I could not believe that my beautiful mother would never open her sweet eyes again. Her breath was gone, and her pale skin was shockingly cold. It was like she was in a cocoon, encapsulated in a white shroud. She would definitely not be wearing her fancy earrings or concert dresses again. No more melodies from Chopin, Debussy, or Beethoven would come from her frozen hands.

My grief was monumental. When I exited the precinct where she was lying before the burial ceremony, my knees gave way. All around, people stepped away from me as if I had some plague they wished to avoid. My grief was raw and brutal. It scared people. My auntie, Sarita, was the only soul brave enough to hold me before I went down full force.

In an attempt to shake this memory, and tired of waiting, I stood up to caress my mother's concert piano. The piano was still there, untouched for years. It seemed so sad, like a beloved pet that stays still and quiet after its master dies.

My mother was extremely talented. Gifted, actually. She was no ordinary person. Music was always playing in her head, and her hands were always moving, as if she was playing a song. Often, I would see her hands move up and down an imaginary piano's keys while she carried on a casual conversation. *Allí iban sus manitas, de arriba para abajo en el teclado imaginario.*

The music she created was beautiful. Not only did she interpret composers, she revived them! She touched people's hearts when she played, and had a brilliant career in front of her. But then she met my father. The end.

SAND FROM JERUSALEM

My parents met at the Jewish sports center. My father had an entourage of women who wanted to marry him. My mother had her admirers as well, many from among her music colleagues.

My father pursued her intensely. She was beautiful. He was handsome. He followed her around the grassy area of the sports center, close to the big Olympic-size pool. He followed her to the cafeteria…the waiting area…the gallery. They eventually went out a few times.

My mother's siblings were getting married, and she didn't want to be left behind. Her respected professor at the Conservatory of Music told her she would have to decide between being married, or following her musical career. My mother panicked. She wanted to have children, and eventually said yes to my father's advances. She made her choice, and there was no looking back.

They married soon after, and went to Acapulco for their honeymoon. The first few days they were there, a giant wave caught my mother and smashed against her right ear. It destroyed her eardrum. She had several operations, but none fully repaired the damage.

Instead of following a brilliant music career, she was left with a white dress she wrapped in tissue paper and put away in a box after the wedding, permanently damaged hearing, and a brusque husband. *Un vestido blanco envuelto en papel de china después de la boda, un oído dañado y un esposo áspero.*

Soon she got pregnant with her first child, and also found herself dealing with a sickly mother, not to mention her demanding and needy sister. Then, like a magician's spell, she got pregnant again and again. With three little children, she had no idea what to do with so many life circumstances at once. Everything left her feeling spaced out. She would forget things right and left, and had no sense of time—except when she played piano at home. In those moments, time made sense to her. Otherwise, she was chronically late for ev-

CHAPTER FOUR

erything and anything, unless it involved a rendezvous with Chopin, for instance. You could not be mad at her, though, because she played innocent, and always had some grace about her tardiness. But still, my father paid no attention to such details. He was very demanding, and expected a perfect wife.

Luckily, she did not stop playing piano altogether after she married my father. She continued to give piano lessons to kids in the neighborhood. She played at home, sometimes for us, but mostly for an invisible audience. The sounds from her piano were my lullabies. *Los sonidos de su piano fueron mis canciones de cuna.* Still, the big concert hall dream was over for her. After she died, I found clippings of news articles in which critics wrote fondly of her brilliance, and affectionately called her *La Novia de Mexico*, the Bride of Mexico.

After we grew up and left home, she attempted a grand return to her music. She was able to play with small orchestras, but her despair for all the years left behind without practicing took a toll. I believe this despair was one of the causes of her heart problems. If you inherit genius as a God-given gift and don't apply yourself to it, your heart begins to quietly deteriorate.

A few months before she died, my mother told me she was hearing the most beautiful music she'd ever heard beyond any composer she'd ever interpreted. She said that it was like hearing *celestial music.* Looking back now, it was a soothing thought. I could picture her playing music with the angels, *tocando su música con los ángeles.* Perhaps she'd picked up the harp in the spirit realm, since that would give her greater mobility in heaven.

Sadly, another component of my mother's heart condition was dealing with my father. The first heart attack she suffered came after a serious argument with him. He was furiously blaming her for encouraging my younger brother to pursue a music career after he graduated college in another field. My father may have been jealous of my brother's creativity, since he had little himself. He spent most of his free time at home reading *Reader's Digest*, or watching TV.

The day my parents argued about my brother's choices, my mother became so angry that she let all of her pent-up rage out, an overdose of some earnest emotion. She went downstairs to the kitchen, opened the cabinets, and slammed every single dish she could find. The kitchen floor was covered with shards of porcelain and glass. Finally, some action! She got *that one* out of her system.

Unfortunately, however, her private ceremony of breaking dishes came with lethal consequences. An hour later, she suffered a severe stomach pain. My father, concerned for once, finally called my mother's brother in the middle of the night. An eminent gastroenterologist, he gave her antacids! I guess there was never a talk between my father and uncle about how upset my mother had been. I suppose they didn't know that the pain was masking someting much more severe. She was misdiagnosed, and got to the hospital too late. She'd suffered a massive heart attack.

She didn't die then, but it was the beginning of the end for her. The heart attack left her with heart failure, and severe health limitations for the next six years until her death. She couldn't play piano for long, and playing with an orchestra was out of the question. And all of that just because my father had disapproved of my brother's musical career? What a waste!

I wasn't around when this occurred. I had just given birth to my daughter, Naomi, and had to leave my mother's recovery in my father's hands. He wasn't very trustworthy, but there was nothing I could do. After all, he was her husband. It was his responsibility.

I don't think he did a good job taking care of her. Whenever I tried to make suggestions about her care, he would snap at me.

"*Ya déjame de fastidiar,* enough! Stop bugging me!"

CHAPTER FOUR

Perhaps his lack of care skills, and his role in precipitating my mother's illness, were also some of the events that had upset Abraham so much as he listened to my father's restless spirit.

Weeks after my mother died, I received a postcard from her. I was in shock! The night she died, she collapsed at the threshold of her bedroom, after her return from a trip to Veracruz with my father. She suffered a massive stroke, and was in a coma at the hospital. Later, the doctors explained to me that the small capillaries in her brain ruptured, probably caused by so many years of taking the prescribed aspirin for her heart condition. But a dark thought occurred to me: Was it possible that my father pushed her, and perhaps she hit her head? I'm afraid I will never know the truth, and maybe I don't want to know the truth. *Nunca voy a saber la verdad.*

Did Abraham learn the truth?

My mother and I both loved Veracruz. I was 11 when we took a family trip there. We went on an overnight train—my first time traveling by train. Its rhythmic motion, the sound of the wheels against the rail, and the way that everything appeared and disappeared so rapidly in front of my eyes enthralled me. The train became a master of illusion for me.

My father told me that the Port of Veracruz was where Cristóbal Colón had first entered Mexico. It was located east of Mexico City, on the Gulf of Mexico. I looked at a map before we left and followed the train route all the way to the coast. I loved geography and knowing where we were going.

SAND FROM JERUSALEM

Veracruz seemed picturesque and delicious to me. I watched the people dance in the plazas while musicians played the *marimba* all around town. The *malecón* was the longest pier I'd ever seen. After a walk there, we went to the main *mercado* where my brothers bought keychains with scorpions frozen in acrylic, and coconuts with funny monkey faces wearing glasses. I searched for miniatures, crafty bags, and boxes made of tiny shells. My mother looked for fancy hats, while my father waited impatiently for us.

People dressed elegantly in white shirts and matching pants, or long skirts, as if they were ready for a wedding. The vegetation was luscious, and the city's narrow, cobblestone streets were beautiful.

Mostly, I loved the Café Parroquia, where people got together in large groups to celebrate life events—baptisms, weddings, business affairs, children's birthdays, first communions, you name it. There were also couples kissing—I closed my eyes!—and friends laughing.

The food was delicious, and the menu had many choices. It was hard to decide what to order, but since we ate there several times I was able to try their mole enchiladas, their specialty hot dogs with chili and avocado, the scrambled eggs with refried beans, and of course, their *huevos a la Mexicana*.

I was mostly intrigued with their coffee service. They had a shiny large Italian espresso machine that they'd been using for more than a century. It was as old as the café. There were endless tables, and our waiter told us that they could serve 400 people at any given time. An unusual chiming sound came from the tables. I looked around to see what was happening, and what was making the alluring noise.

Almost every table had a large glass on it. Our waiter told us that lots of people came to the Parroquia to order the famous *café lechero*, and that certain waiters were designated only to serve coffee. There were two different kinds of coffee servers: the ones who

CHAPTER FOUR

came around with big, old-fashioned tin pots of freshly brewed espresso, and those that carried pots of steaming milk. Our server told us how to call on one of the milkmen to bring milk.

I decided to try it, and ordered a *café lechero*. The first coffee server came to our table and poured three ounces of espresso into the big glass. Then I clinked my spoon on the side of the glass to get warm milk. The second server came and poured steaming milk into my glass from about two feet above it. The effect was a layer of delicate white foam. The scent of fresh coffee was outstanding. I almost clapped with excitement.

I couldn't believe the servers never spilled a drop of coffee or milk. It was like an art perfected by years of practice. The sound of hundreds of people clinking their glasses at different times to call these milkmen over is still etched in my mind. I came home from Veracruz with tons of stories to tell my friends. I even wanted to try the trick at home, calling on our help to bring me milk. Of course, it didn't work like at the Parroquia.

My mother and I had always wanted to go back to Veracruz together and have a *cafecito* at the Parroquia. But for whatever reason, we never did.

In the postcard, she wrote exactly that:

SAND FROM JERUSALEM

Dear little daughter,

I wish you were here, having a cafecito at the Parroquia with me. Veracruz is still very beautiful. It is also very tranquil like in the old times. Remember? It hasn't changed much. There are so many beautiful flowers all around. We also went to Boca del Río to have seafood and a delicious fish. I miss you very much and I hope to see you very soon.

Love from your mother who adores you.

Querida hijita,

Me gustaría mucho que estuvieras aquí, tomando un cafecito en la Parroquia conmigo. Veracruz todavía es muy hermoso. También es muy tranquilo, como en los viejos tiempos. Te acuerdas? No ha cambiado mucho. Hay flores muy bellas por todos lados. También fuimos a Boca del Río a comer mariscos y un pescado delicioso.
The extrano muchísimo y espero verte muy pronto.

Con mucho cariño de tu mamá que te adora.

These were her last words to me. The next thing I knew, I was talking to her fish, then putting Jerusalem sand atop her closed eyelids. I was not having a *cafecito* at the Parroquia with her. We were not enjoying seafood and fresh fish at Boca del Río. We were never going to travel together again.

    The instant I received her postcard, everything became clear to me. She was truly gone. And all I wanted to do was to swim far away with her fish, or be buried beside her.

CHAPTER FIVE

Día de los Muertos

"I felt a Funeral, in my Brain,

And Mourners to and fro

Kept treading—treading—till it seemed

that Sense was breaking through—"

–Emily Dickinson

The brash doorbell shook me abruptly from my daydreams. The pallbearers finally arrived. As the knot in my solar plexus grew tighter, my heart rate skyrocketed. Oh God, now what? Was I having another panic attack? *Ay Dios mío, y ahora qué? Me está dando otro ataque de pánico?*

Luz María ushered them to the coffin. I stood guarding it like a Mayan statue. The pallbearers scared me. They look like crows: long faces and noses, worn-out black suits and ties, pale skin, and dark circles sunk deep around their eyes. *Caras largas, narices largas, trajes negros largos y desgastados, corbatas negras.* These guys could scare you to death.

"Where did *they* come from?" I quietly asked Yosef.

"The temple sent them," he said, then shrugged his shoulders.

I said hello through tight teeth. They didn't say a word back. They were deadly serious. They moved swiftly around the living

CHAPTER FIVE

room, lifting the coffin like a feather and carrying it downstairs. Then they placed it in their dreadfully ramshackle vehicle.

I swear I could almost hear the sound of wings flapping around me as they did their routine. I was painfully aware that the neighbors—*escondidos tras las cortinas*—were watching this spooky crow-dance through the narrow opening behind their curtains.

I went upstairs to gather my purse and a jacket. Luz María was blowing the candles out. *Qué alivio!* What a relief! At least no more candle-chatting. This was the end of it. It was time to go.

My brothers and I drove in a separate car and followed the pallbearers' black vehicle. My father's coffin was inside of it like some kind of prey trophy. We headed to a new Jewish precinct in the *Colonia Roma*, close to where the old Sephardic synagogue was located on Monterrey Street. I had never been to this brand new Jewish funeral home.

The three of us were the first to arrive. We huddled together in a large room with cold marble floors, and rows of church-like wooden chairs that leaned against the walls. We were unusually quiet. It felt like we were at the inquisition waiting for a final verdict. One could hear a pin drop.

Slowly, friends and relatives began to arrive to pay their respects and offer condolences. Cousins and more cousins, aunts and uncles I hadn't seen in years. *Dios mío*…my God…how many people do we share blood with?

We also share the same teeth—*los mismos dientes*. You could see their perfect alignment across any number of broad smiles. This is partially due to braces, but mostly inherited from my paternal grandparents. I've thought hard about this peculiar family trait, and I believe most of us possess a robust upper maxillary. Strong mouth bones, you might say.

DÍA DE LOS MUERTOS

Besides big teeth, we looked alike in other ways too—mainly the shapes of our faces and eyes. It was common for strangers to confuse cousins for sisters or brothers.

There are two cousins with whom I share a strong resemblance, so much that we almost look like triplets. The main exception is that our coloring is a little different. Ariela has red curly hair with lots of freckles, Dora has dark curly hair with no freckles, and I have brown curly hair and freckles. Sometimes I even confuse myself with one of them when I catch a glimpse of myself in the mirror, or look at photographs.

Plenty of guys in the family look alike too, with intense Spaniard eyes, dark beards, and olive skin. Good-looking dudes, I should add.

After mingling with so many look-alike relatives, my brothers and I were summoned into a small chamber to say our last goodbyes to our father before the burial. Before I went into this little precinct, I first had a small talk with my knees: *aguántense chiquitas, porfavor, no se vayan a doblar*. I told them to hang in there, and not to fail me this time around. I was not in any position to faint. I didn't even want to think about the potential of crashing down onto the marble floor, especially since the chamber was so small there would be no room to land without serious harm.

When I entered the little room, I knew that my father was in the simple wooden box, but he didn't resemble my father at all. Was there a mistake? Had someone switched the body? I was confused and almost said something, but when I looked closer, there was no mistake: that was him, looking tremendously stern. Our Jewish tradition allows no makeover for the deceased. *Te vas sin maquillaje*—you go bare to meet and greet your creator. Because his dentures were not in his mouth, his cheeks were sunken in, and his face looked elongated. Where were his dentures? *Adónde está su dentadura postiza*? I tried to compose myself. This was definitely not the time to be distracted by silly things in my head. Still, I

CHAPTER FIVE

could not help it. I became preoccupied with his dentures. Where did they go? Suddenly, a dreadful thought hit me: they were in the garbage bag, and had been thrown out with his medicines and other junk from his bathroom. Was I in trouble? Was this a Jewish sin? I found out later that in the Jewish tradition, dentures had to be buried with the body! Thanks for sharing, rabbi!

The least I could have done was bury them in the backyard, but now it was too late. He was going without them. What would happen in my father's garden if I had buried his dentures? After my mother died, the skimpy, feeble peach tree that had barely produced anything grew four times its size, and gave a crop of peaches like never before. What would have grown from my father's false teeth?

I desperately tried to pull myself together, bring my mind back to the present, and stop my stupid ruminations. I focused on the simple white shroud that covered my father's body, along with his *talit*, a prayer shawl that framed his head and face.

Peaceful enough but very remote, he seemed somehow old and young at once. I couldn't quite make sense of it. Perhaps he was traveling through time, caught in the midst of becoming ageless and timeless. Is that what life is all about? Reaching a Jewish Nirvana inside a white shroud? The only thing I knew for real was that the old man who planted the seed for me to come into the world was no longer in his body.

Grappling with this concept of *nothing* took my breath away.

"If only my racing mind would stop for a second" I begged the Creator.

Not a chance.

One of the holy Jewish men who cleaned and draped the body called my name. I snapped out of it. It was my turn to put the sacred Jerusalem sand on my father's eyelids. I'd been dreading this moment. I swallowed hard and stepped forward, arming myself with all the courage I could summon. *Tragué saliva, y caminé adelante, armándome de todo el valor que podía atraer.*

Since I knew this customary ritual, I didn't freak out when the sand flowed from my fist, little by little, and stayed on the spot where it fell. I was actually surprised at how calm I was. In fact, I was almost catatonic.

"What is wrong with me?" I asked quietly. "*Qué te pasa?*" Maybe I was really out to lunch, so to say. *Ahora sí que estoy medio loca.* Or maybe it was simply a matter of being older and wiser. Was I totally transformed? That would be nice. Or perhaps I wasn't even there. That was it…I'd completely d-i-s-s-o-c-i-a-t-e-d!

Whatever was going on inside my head, it was fine with me. I was not freaking out. Instead, I was standing on my own. The sand ritual worked again: I'd entered the chamber and seen my father's body; I'd placed sand on his eyelids and the sand didn't move. His eyes stayed shut. He was definitely dead. There was no room for denial.

I exited the chamber in a daze. With no time to spare, we had to leave and drive to the Sephardic cemetery. Our relatives and friends followed us. The cemetery was right next to the Catholic cemetery in Mexico City, in an area called the *Desierto de los Leones*—the Desert of the Lions. I always thought it was amusing how we Jews ended up head-to-toe with the Catholics in a place that belonged to lions.

The only thing I objected about this back-to-back cemetery is that Jewish souls were not invited to participate in the *Día de los Muertos* celebration. We missed out on all the fun, and there was no redeeming reconciliation between the two religions at the end of the road. There was no final dance together, no food and music to be shared. Quite disappointing!

Was there any other tradition that invites the dead to come out and dance to the tunes of a mariachi orchestra, eat bountiful dish-

CHAPTER FIVE

es and special breads, and merrily intermingle with their living relatives once a year? I loved the sugar skulls with people's names written on their foreheads. It was so sweet to think of yourself as a little skeleton, sugarcoated with glitter and all.

The half-hour drive to the cemetery was eerie. Prior to leaving, it had seemed safer—so we thought—to drive with Yosef's father-in-law, Moishe. He was neutral territory for three little orphans of two rival families, the Sephardic and the Ashkenazi. Moishe was a kind soul, probably in his mid 80s. He could make the meanest *ceviche* in town. But he was the worst driver. True to form, he almost killed us several times on the way to the cemetery. I thought we were going to keep my father company for good.

Driving in Mexico City was already like surviving an electric shock to my system. Handing the wheel to a spaced-out, octogenarian driver was agonizing. I was certain we were about to dance with the dead, so I held my hands over my eyes.

By the time we arrived, I had no idea how we'd made it. I also had no idea how my brothers gathered their composure after that crazy drive to actually speak their final words to my father in front of the congregation. As for me, I was still pale and dumbstruck. I declined when the rabbi invited me to share some words.

Besides my topsy-turvy stomach, I actually had nothing to say to the people who'd gathered for the memorial—especially not after what I'd heard from Abraham the night before, or from Luz María this morning. This might have surprised people, especially since I was considered the family rebel. In their eyes, I had something to say *about everything*. But now I was tongue-tied, and a bitter taste had planted itself in my mouth. My skin was raw beneath my dark clothes, even if I appeared perfectly peaceful and serene on the outside. I'd mastered a half-beatific, innocent smile, like one you might see on the statues of virgins in Mexican churches.

DÍA DE LOS MUERTOS

I had learned a big lesson in the past: Grief was something I wasn't going to wear on my sleeve, because it was like a dark pit with no end and no beginning. I knew it ran as deeply as an inner river of murky waters, and it couldn't be explained. It disrupted my connection with the immediate world, and swallowed me up into a different time zone. No one would volunteer to go into these deep caverns with me. No one would dare to peek into this ultimate moment of truth. I knew I was alone with my grief, and that I alone had to come to terms with it.

Having been through my mother's funeral, I learned that in the face of grief, people usually want to feed you. But rarely could someone cry with me, or, seeing the despair in my eyes, offer compassion or understanding. Even more unusual was the idea that someone would simply just touch my shoulder to remind me that I was still among the living. No one held my hand quietly as I sank within, or helped me make the ultimate decision to remain alive.

Spared from exposing my heart at my father's funeral, I was relieved when Yosef and Jonatán were able to deliver their speeches with such presence of mind. They both had guts. They were sweet and eloquent, even elegant: two men talking about their father with some sense of pride. Way to go! I tipped my hat to them. *Chapeaux.* I thought for sure that they had better hearts than mine. Somehow, they were able to talk about his positive attributes and legacy. But they didn't know what Luz María had said to me, I reminded myself. Listening to them, my ears were open, but the taste in my mouth was still bitter. *Mi boca sabía amarga.* The words turned into powder on my tongue, and my silence was metallic. Did I have anything good to say about my father? I searched and searched, but the words were elusive. I found nothing. Even my last four words to him had been simple:

"See you later, alligator."

Now, my cynicism was killing me.

CHAPTER FIVE

Perhaps it was the result of the sleepless night I'd spent with Abraham, followed by Luz María's stories in the morning. Whatever the case, I was ashamed that my heart refused to contemplate the positive side of my father. It was hard as a rock.

"Come on, there has to be something!" I said to myself. I was so damn self-righteous! The little mantra in my head wouldn't stop: "He betrayed me. He betrayed us all. Worst of all, he betrayed my mother."

Questioning my father's integrity, I couldn't bring myself to lie in public. I couldn't say he was a wonderful human being. I wasn't sure of a positive legacy from him. I was *so* confused. Let other people talk, I thought. They may know something good about him. Perhaps they knew a nobler person than I did. Indeed, other people talked eloquently about him, but I wasn't paying much attention.

It was better to focus my eyes on the ground, or look up to the sky. I didn't want to make eye contact with anyone. I was afraid they'd see my inner storm. The voice in my head was saying, "Don't look at them. Don't speak. Don't even think about it, little one. Just look up! Find a way to distract yourself."

A giant hawk flew overhead, which was odd. I had seen many hawks in California, but never in Mexico City. It flew in circles directly above us! I stared for a long time. No one else seemed to notice its powerful presence. Was I the only one who could see how out of place this hawk was in the middle of the *Desierto de los Leones*?

Had my father's soul shape-shifted?

I tried to catch the attention of my little shaman-brother so he could check out the hawk, but he was distracted.

"Okay," I thought, "the hawk is all mine." I whispered a private prayer:

"Farewell, my dear *father-hawk*. I can see you. May your soul rest in peace. May your spirit reach the Higher Spirit. I'm sorry we had such a rocky relationship while you were alive. Amen."

DÍA DE LOS MUERTOS

This personal prayer felt better than the Jewish prayers the rabbi recited in Hebrew, half of which I couldn't comprehend. I felt at peace for a moment.

Then the time came to toss soil on my father's coffin, a final gesture that stirred even more emotion. One last *mitzva*, or good deed, towards my father.

When it was my turn, I tried to be brave and strong. I wanted to use the pail gracefully and effortlessly, like the guys, even if the soil was heavy. All my aunties and cousins were sniffling behind their dark glasses. Tears rolled down my cheeks—for my father, for myself, for all of us. I didn't wear dark glasses. I let my tears flow out in the open.

The memorial finally ended. It was time to leave. My parents were together again, underground. My bloodroots had gone back to the earth. The people who created me had vanished under my feet. For a moment, I ceased to exist. I felt vaporized, transparent, and empty. Everyone around me seemed sad; I was numbed. Yet, in a strange way, I felt liberated. *I* existed now, alone. The world at large was my new home. I didn't owe anything to anybody.

At the same time, I didn't feel comfortable with the pitying faces that reminded me of my new title: orphan. I wasn't ready to feel exposed and vulnerable like that, especially not with my relatives. I could feel myself growing a thicker skin on the spot. We were the first among all of the cousins to lose both parents. No one really knew how to deal with us.

As we were leaving, an old friend, a tall handsome man with arms wide open, stepped toward me.

"Thank you for coming, Jorge," I said.

"Don't even mention it. I'm here for you guys. *Ya lo sabes.* You know…"

"You have *no* idea what it means to me that you are here."

He must have felt the tremor in my bones, because he held me

CHAPTER FIVE

for the longest time. He silently understood. With his beautiful presence and embrace, he had the power to dissipate the crowd. I quietly thanked him for surrounding me with his veil of protection. When our hug ended, I wanted to leave the cemetery as quickly as possible.

"*Ya vámonos a la casa, hermanitos*," I said to my brothers. "Let's go home."

Before leaving, we needed to wash our hands. This was part of the ritual. There were a few rows of sinks at the entrance of the cemetery. I dutifully washed my hands as I listened to the rabbi.

"After you wash your hands, you cannot come back inside," he said. "For once you leave the cemetery, you must leave for good, at least for today. You know, this custom has existed since the Middle Ages, when people washed their hands to avoid dark or evil spirits that might bring harm to the living. We want to separate ourselves from the spiritual impurity we attribute to death."

"Weird," I thought. I didn't know Judaism had such superstition attached to death. Nevertheless, I washed my hands again just in case my father's ghost was still angry and wanted to follow me back home.

Drained of my last drop of energy, we drove back to our father's house. Many people followed to start the shiva. There was a *fiesta* atmosphere when people started to arrive with provisions. Someone brought traditional Turkish anise liquor and *borrecas,* a traditional Sephardic pastry filled with pecan paste, mixed with sugar and cinnamon, and glazed with a honey-lemon sauce. Most of the food trays went directly to the care of Luz María in the kitchen.

The old rabbi from our Sephardic community called us to begin the shiva. This same ageless rabbi had presided over my mar-

DÍA DE LOS MUERTOS

riage…and my divorce. Now he'd buried both of my parents. He hadn't aged in 20 years. Was he some sort of Jewish Dorian Gray?

Nothing ever changed for me in Mexico City. It was like being trapped in a still-life painting: the same house, food, scents, friends…even the same rabbi. Like a line from an old poem of Leon Felipe, "*que pena que sea todo siempre así, de la misma manera.* What a shame that everything is always the same, in the same way."

The rabbi rallied us all to the living room. With a pair of scissors in hand, he looked at us.

"The closest relatives to *el señor* Salomón—his children and his siblings—need to tear a little corner of your clothes on your left side, so your heart can be exposed. That symbolizes how much your heart is torn when you lose a parent, a child, or a sibling."

The rabbi passed the scissors around, and we followed his instructions. I was wearing a worn-out shirt my cousin, Ariela, had given me. I was glad I didn't have to tear my fancy clothes. Then he handed each of us a small glass of Turkish anise, mixed with water and ice. He told us a short story about drinking as he poured the anise.

"Do you know that if you drink one glass of wine, you may turn into a lamb? Two glasses of wine, you could turn into a monkey. Three glasses, you could turn into a lion. But four glasses… you could turn into a pig!"

Everyone laughed a little. I took a little sip of the anise to make sure I didn't turn into any of the rabbi's animals and lose my cool. He then gave us each a hard-boiled egg, and told us to eat it on the spot. "*Cómanse su huevo ahora.* In our Jewish tradition, eggs symbolize eternal life, or the cyclical nature of life."

"Rabbi?" I asked. "If we're eating eggs, and we believe in the cyclical nature of life, then why did we have to wash our hands at the cemetery because of death's impurity?"

CHAPTER FIVE

The rabbi ignored my question, which ticked me off. I didn't like these contradictions. They didn't make sense. To him, I was probably meddling with Kabbalistic ideas, which meant I was entering a *forbidden zone* where questions were concerned.

He focused his attention on the room again, and announced that our ritual was complete. We were free to go and mingle with our relatives and friends. I started to walk aimlessly around my parents' living room when the rabbi pulled me aside. I thought he was going to answer my question privately. Instead, he surprised me with a very different topic of conversation.

"*Ya sabes lo que pasó? Sabes lo que hizo tu ex?*" he asked in his heavy *Ladino*—Judeo-Spanish—accent.

"No," I answered somewhat sharply. "I have no idea what my ex did."

"*Tu ex dejó a su mujer y a sus hijos, y se fué de la casa así nada más.*"

"Really?" I said, pretending to sound surprised. "Ari walked away from his wife and children, just like that?"

In truth, I wasn't surprised at all.

"*Sí,*" the rabbi said with gravity.

"I am really sorry for them," I said.

"*Si. Qué pena no?*" he asked.

"Yes, it *is* a shame."

What I didn't say to the rabbi, and what I was feeling inside, was more like, "I knew it. I knew it. I knew it!" I had prophesied this possibility 20 years earlier. I knew that if my ex and I had stayed together, he would have eventually walked out of my life, and would have abandoned our children—had we had any. That is what a narcissist would do! And that is exactly why I left him. And what I *really* wanted to say to the rabbi was, "Aren't you glad *now* that we divorced?" After all, this was the same rabbi who gave

DÍA DE LOS MUERTOS

me so much grief over my divorce. Now here he was, complaining about my ex husband's behavior.

Memories of the *get*—the divorce performed in the Jewish tradition—flooded my mind. It had been torturous. Before I decided on the divorce, the rabbi called us to meet with him in his office. Ari and I arrived separately, and sat down in the rabbi's office after not having seen each other for a long time.

"Children," the rabbi began. "You both come from good families. I know your parents and grandparents very well. They are good people. You should reconsider this grave decision you are about to make."

My reply was blunt.

"With all due respect, even if our parents and grandparents *are* good people, I have been thinking about this for many years. I won't reconsider."

Ari was silent. He didn't even try to say a word. Clearly, he and I were on the same page. Perhaps he was thinking how wonderful it would be to be free to pursue other women—not that he'd stopped pursuing them during our marriage! I was ashamed to expose him to the rabbi's puritanical view of the world.

Then the rabbi said something that stunned me.

"Well, if that's really your decision, and you won't reconsider, then you need to return the wedding ring that doesn't belong to you anymore. You can keep the one Ari gave you, but you'll have to give back the one that his mother gave you as a token of her appreciation."

It was interesting that I was not asked to return the cheap one that Ari gave me. I kept it as a trinket, and gave back the ex-mother-in-law ring, passing it into the rabbi's hand, who then passed it to my soon-to-be-*thank-God*-ex-husband. I could have just given it to Ari, but I guess the rabbi needed us to follow his protocol.

CHAPTER FIVE

Once liberated from the family heirloom, I was ready to sign any document, then leave…happily ever after. Little did I know I still needed to face the divorce inquisition.

Ari and I were escorted to a small room where, in the heat of the day, a group of religious men came in and out to question us. Were we *sure* we wanted a divorce? Yes, yes, and yes again. And every time we uttered the magic word, they would scribble painfully slow on what looked like papyrus, one letter at a time, in ancient Hebrew script.

I wanted to scream out loud.

"Get me out of here," I thought. "*Sácame de aquí*. I just want a divorce, that's it!"

By the second hour of this tedious performance, I could no longer think straight.

I had to continue to repeat that, yes, I wanted this divorce. And every time, I had to move through guilt with renewed efforts. I felt humiliated. Was I really such a *bad* Jewish girl?

I kept reminding myself that this ritual was designed to choke me with shame. I had to endure it, but I felt so alone.

The questioning and scribbling finally stopped. But then came the prohibitions: *I* was not allowed to be under the same roof with a *Kohen*, apparently the purest of the Jewish tribe's members. I was now considered an *impure* woman. Go figure! Ari, however, was allowed to hang out with whomever he wanted. I was fuming.

Okay, whatever, no more *Kohens* for me. I agreed wholeheartedly. I wanted it to be over.

"Can I sign now?" I asked the rabbi.

"Not quite yet," he said.

He handed me the meticulously written document, and instructed me to give it to my soon-to-be-*ex*-husband. Then *he* had to give it back to the rabbi.

DÍA DE LOS MUERTOS

When the rabbi received the document back, he sliced it into pieces with a sharp object. My mouth dropped. What the hell? Why did he do *that*? All this time wallowing in guilt and remorse was for nothing? I was furious.

He told me to stand face to face with Ari in the middle of the room. The rabbi and the religious committee watched as we turned our backs on each other and walked in different directions. Finally! The first reasonable part of this whole deal. *Then* we were allowed to leave.

I bolted out of the temple as fast as I could. No heirloom ring—big deal! I was exhausted, humiliated, hungry, and angry. Ari tried to talk to me outside the temple. I turned around and left without another word. I drove home, free at last.

How had I stayed married to Ari for seven biblical years? How did I fall into this trap in the first place? When I was 18 years old, I became naively convinced I was predestined to marry him. Perhaps I was caught up in some romantic *immigrant fantasy* about marriage. When I met my husband-to-be, and when our respective Sephardic grandmothers heard the news, they were delighted. They had been acquaintances in Europe before coming to Mexico City. Once established in Mexico, they both married and had children. When their children became adults, my father and Ari's mother met at the Jewish sports center and dated for a while. Apparently, there had been some considerations for them to get married, but it never happened. Imagine if Ari and I had been siblings! I dreaded the idea.

One generation later, he and I met on Yom Kippur at the temple. Soon we began dating. After a couple of years, we announced our engagement. That's when I learned about my father and his mother, because our grandmothers proclaimed with pride, "*Si no son los hijos, serán los nietos.* If it's not the children, it will be the grandchildren."

CHAPTER FIVE

I didn't think anything about it at the time, but after the religious divorce, I remembered their prophecy. I felt trapped in a serendipitous matchmaking affair I hadn't signed up for. Had my marriage been a trick of Sephardic destiny, or some Kabbalistic joke?

What if my father actually had married Ari's mother? *Holy guacamole!* Well, it might not have been such a bad outcome. She was a beautiful woman, filled with ambition that knew no boundaries. My father, on the other hand, was more passive, and didn't have her level of ambition. He could have used her business shrewdness. And if my own mother hadn't married him, she could have married a man who would have been the love of her life—perhaps a talented Mexican violinist or cello player. But then, what if the guy hadn't been Jewish? My mother would have been consumed by tremendous guilt. This wouldn't have been pretty, especially if his relatives were the type that would insinuate ignorant things, like my mother belonged to the people who'd killed Jesus Christ. I couldn't bear the idea of my mother having to deal with such accusations from in-laws. She and her love would have had to elope in France, find work with an orchestra, and live happily ever after across the ocean. They probably wouldn't have had babies.

"Where would this leave me?" I muttered out loud.

What a mess. Everything felt like a terrible mistake. Was I a mistake? Was my wedding to Ari a mistake? At 19, I didn't know any better.

During our wedding ceremony, I literally choked on the first sip of blessed wine as we stood under the *chuppah*, the canopy that covered the ceremony. Thank God, I was facing the sacred scriptures when it happened, and had my back to the congregation. My face purpled, and I was about to faint. But no one noticed, not even Ari, who was standing by my side. He was always in his own world. I had to get a grip on myself, and coughed as modestly as I could. This was definitely the beginning of my choked-up marriage.

DÍA DE LOS MUERTOS

Lost in the memories of my marriage and divorce spun from the rabbi's little chat, I realized I was hungry. I reached out for one of the borrecas. It tasted exactly the same as I remembered from my childhood, when my grandma Malka used to make them. She was la reina de las borrecas, the queen of the borrecas. No one had ever perfected her recipe. So, who had made these that tasted so much like hers?

In my 20s, I was determined to make them just like her. One idling day I called and asked her to teach me.

"*Oye abue, quiero hacer las borrecas como tú,*" I said to her.

"*Si claro, ven a mi casa y aquí las hacemos.*"

Yes! I was happy. She said she was going to help me to make the *borrecas* just like hers, and invited me to come to her home.

I arrived in the early afternoon. Her home was in one of the old buildings in the Colonia Condesa, across from the park. It was clean and cozy, with well-kept old furniture and family photos all around. The kitchen was small, but there was room for the two of us.

She had her old bowls and all the ingredients on the kitchen counter ready for our culinary rendezvous.

I followed her every move, watching carefully as she measured the ingredients by sight—she didn't use measuring cups. At some decisive moments during our baking, she would turn away, covering the preparations with her body. I was suspicious that she was adding a hidden *puñito*—a little pinch of a secret ingredient.

The *borrecas* turned out great that day. She sent me home with a good batch of them, which was exhilarating. Soon after, I tried to make them myself, but they didn't turn out like hers. That's when I thought she hadn't quite given me the whole recipe. Something was missing in my *borrecas*, and I never got them right. Besides

CHAPTER FIVE

covering the stove and kitchen counter with her large body, she could also pin you against the wall if she wanted. I once heard my father say she did that to him when he was little.

Luckily for me, Grandma hadn't pinned me against the wall. I was petite, and might have suffocated. I think she actually liked me. She was always sweet to me when I was little, and spent hours at her home playing with *juguetitos*, little toys she kept in a large canvas bag.

The first time I ever went to the movies was with her. I couldn't have been older than five when we drove to Mexico City's old Tacubaya neigborhood, and its big movie theater. I was excited, and felt special. However, when the movie started, I got really frightened. All I saw was darkness, and across the giant screen in front of me appeared scary looking dinosaurs. Imagine an old, black-and-white version *of Jurassic Park*. I didn't understand what was happening. Were these creatures going to eat me up? I kept my eyes closed for most of the movie, and was glad when it was over. After this *lovely* experience, I refused to go to the movies with my grandma ever again.

I also spent a lot of time with my grandpa, Isaac. He used to make strong Turkish coffee every morning and afternoon. He would serve it in a tiny cup, and would dip his pinky in the coffee so I could taste it. When I was a bit older, he would let me sip directly from the cup. Eventually I graduated, and got my very own small cup of Turkish coffee.

He liked to give us children small little sugarcoated pine nuts if we could successfully repeat his impossible tongue twisters. We spent hours trying to repeat them.

"*A ver, dí,*" he would say, and ask us to repeat after him. "*El volcán de parangaricutirimicuaro está muy desparangaricutirimicuarizado, el que me lo desparangaricutirimizare, será un gran desparangaricutirimicuarizador.*"

Sometimes we could pull it off. Most of the time, his hand would close quickly as we reached for the candy, and he'd laugh whole-heartedly at our disappointment. He kind of tortured us.

He was a funny guy though, and loved jokes. But he was scary too, especially when he yelled. And he yelled a lot, sometimes at my grandma, but mostly at his driver, Armando.

"*Armandoooooooooooo, Armandoooooooooooo, ven, ya es hora de irnos!*"

He would yell from the window of his apartment at the top of his lungs to tell poor Armando that it was time for us to leave. Armando was a mechanic who worked at a repair shop around the corner from my grandparents' home. At my grandpa's call, he would have to drop everything and come get us.

Grandpa would get me in the back seat, and off we'd go to who knows where. The car smelled strongly of tobacco and grease from Armando's overalls. And Armando, with his hair stiff with cream, drove like a madman. I tossed from side to side across the plastic-covered seats, like a raggedy doll, as he drove around Mexico City. My grandpa yelled at him the whole way. Soon, he and Armando would settle into a friendly conversation. They would even start laughing and chatting like old friends, or turn on the radio and sing along to romantic songs until their favorite show, *Tres Patines*, started. It was a radio comedy from Cuba about a thief who always got caught and had to go before the judge. We all loved it.

How could the taste of a *borreca* conjure up so many memories? I smiled as they flooded back to me. They provided a reprieve from the shiva, and helped me find refuge among the crowd.

I had another glass of the Turkish liquor and started to feel a bit like a camel, constantly ruminating mementos from my past.

CHAPTER FIVE

The liquor was sweet and warm. My brain began to feel mushy. The Sephardic part of me was deeply enjoying the combination of anise and *borrecas*. Could I keep *just this part* of my heritage?

At sundown, the rabbi called us to gather for evening prayers. The men stood around the large dining room table. The women stayed in the living room, scattered here and there. I felt a moment of trepidation. Years before, when we prayed during my mother's shiva, I was hit with a Jewish prohibition. This same rabbi did not allow *me* to sit at the table with my brothers, father, and the rest of the men. He explained that women were not *allowed* to sit by the men, or to share in the after-prayer discussions. But this was my mother's dining room table! I wasn't going to be humiliated and excluded because I was a *woman*. And, I liked breaking rules. So I didn't budge. I sat between my brothers and stared at the rabbi and all the holy men with a fierce look that said *atrévete a moverme:* I dare you to move me. None of them were up for the challenge. Even the rabbi relented.

That was when I learned to recite the Kaddish, the Jewish prayer for the dead, in Aramaic. The Kaddish sanctifies the name of God in the face of death. The words were difficult to pronounce, but I did my best.

When it was time to recite my father's prayers, I was no longer interested in joining the men at the table. I made my point years ago. Besides, there were too many things swarming in my head. I wanted to stay anonymous, and sat with the women. I would recite the Kaddish for my father on my own. The night before, he'd asked me to do so through Abraham. A promise is a promise, especially if it would help him rest in peace.

DÍA DE LOS MUERTOS

After the prayers, a few people left, and more people arrived. It had been a long day already, and I was sleepless and exhausted. I sat on the low sofa and tried to catch my breath. That's when a woman named Dina, who I was just meeting for the first time, pulled a chair close to me. I assumed she wanted to offer her condolences. She mentioned that she was married to one of my father's cousins. She also happened to be Abraham's cousin!

"*Hola, soy Dina*," she whispered. "*Tú no me conoces pero yo a tí sí. Soy la prima de Abraham y estoy casada con el primo de tu papá.*"

"Yes, you are right. We haven't met. How is it that you know me?"

"I am a *psychic*," she said, emphasizing the word. "Dead people come to me when they are in distress, or they need something. Your father has urgently asked me to come here to see you and your brothers. He needs to explain something very important to you."

I stared into Dina's eyes. My heart began to thump. Not again!

"Are you for real, or am I having a hallucination?" I asked. "If this conversation is a continuation of last night's disclosures from your cousin, Abraham, then I don't think I can sit through it." I excused myself and went into the kitchen to get a drink.

Maybe the liquor was having a funny effect on me. Maybe I was just imagining. Anything was possible.

When I returned to the sofa, Dina was waiting. She asked me to sit next to her. As if in a deep trance, I followed her instructions, dragging my feet the whole way.

"*Tu papá está aquí*," she whispered. "*No se ha ido de su casa y la está pasando muy mal. No se puede ir y necesita tu ayuda.*"

"So, what can I do for him?" The words rumbled inside my spirit like a bird that refused to take flight. I was trying to comprehend what she was saying: my father was here; he'd never left the house; he was having a terrible time moving on. On top of

CHAPTER FIVE

that, Dina said he needed *my* help. I took a peek around. Now I was actually trying to *see* him. But it was to no avail. I was no psychic.

Just the first night of the shiva, and I was already falling apart. Dina could tell I was exhausted.

"*No te preocupes,*" she said. "*Vuelvo mañana y entonces hablamos.*"

"Yes," I agreed. "It's best if we talk tomorrow. I need some rest."

CHAPTER SIX

Defying Gravity

*"Without music, life would be a mistake…
I would only believe in a God who knew how to dance."*

–Friedrich Nietzsche

Thankfully, I got some sleep that night, and was a bit more composed on the second day of the shiva. Getting ready to go to the temple for the morning prayers, I remembered my conversation with Dina. Her frankness felt like a breath of fresh air compared to the rest of my relatives' small talk inclinations, and I appreciated it.

I shivered at a memory from my mother's shiva, when a group of cousins gathered around another older cousin who was sharing pictures of her 50th birthday. It was as if my parents' home was suddenly the ideal scenario for her to show off. The cousins laughed and reminisced, and didn't even have the presence of mind to ask me how I was feeling, having just lost my mother. They only asked about my daughter, or my husband, or the weather in San Francisco.

"*Cómo está tu hijita?*" they chirped. "*Y cómo está tu marido? Oye, que tal está el clima en San Francisco?* How is your daughter… and your husband? How is the weather in San Francisco?"

"She is doing well," I said. "She is happy in school and…."

"*Ay qué bueno…*"

CHAPTER SIX

"Good..."

Cutting me off, they continued with their side conversations. My family definitely had a Ph.D. in pseudo-communication, and an aversion to being authentic. Or maybe they simply weren't interested. Still, they were great at hosting big luscious *fiestas* for any occasion.

When Dina had asked how I was holding up, I considered telling her the truth about what was unsettling my heart. I could have said I was going through a sickening turmoil after the night with Abraham, or that I didn't believe that *los muertos hablan*—the dead can speak. Or, I could have told her what I'd learned about my father from Luz María. But if she was truly psychic, maybe she already knew. Why bother? I could have said that, with both of my parents now dead, I was having this weird sensation of something stuck in my throat about to choke me, while my stomach felt topsy-turvy—a feeling that was definitely *not* the effects of alcohol.

I had no words that could reflect even a tiny bit of what was happening to me. I could sense my childhood roots vanishing from under my feet. The night before, my impulse was to tell Dina that I was tired of *them*—my relatives. Tired of death. Tired of explaining. Tired of being me...of missing my mother...and *especially* tired of talking to my dead father. I wanted to say *"paren el tren que me quiero bajar*, stop this train, I want to get off!" But I wasn't going to take a chance at being vulnerable with a distant relative I'd never met before.

After burying my father, I noticed that my own mortality had come smashing up against me, creating deeper lines in my face. I cheated and peeked behind the mirror's covering, and saw dark bags under my eyes, deeper wrinkles around my mouth. I was pale as a *calaca*, a skeleton. Without doubt, my age was beginning to show. I felt the weight of 44 years on earth, and the distance I was beginning to create between the sea of humanity and myself.

DEFYING GRAVITY

I didn't know where I belonged. Was this what happens to people when they lose both parents?

I have lived in many countries: Israel, China, Italy, and the United States. With my parents dead, Mexico suddenly felt remote and unknown. Once the house was emptied and sold, nothing would hold me to this place. I would be like a kite floating in thin air, at the mercy of strong winds. This was quite a contrast to the days when I would wake up feeling *fresca como lechuga*, fresh like lettuce: young, alive, and ready for life. My energy was on top of the world back then. I felt unstoppable.

When I was six years old, I loved wearing my ballerina shoes and pink tutu, and leaping into thin air! Could I defeat death the same way that I'd once defeated gravity?

My mother understood my desire to fly high. She'd graduated from the National Conservatory of Music, and it was a stroke of motherly genius for her to take me to the National Conservatory of Dance to pursue my passion for dancing.

Every day after school, she took me to dance classes that lasted a couple of hours. She bought me black leotards, pink tights, pink ballerina shoes, flamenco shoes, and long skirts. At the completion of our year training at the Dance Conservatory, we had a big show at a concert hall, El Palacio de Bellas Artes. I didn't care that this renowned performance hall, with all of its white marble, had been sinking for years. I would dance underground if I had to! I had to show the audiences how I could defy gravity.

During those years, I wore many stunning costumes of the finest fabrics. A little old lady who worked in the fine arts building sewed and embroidered them. Surrounded by a troop of workers, she was like a Mother Teresa seamstress of Bellas Artes—she

CHAPTER SIX

seemed as ancient as the marble building itself. Yet her hands were capable of creating astonishing theatrical costumes for us.

The first ballet costume she created for me was an exquisite yellow velvet tutu, with darker yellow sequins all over it. I felt as if I were *La Bella Durmiente o Cenicienta*—the Sleeping Beauty or Cinderella. She also made me a blazing red flamenco polka dot dress with shiny black sequins. The zipper on the side of the dress was so fancy I remember thinking of it as *sexy*—at least a child's view of what sexy was.

The crowded costume room smelled heavily of musk. After I was fitted for my dresses, I was ready to leave. Once the little old lady dismissed me, my mother took me to the stores downtown, in close proximity to the Palacio de Bellas Artes. We had to find some other items for the performances.

We walked down the colorful streets, and went in and out of many stores. Each shop was filled with traditional costumes from every region of Mexico. The colorful shawls, or *rebozos*, displayed outside the shops hung suspended like rainbows.

We finally found the store that carried my size costumes for the Spanish and folk dances that were part of the program. We also found *castañuelas*, castanets, a *peineta*, a curved comb, paper flowers for my braids, *un abanico*, a fan, and *collares de fantasía*, colorful necklaces made with glass beads. I was all set. It was better than Hanukkah! To top it off, once we finished our errands, we went to the Alameda Central, the park adjacent to the concert hall.

I was so excited as my eyes darted here and there. There were dozens of vendors. I liked the ballooners—the *globeros*. They were so lost in the midst of their multicolored balloons, I could only see their feet. Other merchants sold wands for making giant soap bubbles, hand-carved wooden toys, or crispy grilled corn on the cob covered in sour cream, *cotija* cheese, lime juice and chili powder. Fruit vendors sold papaya, *pepinos*, cucumbers or *jícamas* on sticks, or chunks of coconut pieces bathed with *chile y limón*. The scents of food, and the sounds of vendors whistling and bellowing out to customers charmed me. Children played and ran around, while young couples kissed in the grass. Everything that was happening was new in my life's short repertoire.

My mom and I sat on a green iron bench and enjoyed our ice cream cones. She had mango sorbet, while I ate *chicozapote*, my favorite. It was hard to choose that day—all the flavors seemed whimsical to me. I was dying to try them all: *mamey, guanábana, limón o sandía*. My mother said I could only have one, even though the ice cream man let me try a few.

We used to celebrate our birthdays at the Parque de Chapultepec, but that was an enormous park to me, more like a forest. Plus, we had to drive through miles and miles of extensive land to get to our birthday party spot. Sometimes we got lost. In contrast, the Alameda Central was small, quaint, and beautiful. I wanted to have my birthday with all the other kids and the vendors at the Alameda, but my family wouldn't change the tradition.

At the Alameda, I felt like an outsider looking into a treasure store. I was a fair-skinned Jewish girl with freckles, and long, wavy, reddish hair. I looked quite different than the darker-skinned children around me. Shy and quiet, my alter ego loved how the Alameda Central's sounds and multicolored palette enthralled my senses.

It was there that my theatricality was born.

I was lucky as a child to be involved in activities that broke away from our little Jewish community. It gave me a chance to visit and mingle with the *goy*, or gentiles, alongside my mother. I felt an exhilarating freedom being able to roam around and get lost in

CHAPTER SIX

another world, to feel a momentary streak of independence away from the *Jewish ghetto* where I grew up. I loved the park! It taught me how Mexican traditions mingled with the soul of the country. It was also where my love for art began.

I didn't like the word *goy* though. I thought it was insulting. It separated *us* from the *others*. Why couldn't we all dance together at the cemetery, or make soap bubbles with the other children at the Alameda Central? Why did we have to be different, and stuck in an *us, not them* way of thinking?

Throughout my years at the Dance Conservatory, I was the only Jewish kid in my classes. I learned to embrace a double life: one at the Jewish school, and another at the dance hall. With my dance classmates, I became addicted to the big theater, and the scenes behind the scenes: the rush, hush, and whispering, not to mention the mysterious men who pulled the ropes up and down, changed the stage, and managed the sound like they were working the control panel of a spaceship.

Everything felt exhilarating, from the haste of changing costumes and getting ready for dances, to our teacher behind the curtain giving us final instructions and guiding us to our positions. And I loved the amazing light effects on our dresses, and the accelerated heartbeat of anticipation before every number.

There was a moment suspended in time right before the elaborate, stained glass curtain, with its depiction of Mexican volcanoes—*Popocatépetl* (the Smoking Mountain) and *Ixztlaxíhuatl* (Sleepy Woman) lifted. I remember smiling nervously, and actually feeling the prickly dark void beyond the curtain—the quiet breathing of the audience, each pair of eyes shining like a cat's.

When the music started, my body would tremble. Then, after a few seconds, the music moved me almost magically, and infused me with a strange power. I was ready to show the audience how I had learned to defy gravity with a *grand jetté*!

DEFYING GRAVITY

Touched by a force larger than myself, I danced, jumped, and twirled with my classmates. It was like being suspended in a different dimension. And then, when we finished our dance, the thunderous applause sent my blood skyrocketing inside my yellow tutu.

Still drunk with the new experience, we exited the stage after the curtain came down. My mother was waiting behind the stage curtains to take me to our changing room, help me out of my tutu, and into my flamenco dress. She pinned a red clover and a curb comb on my bun, transforming me from a delicate ballerina into a fierce flamenco dancer. I was still shaking with excitement, and fearful that I wouldn't have enough time to dress for the next act. But my mother reassured me.

"Napoleón Bonaparte used to say, *vístanme despacio que tengo prisa*," she said. "Dress me slowly, because I am in a rush." I had no idea who Napoleón Bonaparte was, and could barely comprehend my mother's words. But somehow, they calmed me down. I could see that my mother, for a change, was on top of things.

After the show, our teacher, Miss Bertita, congratulated us. She was beaming with pride, which was not always the case during our lessons. At times, she was strict. She wanted us to do well, but pushed us too hard. If we complained or made mistakes, she would get stern. If someone said they couldn't jump higher, or couldn't remember the steps, Miss Bertita would say something like, "*Si piensas que sí puedes, entonces sí puedes. Querer es poder.*"

I always remembered her words: "If you think you can do it, then you can! When there is a will, there is a way."

Sometimes I thought I could perform a complicated dance step, but the reality proved differently. I didn't care, because Miss Bertita's words stuck with me. At least I tried my best. I loved to dance, and she was on my side. If I thought I could do anything, then that was good enough for me.

CHAPTER SIX

Yosef and Jonatán came down for coffee and a quick bite for breakfast. I was still daydreaming about Miss Bertita, my yellow tutu, and Bellas Artes. It was almost time to leave for morning prayers at the temple.

I was quiet as we drove. I couldn't tell them what was happening to me, or explain the memories and emotions that were flooding my brain.

When we arrived at the synagogue, I was directed to the back of the precinct where the women sat. I didn't know anybody back there, and didn't like being separated from my brothers. I felt distant, so profoundly lost in my thoughts that I didn't even hear the prayers.

As tears rolled down my eyes, I longed for my own temple—my ability to be touched by God through dancing. Instead, I simply sat and stood according to the congregation's cues like a marionette on strings.

Dancing was a much better sanctuary for me. It possessed a mystical and ethereal quality where I communicated with Spirit directly and without intermediaries. I was convinced that God spoke directly to me when I danced—I imagined doing the *Paso Doble* with Him. I laughed, thinking it might sound like blasphemy, but it truly was the way dance worked for me. Let others go to the temple to pray! I just had to dance, and God would smile at me. In fact, the god of Baryshnikov and Nureyev was closer to me than the god of Abraham and Moses.

My best ideas came through as a form of inspiration when I danced. I literally launched out of my body, and into some greater creative realm. Weightless, my heart was alive with different beats. The pirouettes and *grand jettés* liberated me from the physical world. Butterflies fluttered through my belly as my arms became

DEFYING GRAVITY

delicate wings. Music and dance were my best companions, and we existed in perfect unison. Suspended in thin air, I was free.

Dancing taught me a secret: the capacity to understand time, rhythm, space and gravity. So, if I could do this through dance, why couldn't I understand death as well? Wouldn't the same principle apply? Nothing lasts—not my parents, or my ability to dance. Like the girl in the red slippers story—she dances until she dies of exhaustion—I was also worn out. I could no longer dance. Multiple injuries, hip and knee problems, and neck issues were too painful, and challenging to heal. The only thing left for me was to rendezvous with music.

So, whenever I heard music, my eyes projected fantastic choreographies onto an imaginary screen. Perhaps, after all, I'd become like my mother, who moved her hands up and down her imaginary piano keyboard to the sound of music only she could hear.

But my mother was dead. Her piano was mute. My tutus and costumes ended up in an old suitcase. The creative spell was broken. My body aged without my permission. And, since I no longer possessed the capacity to defy gravity, how could I defy death?

I was living in a linear world. One day, I would become ill and die like everybody else. The thought was like a hammer in my ear. I didn't like it! And now, with my parents gone, death was more imminent than ever. Was I next in line? The only consolation was the idea that perhaps when I die, I would be able to dance again. I would pirouette my way around the heavens, my body light and painless.

I was so lost in my head, I didn't realize the service had ended. My brothers came to get me, and saved me from my ruminations. Another whole day of sitting, eating, carrying on empty conversations, and forcing a smile loomed ahead.

CHAPTER SIX

I was bored to death as things moved along uneventfully until late afternoon. That's when Dina showed up again. She came to sit by my side.

"*Tu papá me llamó otra vez y quiere hablar especialmente contigo,*" she said.

"Really? He called you again? And he wants to talk *especially* to me? But I already talked to him with Abraham."

She could hear the complaining in my voice.

"*Sí, ya sé pero está muy nervioso,*" she explained. "*El piensa que tú lo puedes entender y lo puedes ayudar.*"

"But how come he thinks only I can understand and help him?" I asked. "How come he doesn't call my brothers? After all, he owes more apologies to them than to me."

"*Piensa que tú entiendes cuestiones espirituales.*"

"The fact that I am open to spiritual things doesn't mean that I want or need to talk to him. I only talk to God when I'm dancing. Tell him that."

"*Estás siendo un poco testaruda, sabes?*"

"Yes, I know I'm being stubborn. I just don't want to talk to him. Why didn't he talk to me when he was alive? I asked your cousin the same question. He didn't answer me. Can *you* answer me?"

"*Cuando estaba vivo, tu papá estaba en un estado emocional de contracción profunda. Solamente ahora se puede dar cuenta claramente de sus errores terrenales.*"

"Ay Dina, I just don't get it." I threw up my hands. "Why was he in such a contracted state while he was alive, and only now can see his earthly mistakes clearly? What the hell happened to him? Ask him that! Why was he so indifferent to his own children?"

"*Se arrepiente. Cometió errores. Necesita ayuda.*"

"Even if he repents and can see his mistakes now, how can I help him?"

"*Si lo perdonas, estará mas tranquilo.*"

"Dina, even if I want to forgive him so he can be at peace, I don't really know how." I was being completely honest with her. "Besides, your cousin Abraham said that the Seven Jewish Samurai of Guadalajara could help him. What's that about? Who are these guys? Why didn't Abraham answer my question? And what is a Jewish Samurai? Quite frankly, it sounds ridiculous."

"You'll know…" she began, then stopped without giving a full answer. She just smiled and stared into my eyes. I was getting anxious and needed to move, stand up, or run away. Maybe all three.

I excused myself, said I needed more coffee, and went to the kitchen. Once through the doors, I ended up in Luz María's arms. I was shaking, and she hugged me tenderly.

"*Ya no se preocupe. Todo va a estar bien,*" she said.

"How do you know that everything is going to be okay?" I asked. She didn't answer.

Once I composed myself, I asked if the big pot of drip coffee for the guests was ready. I didn't want her to have to prepare more elaborate Turkish coffee for everybody. That would have taken her away from more important tasks in the kitchen. But someone had already asked her to prepare only Turkish coffee. I was furious. Undermining me at this stage—in my own house—was outrageous. I was the commander in chief here.

"Who told you to make Turkish coffee?" I asked.

She rolled her eyes and said with a half-smile, "*su prima Alegre, señora.*"

"And who is the boss in this house? Who pays you? Me or Alegre?" I was laying the anger on a little thick. Really, I wasn't *too* angry about it.

CHAPTER SIX

"*Por supuesto que usted,*" she said, half-smiling. She could tell what I was up to.

"Well, if it's clear to you who the boss is, then *stop* making Turkish coffee immediately. Start a big fat coffee pot with a strong *café americano cargado* for the guests. That's the end of the story. Don't ever bother me again with this stupid coffee shit. And if any relatives come in here and give you orders, let me know immediately."

"*Sí, no se preocupe. Se lo prometo.*"

Then Luz María put her hands on her hips as if to say it was about time, *ya era hora*. She was proud of me. Wow. In my heart of hearts, I knew Luz María was very happy, even with my angry display of emotion. That felt good! She had been waiting for me to stand up to my relatives and put a stop to their intrusions. She hated when they bossed her around whenever my brothers or I weren't looking. But her hands were tied whenever they did—out of respect, she couldn't say anything to them.

I welcomed this kitchen distraction over my pending conversation with Dina. I stomped back out to the living room dramatically. I was ready to put up a fight with any other cousin or aunt who crossed my path.

My sudden state of uncontained fury surprised me. Was this *really* about Turkish coffee? Of course not. It was about not allowing one more person to overstep their boundaries in *my* home. I would die for my boundaries.

"May as well do it today," I said to myself. "*Ahora o nunca.* It is now or never!"

Determined, I marched straight through the short distance that separated me from Alegre. I stood right in front of her with my hands on my hips *a la* Luz María, in a demanding stance.

"*Tú le ordenaste a mis muchachas que no hicieran el café de cafetera?*"

She could sense my anger.

"Yes," she began sheepishly. "I ordered them to stop making drip coffee and make Turkish coffee instead."

"*Y quién te piensas tú que eres?* Who do you think you are? You are a *guest* here. *Tú no eres más que una visita aquí.* I told Luz María to brew drip coffee. Luz María has a lot more to do in the kitchen than one cup of Turkish coffee at a time. If you want to make it, then do it yourself. *Si tú quieres café turco, tú hazlo!* I live here, not you, and I command here. *Yo vivo aquí y tú no y aquí en mi casa, yo mando. No se te vuelva a ocurrir entrar a la cocina y darle órdenes a mis muchachas.* Don't ever go into this kitchen and order *my* maids around again."

She was stunned, and apologized on the spot. She left the house soon after. I didn't care. She probably never expected such a serious display of boundaries or *jutzpa*. I had never done that before—not with everything happening behind my back as it was. How could Alegre know I even *had* boundaries?

That was the day I finally began to gain my relatives' respect. At least I'd sent a clear message: Don't mess with me, because you haven't seen anything yet. Since they gossip with each other, I knew I needed to do this just once; it would trickle down to other relatives, especially *las metiches*, the nosy ones.

My display of *macho* boundaries was for my own sake, but also because I loved Luz María. I would run into the kitchen so she could embrace me before I would ever consider running to any of my aunts. Luz María would sit me down, dry my tears with her worn-out apron and greasy hands, and even cry with me if necessary. Or she would feed me if I was hungry. She was my guardian angel.

With my coffee in hand, and my boundaries well established, I was ready to face Dina while she communicated whatever needed to be translated…or *channeled*…or whatever the right word was. It felt like round three of some unfinished business with my father.

CHAPTER SIX

I went back to my spot on the sofa. Dina looked at me and whispered, "*Tu mamá está aquí también. Está junto a tu papá. Se ve muy linda, con su vestido blanco largo. Se ve muy en paz y está tratando de ayudar a tu papá a pasar al otro lado. Lo está cuidando y es muy dulce con él.*"

"Can you also *see* my mother?" I asked. "I don't see her, but would love to see her looking beautiful in a long white gown. I'm glad she seems peaceful. How is she going to help my father through this difficult passing to the other side? How is she going to take care of him? I'm not surprised she is sweet to him. She was sweet to everybody."

"*Sí, eso lo puedo ver,*" Dina said. She understood.

I was jealous that she could see my parents.

"I thought you die and move on, and that's that," I said to her. "I guess you can get stuck, and not pass on. Is that what's happening to my father?"

"*Sí.*"

She paused a moment, then continued.

"*Tu mamá me dice que quiere pedirte algo importante ahora. Quiere que le digas a tu tío Chaim que necesita perdonar a tu papá.*"

"What?" I almost barked at her. "What are you saying? *My* mother is asking me *now* to tell my uncle Chaim that he needs to forgive my father? Dina, that's impossible. In a million years, he wouldn't do it. Are you kidding me?"

"*No linda, no te estoy tomando el pelo.*"

Dina said she wasn't teasing, but I was out of sorts. What a crazy situation. Now both of my parents were asking the impossible. Couldn't they talk to someone else? Why me?

I was beyond my capacity to breathe normally. I felt hot, shaky, and prickly. *Se me puso la piel de gallina.* It was like Dina, or my mother, or *Spirit itself,* was asking me matter-of-factly to go tell the sun to turn itself into the moon.

DEFYING GRAVITY

Uncle Chaim was pretty detached. A smart and highly educated physician, he would *never* give any consideration to the thought of ghosts. Besides, I believed that whatever caused him to despise my father, was probably for a good reason. I had never witnessed such animosity towards a person, nor such powerful determination to end a relationship that had otherwise been amicable while my mother was alive. After she died, Chaim simply stonewalled my father. Neither of them ever said why.

I was convinced that my uncle knew things about my father, but I never dared to ask what they were. After my mother died, Chaim categorically refused to see or speak to him. Even after my father's big stroke, Chaim not only refused to see him, but wouldn't even offer medical advice to us. His wife, my aunt Sofia, was completely mortified by this situation. She would appeal to Chaim, citing the many years of friendship, kinship, picnics, birthday cakes and family ties. But my uncle *no dió su brazo a torcer*—never gave in. It was almost as if he wanted my father dead, which was quite out of character for a compassionate doctor, not to mention a member of our Jewish family...whatever that meant.

It had been a challenge for him to attend my father's funeral, and to come back to the house for shiva prayers. He was restless and wanted to leave as soon as he got here. I was sure my auntie dragged him to the house. Even if he didn't say anything, I understood that for whatever reason, his integrity was compromised.

Uncle Chaim was a mystery to me. He'd always been remote, aloof, and distant. He seemed to hold his *almighty* power of medical knowledge over all of us, his simple, *uneducated* relatives.

Once, when I was visiting Mexico with my husband, I called him late at night.

"Hi," I said. "My husband is very sick. He's been throwing up all night. What can I do? He needs help."

CHAPTER SIX

"What did he eat?" Chaim asked. His tone was a mix of disdain and anger. "Where did he eat? When did he start throwing up?"

"We had some quesadillas at the farmers market," I said.

"Why the hell did you have quesadillas at the market? You know well enough that you shouldn't eat out in the streets! And why didn't you call me sooner?"

"I thought he was getting better," I said. "But that's not the case."

"That's silly," he barked back. He probably meant to say *stupid*, but somehow restrained himself.

He always made me feel dumb. Every telephone consult ended with him scolding me. At some point, I stopped calling him for medical advice. But then, when I had a surgical procedure, he was angry that I *didn't* consult with him first. Damned if I called him, damned if I didn't. Quite frankly, I didn't like being on the receiving end of his superiority disdain.

Obviously, Dina didn't know any of this. She gave me a sweet, encouraging look, then nudged me to speak to him.

"*No te preocupes*," she said softly. "*Tu mami está aquí y ella te va a acompañar.*"

"Dina, even if my mom is going to be with me, I am worried," I said. Still, I armed myself with courage. "Okayyyyyyyyy," I muttered. "Here we go."

I found Chaim standing apart from the crowd, as was his usual habit.

"*Hola tío, cómo estás?*"

"*Bien chula y tú?*"

"I'm okay, *ahí la llevo*." Taking a deep breath, I went on. The words shot out like bullets.

"*Oye tío te quiero decir algo pero no te sorprendas*," I began. "I want to say something to you but don't be surprised. This lady standing over there, do you know her?" I pointed at Dina. "She is my father's cousin's wife," I went on. "She says that she can see ghosts. She can talk to my mother, and says that my mother is here to help my father move on. She says that she has a message especially for you."

I was out of breath.

Okay, this was usually the moment when Chaim would arch his eyebrows and sneer. And he did, of course! Oh God, *trágame tierra*. May the earth swallow me…la la la…I wanted to disappear. I felt like a speck of sand in the Sahara Desert.

With what little conviction was left in me, I spilled out the rest.

"She is asking you to forgive my father," I said. "*Quiere que perdones a mi papá.*"

I wanted to run for my life! But my feet were glued to the green carpet. I got another big sneer, major eyebrow arch, and a brand-new quizzical look I had never seen before. He had perfected his look of contempt for the stupidity of the entire human race which, in the moment, I represented. Or he thought I was crazy. But, so what? What did I care?

"If you don't want to forgive him, you don't have to."

I thought I heard laughter, but he didn't laugh. I gathered my courage once more to say my final piece.

"This is not my thing. I don't even know this lady. Believe it or not, I don't even care. I know you had your issues with my father. I don't care what they were. If you want to forgive him, that's your deal. Maybe my mother *is* here with this message. Maybe she isn't. I don't see ghosts, okay? And I have my own problems. So, forget it. Sorry to have bothered you with this stupid conversation. It's absolutely ridiculous. I think this lady is a total loony. Just imagine that we didn't have this conversation."

Now *that* sounded sane. I saved my *tush* for a moment, and decided to change the topic.

"*Quieres un cafecito turco tío*? Would you like some Turkish coffee?"

CHAPTER SIX

"Sure," he said. And that was the end of our conversation. Not another word came out of his mouth.

I disappeared again into the kitchen, my one solid piece of heaven. I caught Luz María for another emergency SOS. The best therapist in the world, she immediately saw my agitation.

"*No se preocupe,*" she reassured me. "Don't worry, missus, your mother *is* here. She's standing by your side. She looks beautiful and peaceful. She is wearing the same long white gown I told you about before. Can you see her now?"

"No, I can't see my mother." I was curious about the fact that she and Dina were describing my mother's ghost in the same way.

"Did you talk to Dina?" I asked. "Have you met her?"

"*Quién es Dina?*"

"*Dinaaaaaaa!*" I moaned. "*Esa chava con pelo chino,* that short gal with blond curly hair." I opened the kitchen door slightly, so I could point her to Luz María.

"*No, no hablé con ella y no la conozco. Nunca la he visto. Quién es?*"

"Oh, *olvídate,* just forget about it," I said. I was frustrated because Luz María had never met or seen Dina, and was asking me who she was. Clearly, she hadn't heard Dina's description of my mother's ghost.

"*Cálmese señora, está usted muy nerviosa.*"

"Anxious in an understatement, Luz. How am I supposed to calm down with all that coffee in me?" I looked at her sternly. "Seriously. Don't you let me drink another cup! I think I'm hallucinating."

I was a nervous wreck. *These* people were seeing ghosts, while *those* people thought *I* was crazy for mentioning it. I hated this feeling.

I went upstairs to take a break—and to try to pull myself together. I lay down for a second while my father's nurse, Angélica, cleaned and picked up a few things here and there.

"*Necesita algo?*" she asked.

"Yes. I have a killer headache. Do you have any aspirin?"

"*Por supuesto. Qué le pasó?*"

"What happened? Oh, the usual…everybody is seeing my mother's ghost, and I can't tell if they're serious or teasing me…or if I'm going nuts."

She gave me a serious look, then came to sit on the bed next to me. She handed me a glass of water and aspirin, then held my hand.

"*Sabe qué?*" she said. "You know what? *Le tengo que decir que su papá antes de fallecer en el hospital estaba hablando con su mamá por varios días antes de que entrara en estado de coma. Le decía a su mamá, si chula, ya se, ya se…*"

"You too?" I shot up in bed. "Did you *also* see my mother? Was my father truly pleasantly talking to my mother before he went into a coma? Was he truly saying *yes dear, I know, I know*? That doesn't sound like him."

"*Sí, de verdad!*"

"For real? Did he say anything else? Please tell me! What else do *you* know?"

"*Mire señora,*" she said. "*Yo no la ví pero Silvia, la enfermera de noche vió a su mamá varias veces y me dijo que estaba vestida con un vestido largo y blanco y que se veía muy linda y en paz.*"

"She told you that? Silvia, the night nurse, saw my mother too? Several times? Are you sure she said she was dressed in a long white gown, and looked beautiful and peaceful? Are you sure?"

"*Si señora, se lo juro por mi mamá que eso me dijo Silvia.*"

Angélica swore by her mother that she was telling me the truth. This could not be a coincidence. Too many people were spotting my mother's ghost. Now I had to believe it was true.

I suddenly felt calmer. If this was all true, then the meaning of life and death was something I had not even begun to grasp. Not even a little bit. *Ni siquiera un poquito.*

CHAPTER SIX

If my mother was actually here with my father, then life could truly be eternal. Perhaps love could transcend material life. Maybe they were meant to be together in another realm, even if their marriage on earth had been a big fiasco. Was their marriage just a script in a play they had to perform? And then, after they both died, they would live happily ever after? I wished someone could explain this to me.

If people around me could *see* them, and this was not a fluke, then I definitely had some limitations in my own *seeing* and understanding of a world beyond this one. I was sure, after talking to Angélica, that no one had been teasing me. This was serious business! I needed to get a grip on what was happening—the sooner the better!

CHAPTER SEVEN

Rites of Passage

"I came to explore the wreck...

I came to see the damage that was done

and the treasures that prevail."

–Adrienne Rich

After my conversation with Angélica, I lingered upstairs for a while. I wanted a moment of uninterrupted thoughts to myself. I needed to put order to what was happening inside my parents' house. Once I felt more grounded, I went downstairs to continue greeting the flocks of people still coming in.

A delicious guava scent permeated the home. I went to the kitchen to see what Luz María was up to.

"Hey Luz, what are you making that smells so delicious?"

"*Le compré guayabas en el tiangis y le estoy haciendo dulce de guayaba que le gusta tanto.*"

"You are a dream, Luz. Thank you."

She was so sweet. She was making a delicious guava dessert I've loved since I was a child. She had gone to the *tiangis*, the Mexican farmers market down the street, for ripe guavas while we were at the synagogue. I was so delighted that for a moment I even forgot all about my parents' ghosts.

CHAPTER SEVEN

I went back to the living room and continued to roam around and say hello. But every time the kitchen door swung open, I could almost *see* the mixed scents of guava and coffee traveling in delicate waves toward me. It distracted me from the chattering people who came and went.

I lost sight of Dina, and got pulled into a conversation with old friends. They wanted to know about my life adventures as if I were an exotic museum piece, or a female version of Indiana Jones. I wasn't in the mood to recall events from my childhood or my adult life in other countries. In my head, I heard myself screaming, "Stop it. This is my father's shiva. Can you just be quiet?" *Trying* to be polite was exhausting. Sitting shiva was torturing me. A few more days of this? I'll die!

I tried to concentrate on the guava scent again, and remembered that a tea made from guava tree leaves could settle the stomach. Perhaps I should ask Luz María to prepare me a *tisane*. A sweet infusion of this tea could help me settle, and maybe deal with having to listen to nonsensical conversations that forced me to smile and bob my head up and down like a puppet.

I wished I could hide in a quiet place and sip my guava tea alone. But there was always some commotion in the kitchen. People came in and out constantly, bringing more and more dishes and drinks. There was nowhere to hide except the roof, but I wasn't as agile as when we were children, and could reach the steps easily to get there.

I used to find great places to hide in this big house when my cousins and I played hide-and-go-seek. I considered myself a master of hiding in unusual places. We could play *escondidillas* for hours. Once, I hid my little cousin under the table. She lay on the chairs, and I covered her with the tablecloth. She actually fell asleep! Nobody found her, and she didn't come out of hiding until dinner. Now, when I needed it the most, I couldn't find a place to hide in the entire house. The only safe place was in my head.

The guava scent also carried me into a memory of *mercado de Escandón*, the closest market to my parents' home. As everyone continued yakking their mouths, I tried a new technique: I began talking to old acquaintances as if I was walking through the bountiful fruit and vegetable aisles of the *mercado*.

Most likely, I was in a dissociated state again.

As their lips moved, I offered big smiles in response. But my mind was with Juanita, my old favorite merchant. Ah, where was sweet Juanita now? I remember her being short and chubby, with dark wiry hair. Her eyes were dark like *chicozapote*. She was missing a few front teeth, and always wore a big dirty apron where she'd wipe the fruit to make it shiny before cutting a juicy slice, and offering a piece to passersby.

"*No quiere probar marchanta? Está muy bueno. Andele, pruébelo!*"

She lured every costumer to sample some mango, try an apple, or taste fresh melon. She would chomp down on her own raw vegetables and greet my mother and me with her toothless smile. I was always worried she'd ingest a mouthful of killer Mexican bugs, but she could have cared less.

"*No se apure marchantita, no le pasa nada si lo prueba,*" she would say, assuring my mother that nothing bad would happen to her if she tried the produce.

"*Qué milagro. Cómo está? Qué bueno que trajo a su hija. Quiere probar algo?*"

"Hi Juanita," my mother would say. "We are well, thank you. Yes, I'm also glad that my daughter came with me today. I'd like to try a slice of *sandía*. Is the watermelon sweet? Don't give me any live worms today, okay?"

CHAPTER SEVEN

Juanita would cut a piece of fruit for my mother and laugh at her fear of worms. She sold 100% organic fruits—with worms and everything, as she explained.

"*Ay señorita, no se preocupe tanto, los gusanitos no la van a matar.*"

"I know the worms won't kill me, Juanita. But I just don't like seeing them wriggling around in my fruit."

Then, as if to prove her point, Juanita would find a worm and eat it. I squirmed and wanted to get away. But my mother liked Juanita, and we would stay. After all, Juanita offered my mother the best prices on fruits and vegetables in the market. She even saved the best *huitlacoche* for my mother. Strangely, I loved *huitlacoche*, a black fungi that grows in corn during the rainy season. My mother would sauté it with garlic, and bathe it into a creamy white sauce, which was a sumptuous filling for crepes.

Next to Juanita's stand, the snobbish vendor who sold pristine looking fruits and vegetables always gave my mother dirty looks whenever she bought Juanita's produce. I didn't like this other woman. She was always dressed up, and wore heavy make-up and pearl earrings. She seemed out of place to me.

I liked to meander my way across from Juanita's stand to see the wrinkled old lady who looked like a witch. Besides the candles that had images of the Virgin Mary and Jesus Christ on them, she sold strange looking necklaces, dry herbs, and tinctures that were like mysterious potions to me. My mother would pull my arm quickly if she found me wandering over to her stand.

I went often to the *mercado de Escandón*, usually with my mother, and sometimes with my maternal grandmother too. My *abuelita*

was quite something. She would argue in Spanish with the vendors, with a few stray Yiddish words slipping out in between.

She liked to tease them with things like, "*Oiga, déme aguayón, no engañón,*" to which the vendors would reply, "*Si señora, no se preocupe.*"

She wanted the best piece of meat they had, and didn't like being tricked when a butcher tried to give her a cut she didn't like. The butchers would get a kick out of her Spanish rhymes, her jokes, and her accent—and they cracked up because she was tiny and quirky, but pretended to be ferocious behind her glittery, mischievous eyes.

One time, I heard one of them say to another, "*Ahí viene la viejita chistosa,* here comes the funny little old lady."

Grandma didn't care. She had fun at the market. She would teach my mother how to recognize fresh fish from the old by lifting up the gills.

"The brighter the red color, the fresher the fish," she explained to my mother. "Same with a bright red eyeball." She prompted me once to lift a gill, but it was too nauseating for me. I declined.

"*No abuelita, está horrible y huele feo,*" I cried. "Yuck! It's horrible, Grandma, and it stinks." I wouldn't touch a fish with a 10-foot pole.

Grandma just laughed at me and continued to touch and squeeze everything she could. She'd reach into piles of fresh meat to find the best pieces of beef, tongue, brains, chicken, chicken liver—everything—from under a butcher's piles. It was disgusting, but also enthralling. I loved to just watch her do her thing. We spent hours at the market, and I'd listen to her argue with every single vendor. She created such commotion, but I was happy. Following her around made me feel important and all grown up. I was also learning how to bargain Mexican-style.

She produced some strange meals with her precious goods. We ate *lengua, sesos, chicharrones de pollo, pulpos en su tinta*—tongue,

CHAPTER SEVEN

brains, chicken fats, octopus, and all kinds of pork delicacies. So much for *kosher* food! She was the daughter of a Polish rabbi, but she'd rebelled at a young age and refused to follow all the rules that our religion dictated. After she immigrated to Mexico in the late 1920s, cooking and eating pork was suddenly no big deal for her. She especially enjoyed *tacos al pastor*, pork tacos marinated in spices and *chiles* from the *taquería El Tizoncito* in the neighborhood where she lived.

But when it came time for the High Holidays, if the fish vendors didn't have the exact types of fish she needed for Passover, forget it! Grandma would give them total grief. She needed her *gefilte fish*—a traditional holiday dish made from a poached mixture of ground, deboned carp, pike, and white fish—to be perfect.

At home, I watched her grind her fish for hours. She used an archaic manual grinder, and worked so hard that I could feel my own arms grow tired just watching. She loved to sweat out her cooking—and her mothering, for that matter. She liked to say how she made tomato juice for her children by squeezing tomatoes through cheesecloth, because she didn't have a blender.

After grinding the fish, she mixed it with hard-boiled eggs, salt, and pepper. Then she prepared elongated patties that would simmer with sliced *zanahorias and apio*—carrots and celery. My grandmother's *gefilte fish* was the best.

Celebrating Passover with both families was a mixed experience of Ashkenazi cuisine from my mother's mother, and Sephardic cuisine from my father's mother. One spoke Yiddish, the other *Ladino*. One made *gefilte fish*, the other created meat pies with *matzo* crackers, and *buñuelos de nuez* for dessert—fried dough made of wet and softened *matzo* crumbles, mixed with milk, eggs, and sugar. When the *buñuelos* were ready, we added honey and crushed pecans on top.

RITES OF PASSAGE

Kosher or not kosher, my maternal grandmother was a great cook, but I am afraid she put too much cream in her tacos. Everybody suffered from a heart condition! It was all the rich Mexican food with *schmaltz*: cholesterol in the chicken fat, *chicharrones de pollo*, and tons of thick butter she used for her legendary *spaghetti rojo*, her *huevos estrellados, o revueltos*—red sauce pasta, eggs over easy or scrambled, and everything else she cooked.

I also vividly recall her laughter. She had a good sense of humor, and laughed so hard her eyes watered. Although now that I look back on it, I think a lot of her laughing was really about making fun of people, since she would laugh after she made a remark in Yiddish, a language I didn't understand.

She complained endlessly about all kinds of aches and pains. My mother had to take her shopping, help her cook, keep her company, take her to the park, and run around to endless medical appointments. Grandma got more attention from my mother than all of us children put together. I was completely left in the dark when they talked—they spoke mostly Yiddish. I felt left out because my mother didn't include me in the secret language that only she, her sister, and my grandmother spoke when they were together. They were the *Sisterhood of the Yiddish Mini-Shtetl*, their own little town. I was a foreign kid in their hood.

The only Yiddish phrase I actually learned was "*mine shvigger*," which means "my mother-in-law." I suppose my mother complained endlessly about *her* mother-in-law, and this phrase etched into my brain. I didn't realize that I was a silent witness of a Cold War among different Jews—the Sephardic and the Ashkenazi.

I think my grandma might have felt a bit guilty for taking so much of my mother's time and attention away from us. *Alomejor la abuelita se sintió un poco culpable.* To compensate, she carried little colored packets of gum—*Chicles Adams*—in her black patent purse for us kids.

CHAPTER SEVEN

She also liked to collect delicate pieces of sumptuous fabric. I think her aunt back in Poland was a seamstress, and she knew a thing or two about sewing.

At some point, Grandma urged my mother to find a Haute Couture seamstress who could make dresses for the girls in the family. It was *the chic* thing to do then. My mother took me to Pilar, a Basque woman, who fitted me for a dress she would make out of a pale yellow, chiffon fabric that my grandma bestowed upon me. I hated everything about this miserable situation!

Pilar's hands were ice when she touched my skin. But her house was worse! It was dark and gloomy, and smelled horribly of musk and cigarette smoke. The walls were covered with old portraits of weird-looking people. Pilar herself was old and creepy. She spoke with a deep, hoarse voice. I couldn't believe my mother took me there, but I had to go along with the stupid plan. What power did I have as an 11-year-old child? I was a victim of their sisterhood and their seamstress plot.

But a worse female offense came later, and involved the red velvet fabric my parents had used to upholster the old couch in the family room. Some fabric was left over, and since my grandma disliked wasting anything, she had a brilliant idea: Pilar could devise a red dress out of it for my engagement party! Even though I was a 19-year-old woman with my own opinion, I still felt compelled to go along with their plan—once again agreeing to someone else's idea of what was best for me.

When I tried the dress on at Pilar's, it actually looked good on me—much to my surprise. But when I got home and tried it on again to show my father, I stepped out of my bedroom into the family room, dressed in bright red, and did a double take. My God! It was a terrifying experience: I was one with the red sofa! *Ay Dios mío, quería desaparecer.* I wanted to vanish!

RITES OF PASSAGE

"This is not going to be any fun," I said to myself, almost choking. I felt like a red chameleon. Hot tears rolled down my cheeks. I'd been tricked by the feminine, and betrayed by my own mother. Red was the taste and the color of my shame. With no other pretty dress to wear, there was no alternative—I *had* to wear the red velvet dress.

On the day of the engagement party, I avoided that part of the house like a pest. I didn't want guests to put two and two together. I worried all night about people noticing the *strange similarities* between the sofa's upholstery and my dress.

For all of the betrayals and trespasses by the women in my family, their cooking skills redeemed them. They had incredible gastronomic gifts. My auntie Sofia came up with a recipe for a chocolate cake that we each ate every year on our birthdays. *El pastel de chocolate* carried an embossed promise: Like chicken soup for our entire family's soul, it would sooth and heal what ailed you, and would always taste amazing. It was a slice of eternal familial sweetness.

The rich recipe called for eight large eggs, two cups of flour, one cup of butter, semi-sweet dark chocolate, and one cup of sugar. The filling was made of the same ingredients as the cake, mixed with one tablespoon of Turkish coffee, then chilled for a while before being used for icing.

When I was 13 years old, I had to pass a cooking specialty test for the Jewish Girl Scouts (yes, there was such a thing as the Jewish Girl Scouts in Mexico). I took on the challenge of learning Auntie Sofia's chocolate cake tradition.

For the record, the Girl Scouts were not really my thing. Despite my annoyance, I was going to pass this culinary test. I wanted to enter into the female ring of the traditional chocolate cake makers. Perhaps, I thought then, this could be the rite of

CHAPTER SEVEN

passage that would earn me acceptance into my mother's sisterhood *shtetl*.

In preparation for this special task, my mother spent an unusually long session with me in the kitchen, leading me through all the steps of making the cake. The hardest thing for me was separating the egg whites from the yolks. Once I mastered the task, my mother armed me with the baking utensils I needed—pans, spatulas, measuring cup, and even a mixer—and put them in a big Mexican basket, along with the ingredients. I barely slept that night. The next day, my parents drove me to the home of the woman who was hosting the baking test.

I arrived with pride and honor. Soon all of the girls were ready to start our recipes. I got my utensils out of the basket. Rebeca, one of the other girls, pulled out a big box of *galletas marías y helado de vainilla*. She placed the vanilla ice cream on a fancy plate and decorated it with sugar cookies around it. Then, in a manner of minutes, she proudly declared, "*Ya está listo.*" Her creation was ready. I was in shock.

Then there was Linda, who proceeded to make cranberry Jell-O, with strawberries for decoration. And on and on, one after another, each girl made the simplest and easiest dessert recipe. My heart sunk. I knew I was in for a long haul. Worst of all, within the first half hour, I was alone in the kitchen. The rest of the girls were watching TV and having a good time in the family room.

I swallowed hard and got to work. It was definitely a complicated recipe for a 13-year-old girl to pull off on her own, especially with no baking experience. It was going to take me all of the time allotted for this test—possibly more! How would I separate these eight whites from eight yolks? What if they mixed? What if the whites didn't have the right consistency after I beat them? What had I gotten myself into?

RITES OF PASSAGE

Little by little, I succeeded with every step. But when I took the cake out of the oven, I didn't know I had to let it cool before putting in the filling. The filling melted away, and the cake became a hot, terrible mess.

I was in tears. I still passed the test because of my efforts, but none of the girls understood my dilemma. By the time my parents picked me up, I was the saddest Girl Scout ever. *La niña mas triste del mundo.* I left feeling devastated, and never went back to the Scouts again.

"*Cómo te fue linda?*" my parents asked, wanting to know how it went.

I burst into tears.

"*Qué pasó?*" my mom asked. She was panicked.

"It didn't turn out okay, Mom," I cried. "I don't know what happened. It was really hard to make. The other girls had it easy. Then they had fun watching TV. I was miserable, and no one helped me."

"*No te preocupes,*" she said. "*Ya te saldrá bien en otro momento.*"

"But today was my day, Mom," I cried. "And I failed. I don't know if I can make that cake ever again. I'll never go back to the Girl Scouts."

I was miserable. I failed the family tradition. Why was I born into this family if I couldn't even bake the cake like my mother and my aunties? After all, I was the oldest cousin in my mother's family. I was supposed to set an example. My parents tried to console me. They took me out for ice cream, but I was still upset when I got home.

I locked myself in my room and pulled the covers over my head. Then I began to reason things out. After all, even if the cake wasn't good, I attempted something *way bigger* than the other girls, and I felt a bit of pride in my accomplishment.

With this inner voice speaking, I went downstairs to check on my failure, and dared to try it again. My mom had put in the fridge.

CHAPTER SEVEN

By then it had cooled off, the filling solidified, and it all held together beautifully. When I gingerly took a bite of the cake, to my surprise it tasted like Aunt Sofia's! I took another bite. Nope, it wasn't my imagination! It was *way more* than just edible. It actually tasted like the traditional family cake. I was thrilled. Perhaps they would accept me after all in the bosom of this family? Maybe *this* was the real test I had to pass. Forget the Girl Scouts. I could live without them.

Had any of my aunts or cousins brought a chocolate cake to the shiva? Back in the kitchen, I peeked in the fridge. It was so filled with food that I gave up and asked Luz María instead.

"Have any of my aunts brought a chocolate cake?"

"*No*," she said. "*Pero yo se lo puedo hacer si usted quiere.*"

"You are an angel, Luz," I said with a big smile.

I loved Luz María. Here she was, actually *offering* to bake the chocolate cake for me. I was *so* spoiled! I thought that I could ask any of my aunties to bake it—after all, I was an orphan now, and maybe they would pity me. Yet, I also thought, *mas vale pájaro en mano que cien volando*—better a bird in hand than two in the bush. I happily said yes to Luz María's offer.

The chocolate cake was the only thing I felt like eating—straight from my memory bank and good for my soul. I went back to the living room, comforted with the idea of devouring a large slice.

Dina had been watching me like a hawk, and waiting patiently. No guava scent, market memories, or chocolate cake distractions were going to prevent a conversation about my father or mother, or whoever else was floating around. Nobody was in a hurry to

RITES OF PASSAGE

leave just yet, and I knew it was going to be a long evening—and long days ahead.

Slumping onto the big green sofa, I took a deep breath. I happened to land next to my aunt Reyna. As soon as I looked at her and rolled my eyes, we began laughing hysterically. The springs on the couch were sticking out because the cushions had been removed—our *tushies* were hurting! Despite the fact that immediate relatives had to sit low—thereby closer to the earth, and to the departed—there was still no Jewish tradition that said we had to be tortured by these springs. I adjusted my position, using some small pillows, to make it more palatable.

Still laughing, my aunt held my hand. It was the sweetest gesture. Then she leaned on me, and whispered in my ear that she was actually very sad but couldn't cry.

"*Sabes que yo nunca he podido llorar cuando estoy triste.*"

Wow, what a confession. She said that she had never really been able to cry when she felt sad. This was the very first time *ever* that a close relative talked honestly about *feelings* with me. A new friendship was sealed between us right on that painful spot.

Encouraged by her confession, she proceeded to tell me stories about my father.

"*Sabes? Tu papá era un cuero,*" she said. "He was such a good-looking hunk. *Sabes cuántas viejas se querían casar con él? Eran como moscas muriéndose por andar con él.*"

"Yup. I know," I agreed. "I've seen pictures of him in his bathing suit, chilling at the sports center, surrounded by women. I know he was good looking, and I know how many *chicks* flocked to him like flies, dying to marry him. You have told me that long time ago."

"*Se parecía a Antonio Banderas, no crees?*"

"Well, I don't know if he looked like Antonio Banderas, but he was handsome."

CHAPTER SEVEN

I sadly remembered my father with his sparkling green eyes, charming smile, and a well-kept beard. He cut a Spanish *conquistador* profile, complete with a cute dimple on his chin. His skin was tan with a nice olive tone, and he was in great physical shape. If only his disposition had matched his looks.

I started to feel uncomfortable with our conversation—my aunt was going on and on about all the pretty women that wanted to marry my father until he *ended up* with my mother. She implied my mother was lucky because she was the "chosen one." Did she know that perhaps the *conquistador* never actually stopped his advances towards the rest of the ladies? My father was a flirt. Didn't my mother know that when they met?

When I was a young, I witnessed several of my dad's advances. Children may be innocent, but they aren't stupid. In middle school, I sometimes accompanied him to work, and met my friends there. He co-owned a textile chemical manufacturing plant with two more partners, who had daughters my age. I felt special on these outings with him, but didn't like the way his secretaries or female employees batted their long eyelashes as soon as he entered the office.

"*Cómo está ingeniero?*" Lolita asked with her usual provocative tone. It always rubbed me the wrong way.

"*Bien gracias Lolita, y tú?*" he answered, offering her his broad smile.

Lolita brought him a Coca-Cola, and gave one to me as well. Then he and I went to his office. He had a big desk with a cozy chair, and a large sofa where I sat and watched him do paperwork. Sometimes I played with a small sculpture of a man made out of nuts and bolts. When my friends finally arrived, my father left us alone in his office, and went to talk to his secretaries at the front desk.

Exploring his office, we landed our hands on a *Playboy* magazine that was on top of a cabinet. I'd never seen *Playboy* before, and felt confused, speechless, and downright embarrassed. We hurriedly put it back. We didn't say anything, and I carefully tucked this experience away in a sealed compartment of my memory bank.

Aunt Reyna continued to talk about how *guapo* my father was. After she ran through a number of his *conquistador* stories, she stood up and went to say hello to her sister-in-law. She hadn't said anything about how lucky my father had been to marry my mother—the woman who put aside her brilliant musical career and dropped everything for the *conquistador*. What a bargain she got! It was definitely the wrong chemistry.

Dina spotted me sitting pensively on the sofa. Like a bird of prey descending on a rabbit, she quickly came and sat down on a nearby chair.

"*Cómo te sientes?*" she asked.

"Not great," I said, opting for brutal honesty. "How can I feel good with all the things happening around me?"

"*Tu papá está contento de que tú y yo estemos hablando ahora, sabes?*" she said. Then she began translating his words again. "*Aquí está parado junto a nosotras y quiere que sepas que se siente muy orgulloso de ti.*"

"Come on, Dina," I said. "How could he say that he feels proud of me if he never ever said that to me when he was alive? And what exactly is he proud of? He didn't even know what I did or who I am. And why would he be so happy that you and I are talking right now? This seems ridiculous. Is this for real?"

"*Sí, absolutamente,*" she answered. Then she said that my father was standing right next to me.

I turned my head slowly, and tried to spot his shadow, or whatever it was I was supposed to see.

CHAPTER SEVEN

"How come *you* can see him, but *I* can't?" I asked. "I want to hear directly from him that he was proud of me. Tell him that!"

Dina didn't respond. She became very quiet, and looked down as if she were trying to pay attention to something important.

"*Tu papá no se quería morir,*" she said. "*Estaba muy apegado a su casa y se siente muy triste que no está aquí con todos disfrutando de la comida familiar.*"

"I guess I know he didn't want to die," I said. "I also know he was greatly attached to his home. It was his castle, and he worked hard for it. But Dina, if you have to go, then you have to go. Right? You don't want to get stuck forever in the walls of your home."

"*Bueno sí, pero el continúa yendo y viniendo del cementario a su casa y no quiere creer que ya no vive aquí,*" she said sadly.

She stunned me again, but it made sense: My father was going back and forth between the graveyard and his home. He could not believe that he didn't live here anymore. And, according to Dina, he was sad that he wasn't enjoying a family meal with everybody.

"*No te preocupes,*" she said. "*Mi trabajo aquí es convencer a tu papá que de verdad ya falleció y que eventualmente tiene que irse.*"

"Well, do you think you'll be able to convince him that indeed he died, and that eventually he needs to leave? How are you going to achieve *that*?"

"*Bueno, estoy un poco preocupada si voy a poder porque está tan apegado y es un poco necio así que no sé si se va a ir tan fácilmente.*"

Now I was anxious, because Dina was worried she wasn't going to be able to convince my father to leave. He was so attached to his house—plus he was being stubborn. I couldn't help but to agree with her.

"*Sabes?*" she asked. "*La tradición Judía dice que los muertos se demoran en sus casas por siete días antes de irse. Por eso es que la shiva dura siete días, para animarlos y para que no se sientan solos.*"

RITES OF PASSAGE

"I didn't know that," I said. "I had no idea that in the Jewish tradition there is a belief that the dead linger in their homes for seven days, and that is the reason for the seven days of shiva. That makes sense. But, what if my father doesn't want to leave *after* the shiva?"

"*Por eso estoy aquí*," she said with emphasis—she was here to help.

I was glad she was helping. I didn't want to deal with my father's ghost alone after the shiva, and I prayed that Dina would successfully convince him to go.

Dina said my father was also attached to material things. That made sense too—he never liked sharing his possessions, and got angry if anyone messed with his things.

For instance, he didn't like lending his tools to my brothers, even if Yosef was more adept at fixing things than my father was. My father still kept his tools in his bathroom closet for safeguard. His car was part of the mix as well—he never let anyone borrow it.

I felt fortunate that he had at least shared some good times with me, like when he took me to his office, or when he asked me to dance with him at sumptuous Jewish weddings. He was a great dancer; he danced with my mother mostly, but he also liked dancing with me. On Sundays, he watched football or soccer games with my brothers, but sometimes he liked to sunbathe in the backyard. I kept him company then too, and we would chat about this or that.

Lost again in my thoughts, I was grateful that the evening was winding down. I forgot that Dina was even there—she'd grown quiet, seemingly deep in her own thoughts. Or maybe she was listening to my father. There was a moment of peace. Then, sud-

CHAPTER SEVEN

denly, Dina bolted out of the chair and went downstairs to open the door. I never heard the bell ring, so I was very curious about who was about to enter.

Max Cohen, a man I had never met before, walked in with Dina. He soon introduced himself to my brothers and me as a good friend of our father. I'd known all of my parents' friends, so this was disconcerting. Most of the guests were gone for the night, and only my brothers and some relatives remained.

Dina and Max sat by my side. Dina held my hand. Quietly, Max said, "*Tu papá también me llamó a mí. Dina y yo trabajamos juntos cuando hay una situación que require que unamos nuestras fuerzas para hacer una intervención efectiva.*"

"You too?" I asked Max. "So, all of a sudden, my father's soul needs *yet another* person to have an intervention? I've never heard of anything like this, Max. And who are you again?"

"*Tú no me conoces pero yo conozco a tu familia,*" he began, "*y esta es una situación delicada sobre todo por el deseo tan intenso de tu papá de hablar con ustedes y también porque su espíritu que se encuentra muy inquieto y confuso.*"

"Well, I'm glad you are a friend of our family," I said. "It does sound like this is a delicate situation. Why is my father so intent on talking to us? Why did he die in such a state of restlessness and confusion? And, what exactly are you going to do to help?"

"*Voy a hablar con todos,*" he said.

"Oh shit! Are you going to talk to all of us?" I threw up my arms. "Are you sure you want to do that?" First Abraham. Then Dina. Now some guy named Max calling for a *family powwow*. This was most definitely not a coincidence.

He was so damn serious, and spoke with such distinct authority, that I didn't know what to think. I had to believe this was really happening. There was no room for denial.

RITES OF PASSAGE

"Max, you don't really know my family well," I said. "We are a family of *non-believers*. I don't know how my relatives are going to react to this issue of my father's ghost roaming around. And, to be frank, I'm concerned about my brother Yosef, who has not been in the loop. He doesn't know anything about what's been going on since my talk with Abraham. I don't think he likes the idea of dead people rising from their graves. I don't know if he would believe you guys."

"*Tu papá está preocupado por la salud de tu hermano Yosef y quiere ayudarlo,*" Max said. "*No te preocupes, todo va a estar bien.*"

"How does my father know that Yosef has been dealing with some health issues?" I asked. I was stunned. Better yet, how did Max know to say these things if he wasn't hearing them from my father's ghost? Jonatán and I kept Yosef's situation very private. Yosef was suffering from anxiety, and no one knew. He was also having severe insomnia and nightmares. With my father gone, and so many people around, I was concerned about him even more. I'd been doing my best to shield him.

Not caring about my concerns, Max called on everybody to sit around the living room. He introduced himself as an old friend of our father's. He asked how we were holding on. Everybody was in relatively good spirits, and said we were okay.

He asked if we believed in God. We just looked at each other, puzzled. I didn't feel like sharing *my* beliefs about God with my relatives, so I kept quiet.

"*Les tengo que decir que yo no creo en Dios,*" Max announced. "*Yo sé que Dios existe. Estoy seguro que Dios existe y no tengo ninguna duda al respecto. Gracias por reunirse aquí conmigo esta noche. Tenemos asuntos importantes que discutir respecto al señor Mizrachi.*"

CHAPTER SEVEN

He gave us a long explanation about how he didn't *need* to believe in God because he *knew* God existed, and that he was absolutely certain because he had the *experience* of God, which was the ultimate truth. He also said that we had very important things to discuss regarding Mr. Mizrachi—my father.

I watched to see how my brothers and my relatives reacted to Max's words. To my surprise, they were quiet and attentive.

"*Salomón Mizrachi me ha pedido hablar con todos ustedes en los próximos dos días,*" he said. "*Así que porfavor descansen y empezaremos mañana a dialogar con él.*"

Per Max, my father wanted to talk to each of us individually, starting tomorrow. He suggested we all leave to get some rest.

We sat quietly as our jaws fell to the floor. Max and Dina went upstairs to the family room—they were going to talk with my father together first.

No one spoke. For another moment or two, we just looked at each other. Then, people started to leave. Eventually, Dina and Max wrapped up their private conversation with my father and left.

The house fell into an eerie silence. My brothers and I sat together and stared into space. We were speechless and frazzled. The kitchen was quiet too. It was as if a tsunami had come through, and now we were sitting in its aftermath.

I had enough for another day of sitting shiva. My head was spinning. I needed to be alone. With both my parents deceased, their home vanishing under my feet, and my father's ghost roaming around unwilling to leave, I was drained.

I went upstairs, brushed my teeth, put my pajamas on, and got under the covers. I closed my eyes, and fought against tiny tears inside my heart.

CHAPTER EIGHT

Los Abuelos

*"Never be afraid to laugh at yourself.
After all, you could be missing out on the joke of the century."*

–Dame Edna Everage

After another restless night, I woke up sweating from a bizarre dream. I was driving a blazing red car. Jonatán sat in the passenger seat. We'd just left our mother at a hotel. We were following my father's car; he wanted to visit a special place that my brother and I also wanted to see.

As I drove, my eyes began to close. I was falling asleep at the wheel, and was aware that I was in danger of a major car accident. I tried desperately to wake myself up, but I couldn't. Meanwhile, Jonatán continued to chat from the passenger seat, unaware that I was sleeping. I tried telling him what was happening, but didn't have much luck. My mouth couldn't move, and the words were scrambled in my head. I was surprised we didn't crash, or drive off the road.

Finally, I pried my eyes open in the dream. When we pulled over, the car was balancing precariously on a cliff's edge. A stunning light-blue sea was in front of us. As I was taking everything in, an enormous whale with glittering skin popped up from the water's surface. She was hard to distinguish from the sun's reflec-

CHAPTER EIGHT

tion. It took effort to focus on her shape and the way she shimmered. I began admiring the beauty of the scenery, and enjoying the presence of the whale. Then she locked eyes with me.

I woke up startled.

Disoriented, I turned my head to see what time it was. I tried hard to focus on the clock's fluorescent hands. Three a.m. Why do so many strange things happen at three in the morning? Crazy dreams, ideas, and silly songs from *Mary Poppins* always roam around my head at three a.m. What was a whale doing in my dream in the middle of my father's shiva?

I flicked on the table lamp, found my slippers, and quietly ventured downstairs to get some warm milk. The house was silent, and felt spooky. A strange density in the air scared me. In a particular area of the living room, right between the big table and the kitchen's swinging door, the air was especially chilly. I shivered. I looked left and right to see if I could spot my parents' ghosts, even if I wasn't in the state of mind to actually *chat* with them.

I tiptoed to the kitchen to warm up a glass of milk, then drank it quickly. I armed myself with a banana, and walked back upstairs holding it like a knife. I put the banana under my pillow just in case. I tossed for a while, then finally dozed off.

The alarm woke me at six o'clock.

I jumped out of bed and ran downstairs to take a shower. I dreaded the slow flow of water from the showerhead. I hunted for a new bar of decent soap in the closet, and thankfully found one that showed no signs of being an ancient relic.

The water's temperature alternated between too hot and too cold without warning. I'd had it with this dumb shower! I am generally impatient, but this day I was edgy. *Tenía los nervios de punta.* We needed to get to the synagogue very early for morning prayers. My brothers were generally slower than me. How would they handle this stupid shower? Whatever. That was their problem.

LOS ABUELOS

I grabbed a shabby towel, and dressed as quickly as I could. I woke my brothers up and prompted them to get ready. I guess I was the *big mama* now—and Big Mama hates being late.

Luz María was waiting for me. She had hot coffee ready, and was finishing up the *huevos rancheros*, another one of my favorites: eggs over easy on a lightly fried tortilla, with red and green salsa on top. She separated the two salsas down the middle of her dish.

"*Aquí están sus huevos divorciados para que tenga fuerzas*," she said as she served the dish.

"*Ay* Luz María, I'm not in the mood for jokes," I said. "Why do you think I need *divorced eggs* to gather my strength? I need much more than that! Well…maybe you are right. I'll eat them just because they look delicious, and I love your salsas. Maybe I do need my strength."

I laughed as well. Miserable or not, I enjoyed a moment of Mexican humor when it came to food.

Luz María pulled a chair next to mine, tilted her head to one side, and gave me a quizzical look.

"*Oiga señora, ayer en la noche escuché ruidos en el comedor, aquí donde se sentaba su mami.*"

"What do you mean you heard noises in the dining room last night, right where my mother used to sit at the table. What kind of noises?"

"*Ruiditos así como si alguien estaba llorando quedito pero cuando entré a la sala no había nadie y se sentía muy frío.*"

"You are frightening me, Luz. Are you sure you heard someone crying softly late last night, but you didn't see anybody when you came into the living room? Are you sure it wasn't Angélica?"

"*Sí, se lo juro. No había nadie y hacía frío aquí justo.*"

Then Luz María pointed at the place where she swore she heard someone crying, a place that felt very cold to her. It was the same place where I'd walked into the strange chill.

CHAPTER EIGHT

"Who do you think was crying?" I asked.

"*No sé. Alomejor su papá…o alomejor su mamá.*"

"My mom or my dad? But didn't you say that she was okay, and that she was going to help my dad?"

"*Bueno pues alomejor era otro espíritu pero no se quién sería.*"

"Yeah. Maybe you are right—it might have been an unknown spirit." I rolled my eyes. But then I began telling her what I felt in the middle of the night, how I stood in the same spot and was overcome by a strange coldness.

She grew very pensive, and looked around as if listening to someone who wasn't there.

"*Bueno, ya aquí está su mami otra vez y me dice que de verdad todo va a estar bien y que no se preocupe más.*"

She insisted once again that my mother was standing there, promising that everything was going to be okay, and asking me not to worry.

"*Bueno,*" I said to Luz María. "Tell her I say hello."

If everything was going to be okay, why was I driving like an idiot with my eyes closed in the dream? Why was I asleep at the wheel, unable to see, and about to kill my poor little brother and myself? Driving blindly, and teetering on the edge of a cliff, did not exactly scream *okay*, not in my book at least. Perhaps the dream was telling me that I needed to pay attention to what I couldn't see. I have been angry and disappointed at my parents. Maybe I was just selfish, and needed to see beyond my own stubborn pain, and the way I longed for what I never received from them. Did I even know anything about my parents' pain? What about their own childhood suffering and frustrations? I didn't know anything about that either. Maybe I was blind to everything, and understood nothing.

I wanted to share my dream with Luz María to see if she'd come up with a brilliant folkloric interpretation about the whale. But she was busy preparing breakfast for my brothers. My right foot tapped impatiently on the dilapidated green carpet. I pulled out my cell phone and typed, 'what is the meaning of a whale in a dream?' I scrolled through several answers:

Whales reflect strength and spirituality...they also represent a big event in our lives or a strong feeling of solitude...and can signify that everything will be okay. They relate to spiritual matters of the mind and heart...sometimes may also mean that we are overwhelmed with our own emotions...or an aspect in our lives that has grown too large to be easily handled and we want to escape from the pressures of life.

Bingo! Everything made sense. Perhaps Luz María was right after all. Everything *was* going to be okay.

In the meantime, I was downright overwhelmed.

Memories of my father emerged one after another, without rhyme or reason. I reviewed my life span with him. He was good, bad, and indifferent. Mostly, he confused me. Who was this man I called *Father*?

When I was three years old, I was fond of him. He played with me, and carried me over his shoulder to tuck me into bed.

When I was five, I was terrified of him. I bit my nails when he yelled.

When I was six, he taught me how to swim. He was my hero.

At eight, I was angry with him for making me sweep the feathers out in the street.

As a young teen, I felt proud as we cruised through downtown Mexico to run errands and purchase my first typewriter. And I loved dancing with him at weddings.

By the time I was 17, I was at war with him for the reasons why any teenage girl goes to war with her *macho* father—he in-

CHAPTER EIGHT

terfered with *my* freedom! From then on, I was endlessly taken aback by his indifference.

Finally, at some point in my early adult life, he forgot I existed. His indifference felt like the opposite of love.

Then again, dealing with my mother wasn't easy either. Growing up, I had to compete with my grandmother and aunt for her attention. They sucked the life out of her.

When I was 10, my cousin Deborah and I ran wild between a myriad of racks at *El Palacio de Hierro*, a big department store in the *Colonia Condesa*. We spent a couple of hours meandering the store, unsupervised and creating havoc. We pulled clothes down from the racks, played hide-and-seek, *distractedly* dropped things from tables, and ran up and down the escalator, pushing people out of our way.

Meanwhile, my mother sat with Aunt Rifka and my grandma at a Sanborns restaurant, adjacent to the store. They dragged us to their tea party, but we were not allowed to sit at the table and listen to their gossip. They ordered dessert for us, and after we finished, we had to leave the table and go play in the store. I wasn't having fun, and I didn't like hanging out with my cousin. She was a tale-teller, a spoiled brat, and extremely annoying on top of it all.

I just wanted to go home and play outside, or hang out with Dalia.

Every time I went back to the restaurant to tell my mother I was bored, or to try to join in their conversation, they sent me away to play with Deborah. The hours felt long, and I was tired, but the three ladies wouldn't leave until they finished their dessert and gossip.

Aunt Rifka always had a headache. She had to take aspirin and drink coffee after coffee until she successfully passed the headache on to my mother. She also gave *me* a headache with her incessant chatter about how wonderful she was.

LOS ABUELOS

She used my mother as a driver—she'd had a car accident and decided that driving was not for her. Why bother, since she had my mother as a chauffeur? My mother also delivered groceries to Rifka every so often. My grandma also used my mother as a primary caretaker and driver. She had many obscure ailments and afflictions, and my mother would spend hours taking her to see doctors.

I was 19 when my grandmother passed away. That's when my mother woke up from a long reverie and bitterly realized that she had been absent from our lives. She began psychoanalysis, and after several months of treatment—and with her newly discovered self-awareness—she asked us to forgive her for her shortcomings as a mother.

One day, she invited me out to lunch.

"*Siento mucho que no les presté atención cuando eran chiquitos,*" she told me. "*No sabía bien lo que estaba haciendo y tu abuelita y tu tía me quitaron todo el tiempo que tuve que haber dedicado a mis hijos.*"

"Mom," I began, "thank you for telling me this. Yes, I was aware that your mother and Aunt Rifka took all of your time away…time that you needed to dedicate to us. I'm sorry you didn't know what you were doing, and missed out on being with us. It's a shame, but it's now in the past."

"*Lo siento en el alma,*" she said. She had tears in her eyes.

"I'm very sorry too." I swallowed hard. What else could I say to her?

"*Te prometo que voy a ser mejor madre ahora. Quiero mucho a mis tres hijos y voy a tratar de rehacer el tiempo perdido.* I promise you I'll be a better mother now. I love my three children and I'll try my best to make up for the lost time."

"I believe you, Mom," I said. My eyes filled with tears.

She fulfilled her promise of becoming a better mother, and making up for lost time. We were able to rebuild our moth-

CHAPTER EIGHT

er-daughter relationship, and I forgave her—how could I refuse her heartfelt apology?

Perhaps no matter how old we get, we *live* to hear our parents apologize to us.

To my delight, she and I discovered how much we had in common. We liked similar foods and restaurants, and equally enjoyed nature as well as window shopping. We even held hands as we walked down the streets of my Noe Valley neighborhood in San Francisco.

At Muir Beach, we watched sunsets together. We relished our visits to the Dipsea Café in Mill Valley, and Café Mario in North Beach, where we had authentic Italian cappuccinos. We loved to stroll down Lombard Street with its curvy elegance and flowers. We relished dim sum by the waterfront in Sausalito, where we loved shopping for *chachkes*—sweet little nothings. Her laughter was like a waterfall, so quick and easy, as we talked about life, books, music, dance, and art.

"*Mira los pajaritos, les tiramos pedacitos de galletas de la suerte?*" she asked.

"Okay," I said. "Let's see how many come to us." We threw pieces of fortune cookies to the birds that flew around the pond at the Japanese Gardens, while we sipped tea from tiny china cups.

In the stillness of the moment, she began confessing about an old love she'd known in her performance days.

"*Sabes? Estoy tratando de encontrar a un antiguo amigo mío. Un violinista famoso con quien tocaba música de cámara.*"

"Really? Where is he?" I was curious about my mother's desire to locate an old friend, a famous violinist with whom she played in her younger years.

"*Vive en San Diego.*"

LOS ABUELOS

"Are you sure he lives in San Diego? How do you know? How did you find him? Were you in love with him? Did you play many concerts together?"

"*Pues sí, creo que sí pero no era judío y no pudimos tener una relación porque su familia no me aceptaba.*"

"But if you were in love, how come you didn't elope? Your parents wouldn't have accepted him either, the same way his family didn't accept you because you were Jewish."

"*Sí, tienes razón pero eso ya está en el pasado. Ahora que tengo esta condición no tengo nada que perder. Alomejor hubiésemos sido felices pero no lo sé.*"

"I guess you are right," I said. "It's all in the past. With your heart condition, you have nothing to lose. You may have been happy together. Who knows? But I'll be happy to help you find him now if you want." And just like that, I became my mother's accomplice in finding a long-lost lover.

"Do you think you made a mistake by marrying Dad?" I dared to ask.

"*Posiblemente,*" she admitted. "*Extrañé mi carrera y cometí muchos errores como madre y también como esposa pero eso ya también está en el pasado. Si no me hubiera casado con tu papá, no tendría a los hijos maravillosos que tengo.*"

"I am sorry, Mom. Sorry that you missed out on your career, and sorry for all the mistakes you feel you made as a mother and as a wife." But then she said she wouldn't have had her wonderful children. What could I have said to her?

I looked out into the beautifully manicured garden, and pondered my mother's revelations. On one hand, she was full of regrets, but on the other hand, she was filled with joy for having had us, her children, on account of marrying our father. It had been a terrible dilemma for her as a young woman.

CHAPTER EIGHT

Now that she was confessing, I was perhaps more of a sister to her than a daughter. Nevertheless, I was living in another country, and she was living on borrowed time in Mexico City. Her heart was weak, and she refused risking a heart transplant. Our healing time together as mother and daughter was limited—we both knew it.

Sure enough, her heart eventually gave up prematurely. She was relatively young when she died, and the mother-daughter bond we were just starting to form was severed. I had grown up feeling motherless. At 37, I was motherless again, this time for good.

I was quiet. Tears fell into my *huevos divorciados* as I reminisced about my parents' choices. My brothers showed up for a quick bite to eat before we left for morning prayers. Their presence snapped me out of my bittersweet memories, none of which I shared with them. Just like in my whale dream, I was unable to speak. Did they share the same feelings and memories? I didn't recall them being at *El Palacio de Hierro* playing with Deborah and me. Where were they during the ladies' escapades to Sanborns?

I kept my brothers company at breakfast. They seemed to be in good spirits. Like always, I was the one who was thinking too much, and I was glad they were chatty and witty.

When we were ready, we jumped into my father's car. Jonatán decided to drive. I was relieved! I didn't want to repeat my dream. In absentia, my father would have to finally give us his blessing and let my brother drive his fancy car.

We arrived at the old *Templo de Monterrey* in the *Colonia Roma* for the morning prayers. The synagogue had been a fine-looking building in its day. It was built between 1941 and 1942, and was similar in its neo-gothic style to a temple in Vidin, Bulgaria. It was named *Yehuda Halevi* in honor of the Sephardic philosopher, who

LOS ABUELOS

was also a doctor and a poet. Years later, the community built a *bigger, better* synagogue in a fancier Jewish neighborhood. Now the old synagogue was like a first child—all grown up and left to its own devices.

I was 11 years old when I sang with the synagogue's choir during Sabbath services, and also at weddings. I liked singing at weddings better—they gave us almond-covered candies when we did. Once, my friend Maggie spread a rumor that at night the synagogue was haunted. She told stories of how the ghosts of lovers who were not allowed to marry came back and reunited after dark. We were all convinced that the stories were true. When we sang, I would look warily at the enormous chandeliers to see if they were moving, or would focus on the stained glass to try and catch a glimpse of the ghosts. If I didn't see anything move, I would get distracted by the imposing marble lion sculptures that stood guard on each side of the Torah's arch, under two immense golden menorahs, one candelabra on each side. Most of my friends from Jewish school were part of the choir, and we were always together—school, temple, the Jewish sports center…everywhere. The stories of lovers and ghosts followed us from place to place, and different people embellished them over time.

Even if we were not singing, I was thrilled that we were allowed to sit together unsupervised in the choir loft during the High Holiday services. The cantor alone was in charge of the religious prayers in the main sanctuary. Looking down, I was curious about why men and women sat separately across aisles of the synagogue. But as long as I was with my friends, I didn't care much, especially because I liked sitting next to the boys. Sometimes during prayers, the rabbi gave us the evil eye because we created such a ruckus up there. Evil eye or not, nothing prevented us from chatting and carrying on with our incessant debates about the souls of dead lovers lingering in the synagogue.

CHAPTER EIGHT

Eventually, once puberty hit, we moved on from ghosts to gossiping, then to flirting.

I was sad that the early morning prayers did not take place in the main sanctuary, but in the small precinct downstairs by the kitchen. I wanted to sit by the lions so they could escort me through my difficult emotions. Still, in a way I liked this sanctuary. With its red carpet and wooden wall paneling, it felt soothing and warm, like a Jewish womb. I sat all the way in the back with the other women, and relished a moment of being alone.

We had to recite the Kaddish twice daily: once in the morning at the temple, and once in the evening, at my parents' home. It had become almost like a lullaby for me, swaying my soul slowly into a place of peacefulness. The Kaddish prayer was ancient, written in Aramaic—I had to pay attention to recite it correctly. If I was tired, the words felt heavy on my tongue, and it was hard to pronounce them.

After the service, the rabbi told a story about my family that took me by surprise.

"*Yo recuerdo muy bien al papá de el señor Salomón que en paz descanze*," he began. "*Recuerdo que le gustaba caminar todas las mañanas al templo y fumaba sus cigarritos que cortaba a la mitad porque siempre estaba tratando de parar de fumar. El era un buen judío que se sentía cerca de Dios y también era muy simpático.*"

I perked up when the rabbi described my grandfather. I didn't know he walked every morning to the synagogue, smoking his cigarettes that he routinely cut in half because he was always trying to quit. Nor did I know that my grandpa felt close to God, or that he was a "good Jew," according to the rabbi. I was curious as the rabbi talked about Grandpa's humor and easy laughter, and I got

LOS ABUELOS

the sense that he really knew him. Sadly though, the rabbi didn't know much about my father, so he didn't have much to say beyond "may his soul rest in peace."

I smiled. My grandpa had been a funny guy. He loved to play tricks on us, particularly during Passover. He had a crystal glass that he placed on the Passover table, mixed up with similar looking glasses. The glass had small holes etched into it that were impossible to detect. Eventually, someone would get the glass and drip water all down their chins, but they could never figure out what had happened. Grandpa would laugh so hard, it was contagious. It was also impossible to get mad at him. *No te podías enojar con él.*

His most notorious joke was his fart balloon that he would place under a chair cushion and wait for someone to sit on. Then he'd laugh wholeheartedly as he tricked another fart victim. We kids would join in the laughing too, even if we knew the joke by heart.

The rabbi was also right about my grandpa being a good Jew. When it came to his religion, he was serious, especially the way he conducted our traditional holidays. In contrast, my father seemed distant from his religion. He never talked about God, or about being Jewish, or about any other spiritual beliefs for that matter. I had no idea if he even believed in God. Did he like being Jewish? Was he resentful about it? I only knew that he liked the evening prayers of Yom Kippur—the Kol Nidre. So, when the rabbi was done telling stories about my grandpa, I decided that perhaps reciting the Kaddish would help my father's soul find his way back to a Jewish God—whether he liked being Jewish or not.

After the service, my brothers and I were invited to sit in the front row. Everyone who had attended the morning services could shake our hands and express their condolences. I was deeply moved by the sense of sincerity in this simple ritual. I held back tears, and realized for the first time that I felt a deep loss at no longer being a part of this community. All of these people had known

CHAPTER EIGHT

our grandparents and our parents. They held our family tree in their backyard, and were bearing witnesses to our loss. They knew who we were and where we came from.

Who would know my history when I died?

We left the synagogue and returned to my parents' house, ready to repeat the same ordeal as the day before: late morning visitors, family meals, afternoon visitors, more coffee and sweets, and more prayers in the evening.

I couldn't stop thinking about my identity tied to this community. The loss hit me hard. What was I doing living in another country? Where was my community now? Was it anything like the one I'd left behind?

My feet felt light. With my parents and grandparents dead, I was rootless…anchorless. Nothing kept me tied to the ground. The image of my maternal grandfather, Gabriel, flashed through my mind. It made me smile. I had a special kinship with him, the family's philosopher.

He would say things to me like, "*Ay mi'hijita, qué no te puedes reír de todo?*"

"*Ay*, Grandpa, how can you say that we can laugh about everything? Don't you think that is a bit cynical?"

"*No linda, sí que te puedes reír de todo.*"

"But…how can you *really* laugh about everything, Grandpa?"

Then he showed me a half smile, half laugh. It was a bit strange, a bit cynical, and I didn't understand him.

"Did you mean letting go of everything so nothing bothers you?"

"*Algo así. Solamenteríete de todo.*"

"What do you mean, something like that? Just laugh about everything?"

He was mysterious that way, and never quite answered my questions. To this day, I haven't gotten to the bottom of what he was trying to say. Maybe he meant that in the larger scheme of things, nothing much really matters except laughing, which keeps you young and detached. Maybe *that* was the key to living in the present. Had Grandpa discovered *the power of now* long before Eckhart Tolle wrote a book by the same title? Was it his *laughing Buddha* attitude that helped him get up and move on with his life every day?

Grandpa Gabriel was also a creative spirit. He taught himself several languages, and studied philosophy and Jewish history. He also taught himself to draw, and play mandolin. He developed a taste for Turkish coffee, despite the fact that he was Ashkenazi, and born in Poland. And he loved black beans with sour cream, which he ate religiously after every meal. He called it his dessert.

He was a bit eccentric to say the least. After my grandmother died, he would dress up in colorful shirts and suits to go to the *Parque México* in the *Colonia Condesa*. There, he'd flirt with the ladies who sat on the green iron benches around a fountain—the one with a sculpture of Einstein's head. He wore fancy hats with colorful feathers, and bathed himself in a strong men's cologne. Armed with his most charming smile, and a whiff of that powerful scent, he would march straight to his spot, just a few blocks away from his apartment. Sometimes I chaperoned him to the park, and met some of his friends. They all spoke in Yiddish, and they literally owned this little pick-up place of theirs.

"*Mira, te presento a Golde*," he would say, introducing me to a woman. Or, "*aquí está Elkie. Ven a conocerla*," as we walked to a different bench to meet another woman.

"*Esta señora es muy linda. Déjame presentarte a Shayna.*"

"Okay," I would reply, as he took me to meet yet another woman.

He was so happy introducing me to all the ladies. There was Feiga, Blume, Libke, and dozens of others. He was like a 15-year-

CHAPTER EIGHT

old boy, all excited about the girls. I thought it was cute. I relished watching his interactions as he went from bench to bench, making sure to say hello to everybody.

But Grandpa Gabriel was a bit naïve at times. On one occasion, he came home from the park very excited. He said he'd met a captivating woman who supposedly was visiting relatives in Mexico City. She was a Jewish woman from Russia who now lived in Florida—apparently, she'd fallen in love with my grandfather. That's what she said, at least. She invited him to visit her and her daughter in Orlando. He accepted the invitation, and soon booked a flight to Florida. He took off excitedly with the blessings of his children.

When he arrived at her address, she locked him in a room in her house and demanded a ransom from my uncle Chaim. Yes—this woman actually kidnapped my grandpa! But my grandpa, who'd escaped the Nazis, was not going to let this stupid Russian woman get away with it. Taking matters into his own hands, he left by the fire escape, and asked a bypasser to help him. The police came to rescue him, and he somehow found his way back to Mexico City. She ended up in jail!

Of course, this incident didn't deter him from visiting friends at the park. They greeted him like a hero, and he delighted people with his story of the *Super Polish Man* who'd escaped from the *Russian Enemy* in Florida.

I was in my early 30s, living in California, when I heard the news that my grandpa died. It broke my heart. I took a long walk on the Tennessee Valley trail in Marin County, all the way to the cove. I climbed up a large rock that overlooked the ocean, and tried to conjure his spirit. I was sad to lose him, along with his stories and adventures. I sat on the rock until dusk, crying.

The night he died, he visited me in my dreams, smiling and singing like always. He was playing his mandolin and said that he wanted my daughter to have it.

LOS ABUELOS

"*Mi'hjita, quiero que le des la mandolina a tu hija.*"

He was emphatic about it.

I called my mother the next morning and mentioned the dream to her. I asked if she had the mandolin.

"*La acabo de recojer de su casa y aquí la tengo conmigo y cuando vengas por supuesto que te la puedes llevar,*" she said.

I thought the mandolin has been sold, but my mother said that she had just picked it up from Grandpa's apartment. I could come for it the next time I visited México. I was thrilled.

Years before my grandpa died, I had a similar experience involving my grandmother. I was 19 at the time. A few months after she died, she came to me in my dreams.

"*Mi'hjita,*" she said, "*quiero que tú te quedes con el anillo de diamantes.*"

"What diamond ring do you want me to have, *abuelita*?"

"*Te lo voy a enseñar.*"

Then she showed me a detailed picture of her ring: a white gold band that was thick in the middle, narrow on the sides, with small diamonds incrusted throughout. It was a beautiful ring in my dreams, but I didn't remember ever having seen it on my grandma's hand.

The next day I told my mother about the dream, and described the ring in detail. She grew pale and distressed almost immediately.

"What's happening to you?" I asked. "Mom, are you okay? You're scaring me. Do you need some water? You are super pale."

"*No, estoy bien,*" she said. "*No sabía que las personas cuando fallecen te pueden visitar en tus sueños. Yo nunca he soñado con mi mamá.*"

"I didn't know that the dead can visit in dreams either," I said. "I'm sorry you haven't seen your mom in your dreams yet."

"*El anillo ha sido razón de un pequeño conflicto entre tu tía, tu abuelito y yo.*"

CHAPTER EIGHT

"Why? What is the problem? Why are you, Aunt Rifka and Grandpa arguing about the ring?"

"*Tu abuelito no sabía bien que hacer con el anillo o a que hija dárselo así que el anillo va y viene de mí a tu tía y viceversa.*"

"I didn't know this caused so much trouble, or that Grandpa didn't know which daughter should get the ring."

As my mother explained, the ring had been going back and forth between her and Aunt Rifka for months.

"It doesn't sound fun," I said.

"*No*," she agreed. "*No es muy divertido. Tu abuelita me dió el anillo para tí antes de morir pero tu tía lo quiere porque su esposo se lo dió a tu abuelita y era un regalo especial. Tu tía quiere dárselo a Deborah.*"

"*Ay*, Ma," I sighed. "This is too convoluted for me." As I understood things, my grandmother had given my mother the ring before she died, and she'd asked that it eventually go to me. However, my Aunt Rifka wanted it for Deborah, because her husband gave it to my grandma as a special gift.

I replayed this back to my mother, and asked if I understood everything correctly.

"It sounds like a *telenovela*," I said. What a crazy soap opera, I thought.

"*Sí, así están la cosas. Ciertamente de telenovela.*"

"But if someone gives you a gift, isn't it yours to do with it what you want?"

"*Sí, tienes razón pero qué puedo hacer?*"

"Okay," I said. "You and I are right, but I'm getting dizzy with this story. Why don't I relinquish the ring, even if my grandmother wanted me to have it? I don't care if Deborah inherits it. That's what you should do. Give it to her."

"*Bueno linda*," she said. She agreed with my thinking and seemed relieved.

LOS ABUELOS

With the ring dispute resolved, my mother settled down. There was no more discord between sisters, but perhaps my grandmother disapproved of my decision—she never came back to visit me in my dreams again.

These two vivid dreams involving my grandparents didn't come close to my mother's visits after she died. She haunted me in dreams for months, and the dreams themselves became frightful nightmares. Often, she looked dreadful and ill, and as much as I tried to convince her that she was dead, she kept denying it. She insisted that I give her some kind of medicine to help her recover. The dreams tormented me until a friend, worried about my sunken eyes and obvious distractibility, suggested I see a psychic—the famous Clarissa Johnson with an office in Fairfax, California. My friend swore that Clarissa was *for real*.

The day of my appointment, I dragged my feet to her office. I wasn't expecting much—I didn't quite believe in psychics back then, and I had never seen one.

Clarissa greeted me with an open smile and unexpected warmth. Once I realized that she wasn't just some weird hippie lady, I felt at ease. This tall, well-dressed, soft-spoken woman reassured me with her calm demeanor, along with her description of how our session would go.

"Imagine you invite me into your home, but I only have permission to enter into the rooms you allow me to see," she said. "You are the only person who can open a door to other rooms, and allow me to explore different aspects of your life."

"Okay," I said. "Sounds fair."

She began to pray for guidance, invoking all kinds of spirits—*los santos, los ángeles, la Virgen María, Dios Todopoderos*, all the

CHAPTER EIGHT

saints, the angels, the Virgin Mary, and even Almighty God. She called on other spiritual teachers and guides as well.

I was getting dizzy with all of these spirits around, but Clarissa stayed calm and peaceful. There was no wriggling in her chair, spinning of the head, or rolling of the eyes in a weird way. So far, so good.

Suddenly, without me even inviting her into any of 'my rooms,' she opened her eyes.

"I'm sorry to stop before we even begin, but your mother is here. She wants to talk to you."

"What?" I squawked.

"Yes. She is here. She desperately needs to talk to you."

I was jolted as if stricken by lightning. I hadn't mentioned anything about my mother. Clarissa didn't know about the issues I'd been wrestling with, or why I'd contacted her in the first place.

She went on without further invitation.

"Your mother is very distraught," she said. "She has been coming to visit you in your dreams. She has been trying to communicate something to you, but she doesn't know how to do it in a way that won't scare you. She's sorry. And she's happy that you are here."

"Okay," I said, but hardly heard my own voice. I was petrified. My mind went blank, as if in a deep trance.

"Your mom says that she feels terribly sorry for all the years of your childhood when she treated you cruelly," Clarissa said.

"What does she mean by *that*?"

"She feels terribly sorry, specifically, about how much she abandoned her children, and neglected you for the sake of being with her mother and her sister. She didn't know how to handle a married life. She also missed her music and her piano career. She says your father was very demanding, but also, her mother didn't encourage her to take care of her husband or her children.

LOS ABUELOS

Your grandmother was selfish. So was your aunt. Your grandmother always told your mother to let your father wonder where she was."

My mouth dropped. How could Clarissa know these things?

"Your mother had been kind of *curious* about you," she continued. "But she really didn't want to bother paying any attention to you when you were little, and didn't show up for you. She says she feels sorry she didn't give you the roadmap or the compass to navigate life."

"I guess you are right, now that you mention," I said. How many hours had I waited for my mother to show up at school events, or to pick me up from dance class? She wasn't there for any of my milestones in childhood. I had to make it by myself.

"She was also aware of the endless hours she left you alone to fend for yourself," Clarissa went on, just as that very thought crossed my mind.

"Now she wants to make it up to you by becoming your spiritual guide. She is asking *your* permission to let her be a guiding light from the spirit realm."

I took a deep breath, then asked Clarissa how such an arrangement would work.

"Well," she began, "she can be close to you, and guide you in your adult life. She can also protect you. But, you have the right to refuse her proposal. She says she would be perfectly okay with your decision, even if you don't want her to be your guiding light."

"So, what would happen to *her*? Will she still be coming to see me in my dreams?"

"No. She would just move on and be a guiding light for other people. Other spiritual beings would guide you for the rest of your life."

I thought about it for a while. I wasn't thrilled about the idea of having my mother be my guide, since she had been so flaky and

CHAPTER EIGHT

distracted in her life. However, I felt guilty to send my mother into the ether without accepting her offer. I made up my mind.

"Clarissa, please thank her for her offer…but I cannot accept it. I am ready to move on, and I think she needs to do the same. Even if I feel bad with my decision, I think it is the best one. Sometimes, mothers and daughters need to part ways."

I thanked Clarissa for her intervention, and we ended the session on that note. The visit to Clarissa's proved to be the best remedy to my nocturnal disturbances. My mother never came back to my dreams. Maybe when I die, we'll reunite, and she'll be there in her white nightgown to guide me into another realm.

CHAPTER NINE

Acapulco Tropical

*Thunderous tidal waves crash without mercy
on the rocks of my childhood memories.*

The drive home from the synagogue seemed eternal. Memories continued to flood my mind. When we arrived at my parents' house, I paused for a moment to look at our street. Everything looked old and disheveled, just like our childhood home. The road and sidewalks were cracked from overgrown tree roots. Cars crowded every inch in the cul-de-sac. There were no kids playing in the street like we had when we were young. They were probably playing video games, or sitting glued to their computers or TVs.

My friends and I had been happy when we were kids. We lived close together, and practically took over our cul-de-sac for entire afternoons. We were a pack of about 15 kids with a nice range of ages, and a good mix of Jewish and non-Jewish backgrounds. We played for hours until we were exhausted and ready for dinner. Mostly we got along well. None of us wanted to miss the fun, like when the guy with a pet black bear came down our street.

He led his bear on a leash, and shook a tambourine with his other hand. *El oso* seemed harmless—it danced to the sound of its master's tambourine. Delighted with the acrobatics of this giant pet, we formed a circle around him, clapping and dancing along. I

CHAPTER NINE

had always wanted to pet the bear. He seemed so soft and furry, but his owner wouldn't let us come close to him. Yosef always gave me the *don't be a silly girl* look, essentially saying, "don't touch the darn bear!" with his eyes—*no seas mensa, no lo toques.*

Lots of other vendors came down the street too. There were guys selling *nueces de Castilla*—whole pecans from Spain—and sweet roasted yams, announcing their arrival with a loud whistle. Other solicitors wanted *ropa usada, periódico viejo, o zapatos para bolear*—used clothes, old newspapers, or shoes to shine for a few coins.

I always waited anxiously for the bicycle guy—*el cuate de la bicicleta*. All kinds of toys spilled out of the big cardboard box tied to the rack on the back of his bike. Once, when I was in sixth grade, he brought yo-yos. Everyone got one. I got a yellow one. We started a yo-yo competition that lasted for months. We practiced for hours the 'little dog,' 'the swing,' and the 'journey around the world'—*el perrito, el columpio y la vuelta al mundo*. I got carried away practicing one day at school. My teacher, *el maestro Solana*, caught me practicing *el perrito* during a lecture. He took my yo-yo for good. That was the end of the competition for me. He never returned my yo-yo.

Other competitions would come about spontaneously, like bike and roller skate races, or relay runs. We played a game called *stop*, declaring a war on different countries, and running for our lives. There was hopscotch, hula-hoops, kick-the-can, hide-and-seek behind parked cars, and freeze tag—*encantandos*. We climbed up on rooftops and played war by throwing rocks or loquats as projectiles. Our parents had no idea where to find us. They were clueless about what was going on outside.

Getting older in our neighborhood was fun too. As teenagers, we went to many birthday parties, and of course to the *quinceañeras*—a celebration of a girl's 15th birthday, and her transition from childhood to adulthood. Most of the parties took place in people's garages. Big bands played music, and we danced until the early morning. Don Isidro, with his famous freshly made quesadillas, was invariably hired for these parties—we all loved him. An array of relatives helped him make his quesadillas. We talked to him as if he were our favorite uncle.

"*Oye Isi,*" we would say, "can you make me a quesadilla with mushrooms and green sauce—*me das una verde de hongos con queso?*"

"*Espéreme señorita, aquí se la preparo en un momentito,*" he would reply.

"Thanks Isi. Sure, I can wait for a moment."

The line was always long, but the quesadillas were worth it. Plus, waiting was a good excuse to flirt with the guys.

There was no alcohol or drugs at these parties. We got high on *salsa verde picante*—spicy green sauce—along with the quesadillas, sodas, and of course the dancing. Once in a while, tempers got heated. Fights between guys for a particular girl were mostly entertaining—they never got completely out of hand, and the guys were always silly and amusing in the end.

If there were no parties on a Saturday night, we would eat tacos at the *Kalimán*, or the *Tizoncito*, then hang out at the park or the movie theater.

Another great stage for our endless entertainment was the Jewish sports center. It was like its own city, and we'd go there during the day to get lost. Its grounds extended for miles and miles, with numerous tennis and squash courts, plus several gyms, playgrounds, theaters, event spaces, and art studios. There were restaurants and salons, not to mention the biggest swimming pool I had ever seen. In fact, I still haven't seen a bigger swimming pool.

It was where my father taught me how to swim.

CHAPTER NINE

"*Pon tus brazos así como flechita,*" he'd say to me. And I'd try my best to put my arms over my head like a little arrow as he held me in the water.

"*Ahora tomas aire así, con tu cabeza de lado y no respires cuando metas tu cabeza derechito en el agua.*"

"Like this, Dad?"

I tried to follow his instructions: breathe with my head to the side, hold my breath when I put my head in the water, then kick hard as he held me.

"*Patalea fuerte,*" he'd say to me. And he'd hold me until I was able to float while I kicked.

Little by little, I learned how to breathe and hold my breath under water.

"*Ahora te voy a enseñar como nadar bien,*" he'd say.

Once I learned how to do what he was instructing, he taught me the breaststroke, and the freestyle technique.

In those years, my dad was patient and loving. Then he disappeared under water.

A barking dog startled me back to reality. Everything looked barren now—no children anywhere. A nostalgic sigh escaped my mouth. I hadn't seen my parents' shortcomings when I was a child because it didn't feel like I lacked anything. The street and the people were everything I needed back then. And like a good daughter, I wrote special cards on Mother's Day and Father's Day, and told my mom and dad they were *the best parents* in the world.

Back then, I simply didn't know better. My street was fun and safe. There were dozens of games to play at any moment. I went to a private school, and we even had our own driver who dropped us off and picked us up so we didn't have to take the bus. Every year we had new leather bags filled with books, notebooks, sharp pencils, compasses and whatever other tools we'd need. My uniform was always clean and starched, ready for each new day. At home, the pantry was full for the cook, and the maid was there to clean up. Every December we traveled to Acapulco for vacation, and occasionally we ventured to the U.S. in the summer.

According to my calculations, there was nothing wrong with my perfect little world. But I felt my happy childhood crushing under my feet as I walked back into the house. With my parents gone, the memories seemed confusing. Where did everything go? Had my childhood really been that good? Or had something gone wrong without my noticing?

I needed to hold on to something, anything. All of the nostalgia was turning bitter.

I ran upstairs to join my brothers on the low sofa.

"Ouch, this darn sofa," I cried. "Can you guys feel the wires?"

"Yup," they said. "*Tú qué crees?* What do you think?"

We were in stitches squirming on the sofa—maybe out of pure anxiety.

"I love you guys," I said, and reached to hold hands with both of them.

Luz María came in to check on us. She offered Turkish coffee again and *rosquitas de anis*, my favorite anise cookies. It was like aromatherapy for me.

"*Les hago un cafecito turco?*" she asked. "*Quieren rosquitas de anis?*"

"Sure Luz," I said. "Let's do it."

For the next hour, we enjoyed a sweet, quiet moment to ourselves. But it didn't last long.

People came and left, and soon it was time for our family meal. Cousins and aunts arrived, and more food piled up in the kitchen.

CHAPTER NINE

We all sat together at the dining room table. We ate and ate, talked and talked, ate and ate and talked some more. And we laughed too, mostly at nothing—but at least we were laughing. To an outsider, it might have seemed like a perfectly bucolic Sunday meal. But with so many unsettling things I couldn't speak of, I began to sink in the pool of food and laughter.

After the meal and more coffee, we took our positions again on the designated low seats. We were quiet for a moment, almost dozing off in the sunny afternoon. But soon, the doorbell began to ring incessantly. People paraded through the house non-stop until evening prayers, when they finally began to leave.

That's when Dina and Max showed up together.

They ushered us to sit around a circle in the living room with other relatives, including my father's brother and sister.

Max began talking about his *long, personal spiritual trajectory*. He'd studied the Rosicrucian, the Kabbalah, and a number of other mystical texts. He asked us if we believed in God. We all nodded without conviction. He emphasized how he *didn't believe* in God, but that he *knew* God. He went on and on talking about his personal faith in God. I wanted to roll my eyes.

He looked sharply at my brothers and me. I straightened up, ready to put up a fight.

"*Cómo están. Cómo se sienten hoy?*"

"We're okay," Jonatán and Yosef responded. I just nodded.

"*Cuéntenme un poco de sus familias. Adónde viven? Tienen hijos?*"

I was thinking that, if he was a psychic, shouldn't he know things about us? Like, where we lived, or if we had children. Questioning us about our own families in front of our relatives made me feel vulnerable and exposed. My brothers began telling him about their lives, but when it came to me, I decided to answer him nonchalantly.

"Oh yeah, I live in California," I said. "I love it there. Yes, I have a daughter. Yeah…I'm happy. Yeah, everything is okay." Yadda yadda yadda. Of course, I wouldn't dream of disclosing anything more personal than that right now.

"*Están contentos con sus vidas?*"

Who asks such questions? Maybe my brothers were thinking the same way I was, because they seemed similarly annoyed, and began answering casually as well.

"Yes, sure," they said. "We are happy with our lives. Why do you ask?"

"*Me gustaría saber cómo se sienten respecto a la muerte de su papá y si les es posible perdonarlo.*" His bluntness wasn't going away. Now he wanted to know how we felt about our father's death, and if we were able to forgive him.

I felt like someone slapped me across the face. I probably blushed. Hearing it took the air from under my belly—*me sacó el aire*. My feet felt wobbly. What was Max getting at? How could I possibly answer him honestly in front of my relatives? After all, he was a perfect stranger to me.

I needed some time and perspective, and I definitely needed to catch my breath—*recuperar el aliento*. I let my brothers speak as adrenaline flooded my thoughts. Then they both stopped and looked at me. I could sense that they were surprised by my silence.

Sweating, I finally conjured an answer.

"Well, I think my father is okay now," I said. "And I'm glad he is not suffering any longer because of his illness. I'm pretty sure he will move on peacefully. Probably the best gift we can offer him now is to be happy in our lives. Don't you think, Max?"

What a bunch of lies!

There was tension in the air, but Max didn't seem to notice. He continued his questions, and we just stared back and forth between our shoes and at each other. I wanted him to leave. I was

CHAPTER NINE

tired of being polite. I wanted to scream, but somehow managed to stay composed, pretending that Max was just talking about the weather or the most recent Alfonso Cuarón movie.

My auntie Reyna spoke up.

"*Mi hermano era una persona maravillosa, muy querida y respetada por mucha gente y estamos tristes que falleció.*"

Really? Does she *really* think my father was a wonderful person, and that lots of people loved and respected him? Who exactly is sad to see him go? Had we all been watching a different movie during his lifetime?

I felt like I was going crazy. Maybe we were all actors in a big theater plot. How many roles do we play? How long could we continue to fool everybody else? It seemed appropriate that we were all speaking about my father now—he was the most superb actor of all. I could feel the void in my belly again, and a bitter taste in my mouth. Was I a liar, or were they?

Then my uncle Rafael spoke.

"*Yo la verdad siento resentimiento hacia mi hermano,*" he said. "*Yo quería estudiar medicina y el convenció a mi papá que no era una carrera buena para mí. No había mucho dinero en la familia así que tuve que elegir otra carrera.*"

Wow— finally some sanity. A little piece of authenticity was bubbling up. I hadn't known about my uncle's resentment towards my father. Apparently, my father had told my grandfather that Rafael shouldn't study medicine because there was no money to support him while he studied. Now I felt bad for my uncle. It reminded me of how my father wanted me to become a secretary, rather than follow my creative passions.

What other family stories were buried?

ACAPULCO TROPICAL

Once Max ended his spiritual examination of our family, I felt relieved. He seemed satisfied with our answers, at least for the moment. It was getting late, so everybody left. The house settled back into a creepy silence. I was actually grateful for any kind of silence, even if it came with a chill.

My brothers and I dragged our feet upstairs to get some rest. Tomorrow, we'd have to perform the same song and dance again.

In the morning, I endured another slow shower, then an uneventful breakfast. No surprises from Luz María, no skeletons popping out of closets. At the temple, the morning prayers started and ended without my stomach spinning around. The frantic events from the last few days had settled. My heartbeat was normal, and miraculously, it seemed as if my skin had thickened. I was able to brush off tales of my parents' ghosts floating around whenever Dina or Max, or even Luz María mentioned them. In fact, I was resigned to *mingle* with their ghosts now, even if I couldn't see them.

Visitors dwindled down during the morning hours, and at our family meal—even with all the aunts, uncles, and cousins, not to mention the endless parade of dishes—a sense of peace flooded my brain. Was I successfully *faking it*? Or was this real?

Things kept along their smooth course until Max and Dina came back *again* in the late afternoon. I thought they were appeased by our answers the day before.

"*Buenas tardes*," Max said. "*Hoy es el día en que vamos a tener audiencias privadas con el señor Salomón. Les voy a llamar arriba a uno por uno de sus familiars para decirles lo que él desea.*"

Yikes! He wanted to call each family member to sit for a personal *audience* with my father. We had to go upstairs one at a time, while the rest of the family waited in the living room. We all

CHAPTER NINE

nodded in agreement. Even my agnostic relatives went along with Max's mystical plan.

I sank lower into the green sofa's stupid springs and tried to disappear. I was dreading a solo *chat* with my father. I tried hard to conjure a pleasant memory of him, and let my mind drift. How did I know it would take me back to roasting chestnuts with him in Acapulco?

I was three years old, barely tall enough to reach the stove. My father, tall and handsome, smiled at me. We were at the table in the kitchenette of our bungalow. Outside, the leaves of giant palm and mango trees swayed, while parrots sang their non-stop loud noises.

My father meticulously cut a small cross into the tough skin of each chestnut. What delicate work! Then, we walked to the stove, and he put the *castañas* on the *comal*, the flat iron pan usually used to warm up tortillas.

Even if I couldn't see the chestnuts roasting, I could smell them. It was a glorious scent. I balanced on my tippy toes and tried to catch sight of at least one of them. I loved how they crackled noisily when they popped. Sometimes, if my father had forgotten to puncture one of them, a chestnut would jump off in a delightful explosion of sound and scent, the soft, light color of their insides poking out just enough to give a taste of what was to come.

In the heat of December, the soft, warm breeze of the tropics mingled with the scent of the roasting *castañas*. My father and I sat quietly and ate as many as our tummies allowed. With Yosef still asleep, and my mother in another room taking care of baby Jonatán, this was my *special time* with *my daddy*.

ACAPULCO TROPICAL

Our bedroom faced the street. Sometimes, a rumbling would wake me up—cows running madly on the dirt road behind the hotel. I was dying to go outside and ride a brave horse to steer them, but then I got sleepy and went back to bed.

In the morning, before chestnuts, I would ask my father if he saw the cows too.

"*No linda,*" he chuckled. "*No las ví pero hay muchas vacas en Acapulco.*"

"How come you were asleep, *Daddy*? Is that why you didn't see them?"

"*Sí, me quedé dormido,*" he agreed.

"Why are there so many cows here?" I asked.

"*Acapulco es un pueblo y necesitan las vacas para comer y también las vacas les dan leche.*"

"What is a *pueblo*, Dad? Why do they need the cows to eat? How do they get milk from the cows? Can I go out and pet them?" Question after question as I tried to make sense of things. And my father just smiled and continued to prepare the chestnuts as I asked away.

For nearly two decades, we took off to Acapulco for a family trip around Christmas and the new year. During those years, my father remained a creature of habit. On the morning we'd leave for Acapulco, he would wake us all up at 5 a.m. so we could be ready in an hour. Not a minute later.

"*Ya levántense niños, y vístanse rápido que nos tenemos que ir tempranito.*"

"Dad, I'm sleepy...why do we have to wake up and get dressed so quickly? Why do we have to go *so* early?"

"*Para que no nos agarre el calor tan fuerte en el Cañón del Zopilote!*"

"What's the vulture's canyon?"

"*Un cañón con cactus y zopilotes adonde hace mucho calor.*"

CHAPTER NINE

"Is it really that hot in the canyon?" I would ask. "Are there really big cactuses there?"

"*Si señorita. Ya déjame de preguntar cosas y apúrate.*"

He'd finally lose his patience, and tell me to stop asking questions. Then he'd send me off to go get ready.

Once I dressed, I wanted to be the first one to the car, so I could sit up front between my *mami* and my *papi*.

I cozied up with a red blanket wrapped around my legs, and waited for everybody else to come down. Sitting in the front seat was not going to last forever—I had to take turns with my brothers. But the first portion of the trip, as we pulled out of the garage and drove through the chilled empty streets of Mexico City, was soothing for me, and I enjoyed watching the Christmas lights.

The drive was easily six hours long, usually more. The winding roads seemed eternal to me. At the *Cañón del Zopilote*, the sharp turns and curves were sickening. By the time we reached it, the temperature would be very hot. I had to concentrate quite a bit so I wouldn't throw up while my father attempted to distract us with random math questions.

"*A ver niños, cuántos kilómetros nos faltan si viajamos a 60 km por hora?*"

"Let me see, how many kilometers from here to Acapulco if we are traveling at about 60 kilometers per hour?" I would repeat it back, to make sure I understood.

"Maybe like about 100, right Dad?" Yosef would guess quickly.

"Yeah, or maybe like 120," Jonatán would reply when we were all old enough to play the game.

"*Los dos están bien, son mas o menos 110 kilómetros.*" And my dad would praise my brothers for coming so close, while I was still trying to figure it out.

I never understood how they could do math in their heads like that. Whenever the three of them carried on about numbers, I felt

ACAPULCO TROPICAL

left behind. Why hadn't I received the same mental math engine as they had in their brains?

To distract myself and not feel so dumb, I would count the Volkswagens that passed us on the road.

After the *Cañón del Zopilote*, we usually stopped for lunch at *Lupita*, an old café with pale yellow walls and a tired looking server. The place was strategically set along the side of the road, and served delicious hot cakes and *huevos a la Mexicana*.

After lunch, we would continue with our journey with less curves ahead.

One particular trip stands out in my mind, starting with the moment I yelled from the backseat, "Dad…Daaaad! I can see the ocean now!" We were rounding the final curve on top of the last hill. The Pacific Ocean glistened in the distance. I might have been hot, sweaty and tired, but I forgot about everything when I saw the ocean.

As we arrived at our hotel, Pilar, the owner, welcomed us like old friends. We checked in, left our baggage in our room, and quickly changed to our bathing suits. Then, we walked across the street to the *playa hornitos*, the "oven beach" where the sand could sometimes feel too hot to walk on.

We sat under a *palapa*, a palm roof structure that protected us from the sun, and ordered *Yolis*—fizzy lemon sodas they only sold in Acapulco. Then we jumped in the water as fast as we could. After a little while, we were back under the *palapa*, dripping salt water everywhere. And we were suddenly starving!

"*Quieren agua de coco?*" asked the waiter of the *palapa* restaurant.

"Daaaaad," we pleaded. "Can we have coconut water?"

"*También tenemos tostadas de camarones al mojo de ajo, huachi-*

CHAPTER NINE

nango a la parrilla, pulpos en su tinta, ceviche de pescado, tostadas de camarón," the server said. "*A ver que van a querer.*" He offered the day's menu: shrimp tostadas, grilled red snapper, octopus in ink sauce, and fish ceviche.

Jonatán and Yosef ordered shrimp tostadas. I ordered grilled red snapper. My mother ordered octopus with rice, and our father ordered the ceviche. He was happy and agreeable. Every time he spoke, it seemed like an unusual *yes* was the first thing out of his mouth. I was happily dangling my feet under my *palapa* chair.

We cooled off under the *palapa*, and sipped coconut water until the seafood arrived. After we were done, we went straight to the hotel for a *siesta*. We'd have supper at the hotel under a bigger *palapa* later. Pilar supervised the service at the restaurant, and nothing escaped her eye. She was short and plump, with a round face, and a potently high-pitched voice. She was married to a tall, lanky Swiss-German guy with dorky glasses. They mainly catered to European tourists, especially Swiss and German, and the food was a combination of Mexican and European cuisine.

Once I overheard a discussion between my parents about the guests.

"Salomón, I think Pilar's husband is an ex-Nazi hiding in paradise," my mother said. "I heard him talking to his guests in German. Once they sip enough *Pacífico* beer, they start singing war songs and praising Germany for its heroic actions. It rubs me the wrong way."

"*Ay Shayna,*" my father said. "*Estás exagerando.*"

"I'm not exaggerating! I can understand them. I speak Yiddish, and it's very close to their German. I'm telling you, they are ex-Nazis."

"*Bueno, qué quieres que haga,*" he said. "*Los niños están contentos aquí y nunca se enferman. La comida es buena y nos tratan bien. No les hagas caso.*"

My mother walked out of their room, lifting her nose indignantly. She had no comeback to my father's argument: we children were happy here, no one ever got sick, and they treated us well. She simply had to give up on her grievances and pay no attention to what she heard. As for my father, he just shrugged off the situation—like he always did. After all, he was a man of habit, not of principle. If we were stuck in a hotel full of ex-Nazis, but the owners were treating us like royalty, so be it. As long as we were going to Acapulco, we would stay at the Hotel *Papagayo*! End of story.

I didn't understand anything about the war or the Germans. I just loved all of the Christmas decorations this time of the year. Two enormous, star-shaped *piñatas* hung by high ropes from a colossal mango tree. We knew they were filled with great treats—sugar cane pieces, tangerines, peanuts, chewing gum, and a myriad of colorful Mexican sweets and candies. *Cañas de azúcar, mandarinas, cacahuates, chicles y dulces de colores*. One would be broken on Christmas Eve, the other on New Year's Eve. And since my birthday was *also* on New Year's Eve, I couldn't wait to celebrate with the rest of the children in the hotel. There would also be an enormous cake for me, and everybody would sing happy birthday and *Las Mañanitas*. The flamboyant birthday celebration suited my personality just fine, and the wedding-style cake *did not* feel excessive at all.

One time, my friend Dalia and her family joined us at the Hotel *Papagayo* for our winter holiday. We were 10 years old and impish—we just cruised and explored different parts of the hotel, and looked for ways to create a little playful havoc.

The hotel's giant Christmas tree left us awestruck. There were so many ornaments, especially bright colored glass spheres. Curious about what was inside the spheres, we *casually* dropped a couple, and were enthralled by the tinkling sound they made when they hit the ground and broke into hundreds of pieces.

CHAPTER NINE

Once we got bored with the ornaments, we went to the little zoo that Pilar's mother kept at the back of the hotel.

"*Oye, cuántos años crees que tenga la viejita?*" Dalia asked.

"How should I know?" I shrugged. "Maybe she's 100 years old!"

"*Sí, creo que sí. Alomejor tiene como 105 años.*"

"Yeah, maybe 105 years old. Maybe more. Who knows?"

The crotchety old lady collected a number of equally ancient and alluring animals, and kept them in makeshift cages.

Dalia wanted to go see the crocodile first.

"*Oyes, vamos a ver al cocodrilo primero.*"

"Okay," I agreed.

We looked around for the longest stick we could find, then marched to the crocodile cage. Dalia, with a mean look in her eyes, began poking mercilessly at the poor croc with the stick. I copied her when I took my turn with the stick. I don't know what evil force drove us to do it, but we went on and on because the crocodile didn't move. I thought it was dead. Then, suddenly, the crocodile turned so fast, and bit the stick so hard, that the whole cage rattled. We were scared to death and ran for our lives. When we were able to catch our breaths, Dalia proposed we go see the parrots next.

"*Vamos a ver a los pericos.*"

"Okay," I agreed. "But we are not going to poke at them."

"*Bueno. Está bien.*" She agreed.

Off we went to see the parrots and the cockatoos. We gathered long leaves from mango trees, and tickled their bellies until they grabbed at the leaves with their talons and chewed on them. We tried to teach them our names, and repeated ourselves over and over. But we were unsuccessful, got bored, and left.

"*Estos pericos son tontos,*" Dalia said. "*Vamos a ver a la marta.*"

"Maybe they are not *that* dumb," I countered. "Maybe we just don't know how to *teach* them how to speak. Let's go see the marten."

ACAPULCO TROPICAL

The marten seemed like a cross between a monkey, a squirrel, and an opossum. It looked soft, but we were afraid to touch it—we both thought it looked suspicious and unpredictable. And how come it lived in a tree with a swing, and not in a cage? We offered it pieces of fallen fruit, then watched it quietly, waiting for it to eat. Maybe it would curl its tail and swing back and forth from its swing bar. We knew that people made expensive art paintbrushes out of marten fur, and that made us want to touch it even more. How soft was it? But we never quite gathered the courage to do so.

After that, we were off to see the peacocks. We chased them around, trying to get one of their colorful feathers, but were never lucky enough to pluck one out.

As we grew up, Dalia's family moved on to higher-end hotels. We remained at the *Papagayo*. My childhood adventures shifted to new teenage endeavors. By then, I longed to escape to the beach for evening bonfires, to sing to the guitar tunes of Joan Manuel Serrat with friends, or maybe make out with a boyfriend. And naturally, as soon as I turned 15, my father started watching me like a hawk. Occasionally, he would let a guy take me on a *paseito en las calandrias*—a romantic ride on a fancy, horse-pulled cart. We would scuttle along the coast, but not for too long—I had to keep a strict curfew. Meanwhile, Yosef did not have the same time constraints, a fact that didn't sit well with me.

I learned to manage the situation as best I could, and used my sneaky intelligence to dizzy my father with inventions and lies.

"Yes, I'll be with Dalia at her hotel. They'll bring me back later." Of course I wasn't with her, but she covered for me.

He never knew *adónde quedó la bolita*—what the heck I was up to. In the end, his perception of me was right: I was a mud rat, *a mos-*

CHAPTER NINE

ca muerta. I loved boys, and I was not going to let him get in my way, especially as I was just beginning to explore this brand new world.

I was truly my father's daughter—since he was a conquistador, how could I be anything but a *conquistadora*?

Maybe we had more in common than I thought.

But there was something wrong with this picture. Had he actually continued his *conquistador* escapades all throughout his marriage with my mother? This raw thought took me away from the sweet memories of Acapulco, and thrust me back into my present reality.

How could I make peace with my father's ghost while these fumbling thoughts ran through my mind? How could I reassure Max that I had forgiven my father, or that I was filled only with sweet love for him?

At some point, long ago in my past, my *daddy* and I had stopped roasting chestnuts. The dirt streets where cows once ran wild were paved over. The *pueblo* charm disappeared. And I grew up!

I was at a loss for what to say.

CHAPTER TEN

Las Amantes

*"We meet ourselves time and again
in a thousand disguises on the path of life."*

–Carl Jung

Before our individual *chats* with my father, Max was taking a long time talking to Dina upstairs, and my thoughts began to spin out of control like a river barreling toward the ocean. A disquieting image of a voluptuous woman with large breasts, dressed in a tight red dress—like women in Fellini movies, complete with piercing eyes—assaulted my already fragile state of mind.

Sadly, she wasn't just a figment of my imagination. She was real, and my first encounter with her was by phone, when I called the hospital after my father's stroke. Before then, I knew nothing of her existence.

"*Bueno?*" she answered. She sounded kind and caring. "*Ah. Eres la hija de Salomón*," she went on. "*Mucho gusto. Me llamo Beatriz y lo siento que no nos hemos conocido pero no te preocupes, tu papá está bien y ya se va a ir a su casa pronto.*"

"Oh," I said. "Thank you for keeping my father company, Beatriz. I'm glad to hear he's doing well, and that he's going home soon." Whoever she was, I was happy she was at the hospital taking care of him.

CHAPTER TEN

"I know we haven't been introduced," I went on. "But I'm glad you're there."

"*Oh, sí. Aquí me quedo con él hasta que salga del hospital.*"

"Thank you. I'm grateful that you are staying with him until he leaves. I'll get down to Mexico as soon as I can."

Once I arrived in Mexico City, I went straight to my father's home. Beatriz was there. I got goose bumps when I met her in person, and my blood ran cold. Where the hell did this woman come from? She seemed to have emerged straight out of a Mexican vaudeville. She wore heavy red lipstick and makeup, and fake eyelashes. I had a vision of an octopus! Where did my father meet *her*?

I went downstairs for a moment to compose myself. I must have looked pale, because when Luz María saw me, she said, "*ay señora, qué le pasa? Se ve muy mal.*"

"I'm okay. Nothing is happening to me. But who is *that* woman upstairs with my father? Please tell me the truth, and don't lie to me."

With a sheepish look, Luz María said, "*esa señora viene muy seguido a ver a su papá y aquí se queda. Se llevó los vestidos de concierto de su mamá que quedaron en el closet y también el coche de su mamá.*"

I felt a dagger in my heart.

"How come you never told me this? Are you sure that she comes often, and stays with my father? And are you sure she took my mother's concert dresses from the closet upstairs…and also her car?" I was dumbstruck.

"*Si señora. Su papá me dijo que no les dijera nada. Pero no sé quién es ella. Es muy fea verdad?*" Luz María didn't know who Beatriz was, and my father had asked her not to tell anything to us. She clearly didn't like Beatriz.

"Yeah Luz, she is ugly," I said harshly. I was fuming, and didn't care that I was being mean. "Has Jonatán met her?"

"*Creo que sí, pero no estoy segura.*" Maybe, she said, without giving me a definitive answer.

Lost in this memory, my body jolted when Max called my brothers and me to join him in the family room.

"*Cálmate,*" I whispered softly, reminding myself to keep calm. By now, I was having major indigestion. From the sweet memories of Acapulco, to the images of Beatriz, my mind was in overdrive, and my stomach was having trouble with the ride. Who was my father? Why did I have to talk to him now? Damn him! He owed *me* an explanation. Who the hell was Beatriz?

Max began a new litany of spiritual lectures: "*Conocer a Dios es muy importante,*" he said. "*Yo no creo en Dios porque creer en Dios es realmente el verbo incorrecto. Yo conozco a Dios. Yo sé que Dios existe.*"

We sat and listened to him. I was thinking to myself, "Yes, just go along with Max. *Believing* was the wrong verb. Max *knew* God existed."

"*Saben muchachos? La Kabbalah habla de la existencia de Dios sin ninguna duda. También habla del principio de reparar el mundo, o Tikkun Olam. Y eso es lo que deben hacer ahora. Me entienden?*"

"I think we get it by now," Jonatán snapped. Good—he was as annoyed as I was. Repeating back to Max, Jonatán said, "You say that the Kabbalah talks about the existence of God without doubt, and about the principle of repairing the world. And this is something that we have to do now, right?"

"*Exactamente. La manera de hacerlo es perdonando a su papá.*"

"So," I chimed in, "I want to make sure I understand correctly. You are saying that we could *repair the fabric of the world* if we forgive our father? But what exactly is he asking forgiveness for?"

CHAPTER TEN

Would we finally get to the bottom of this already? If our father wanted forgiveness, I needed to know what he'd done wrong. Maybe then I could corroborate the stories that were swarming in my head like a beehive.

Max disregarded my question, which annoyed the hell out of me.

"*Saben? Existió una secta muy importante the judíos Mexicanos que estudiaba Kabbalah y que vivía en Guadalajara. Ellos hicieron un pacto que al morir, su trabajo sería el de ayudar a las almas de judíos que al morir estuvieran angustiados. Su propósito ha sido el de ayudar a estas almas a alcanzar su morada eterna.*"

I was speechless. According to Max, there was a Mexican Jewish Kabbalistic sect of studious people in Guadalajara. They made a pact that, after they died, they would help Jewish souls in distress reach their eternal dwelling.

"*Nosotros los conocemos como los Siete Samurais Judíos,*" he added.

"The Seven Jewish Samurai?" I asked. Them again! The same group Abraham had muttered about a few days ago.

"*Si, exactamente. Los Siete Samurais Judíos.*"

"And who exactly were they?"

Abraham hadn't explained. Neither had Dina when I asked her. Would Max? Or where they just some part of an in-joke among two-bit psychics? This was the third time I'd heard about them since my father's death—maybe they *were* real. I kind of liked the idea of being escorted to heaven by seven good-looking Jewish guys.

"*Los Siete Samurais Judíos estan dispuestos y listos a ayudar a su papá a desprenderse de este plano y seguir hacia su morada eterna,*" Max said.

"And how do you know they are willing and ready to help my father move on towards his ultimate soul dwelling?" Jonatán asked.

"*Porque yo mismo los llamé, a petición de su papá, para que hicieran esta mitzvah para el señor Salomón.*"

Had my father's spirit truly called on Max to bring the Seven Jewish Samurai forward, so they could perform this *mitzvah*, or good deed? If so, then I was off the hook! They could do what I couldn't do. I was thrilled.

"If these spirits are here to help him, I don't think our father really needs us now," I said.

"*Te equivocas, su papá los necesita y necesita también su perdón.*"

Oy. I guess I *wasn't* off the hook. Max said that we still needed to forgive him even if these spirit guides were around.

My own spirit deflated.

"Do these Jewish Samurai have names?" I asked.

"*Por supuesto. Tienen los mismos nombres que tenían cuando estaban vivos. Eran muy buenos amigos y todos crecieron en Guadalajara. Se llamaban: Jacobo, Issac, David, Nathaniel, Ezequiel, Rafael, and Aaron.*"

I was a bit skeptical of the idea that their names were the same as they'd been during their lifetimes—not to mention that they had been best friends growing up in Guadalajara.

Max went on with more details.

"*Rafael era médico cirugano del corazón. Aaron tenía un negocio de mueblerías. Ezequiel era un arquitecto muy reconocido. David era artista y pintó algunos murales en Guadalajara. Nathaniel era comerciante de telas. Issac era dentista y Jacobo era profesor de ciencias en la Universidad de Guadalajara.*"

They sounded like a fantastic bunch: a cardiologist, the owner of a furniture store, a renowned architect, an artist, a fabric businessman, a dentist, and a professor of science.

"*Todos ellos eran muy buenos amigos y fueron a la escuela juntos. Estaban interesados en la Kabbalah y decidieron formar un gru-*

CHAPTER TEN

po que estudiaba todos los domingos desde la tarde hasta altas horas de la madrugada."

I tried to imagine these good friends moving through life together. First, they were schoolmates. Then, they immersed themselves in Kabbalah. From there, they formed a weekly study group, met every Sunday, and studied until very late. Fascinating, but how much of it was true?

"*En el transcurso del tiempo descubrieron algunos principios esotéricos que les llevó a entender que la muerte es solamente un portal hacia la vida enterna e infinita*," Max continued. "*Así que no le tuvieron miedo a la muerte y entonces hicieron un pacto de permanecer juntos cuando murieran y ayudar a otras almas judías a pasar sin temor hacia el universo eterno.*"

Over time, these Jewish Samurai came to understand the mystical texts, which explained that death was only a portal to an eternal life. They were not afraid of dying, and they made a pact to remain together after they died—and to help Jewish souls move on fearlessly towards an infinite universe.

How was my father capable of summoning these living psychics and mystical Jewish warriors to his aid? His soul must truly be in deep trouble.

Max closed his eyes and grew quiet. When he opened them, he seemed brighter.

"*Los Siete Samurais me están hablando. Dicen que el señor Salomón era un Buddha de Oro.*"

"Are they talking to you right now?" I gasped. "What do they mean when they say that our father was *a golden Buddha*?"

"*Me dicen que su papá toda su vida fue un Buddha de oro, pero desafortunadamente estaba cubierto en lodo y esa fué la razón por que que fué incapaz de dar.*"

LAS AMANTES

Max said the Samurai *told him* that our father was some kind of golden Buddha—shiny underneath, but covered in mud. That was the reason he was incapable of giving during his life.

This made sense to me. I'd seen glimmers of gold at times.

Was this whole thing an exorcism to remove the mud that covered my Buddha-like father? Could he shine like the real Buddha that he was deep down? What could I do with the darn image of grotesque Beatriz—her octopus lips and tight red dress—that had taken over my father's life before he died?

Everything in my head was scrambled. How could the sublime mingle with the absurd like this? I tried as hard as I could to be present in our conversation, but it was almost impossible. I kept coming back to Beatriz, and felt lost in the mess of my brain. I tasted the same repulsion as when I'd first met her. I was floating towards a vortex of more disturbing memories.

After Luz María explained who Beatriz was—and what she'd been up to—I marched to my father's room. Beatriz sat at his bedside, spoon-feeding him some sort of ghastly looking soup. She was actually forcing him to eat it.

"*Andale Salomón*," she cooed. "*Come un poquito de sopa, te va ha hacer bien. Tiene yerbitas que me dio un curandero.*"

She said the soup was good for my father, and that it was made from rare herbs she'd gotten from her *healer*. It would give him strength. I gasped for air and almost threw up. I was certain that she was trying to poison him.

Beatriz stood up and went to the bathroom. I examined the soup. It had a strange consistency and looked awfully murky. That's when my father, who'd seemed so passive and remote a few seconds earlier, turned to me abruptly.

CHAPTER TEN

"*Yo no me quiero comer esa sopa.*"

"No, of course not," I said softly. "If you don't want to eat the soup, you don't have to. Did she actually *make* that for you?"

"*Sí. Eso dijo,* that's what she said."

"Let me get rid of it." I took the soup to the kitchen and threw it away. When I came back upstairs he asked me, "*qué piensas de ella?*"

He wanted to know what I thought about her.

"Mmmmm…" was all I could get out of my mouth. So many answers rattled around my head. I almost started choking.

"About what exactly?" I asked, looking for some clarification.

"*De ella,*" he said.

"About *her*. Well…" I took a deep breath. A moment ago, I wanted to strangle her…and him, for that matter.

"*Pienso que la cosa esta terrible,*" I said. "I think this is terrible."

"*Si verdad?*" he said.

"Yes," I said. "Truly terrible."

For a split second, we shared some father-daughter complicity.

"What do you want me to do about her?" I asked.

"*Lo que quiero que hagas ahorita mismo es decirle que se vaya,*" he answered.

He wanted me to get rid of her right away.

I waited for her to come out of the bathroom. I felt empowered by my father's desires, and my own sense of righteousness.

"*Mi papá quiere que te vayas en este momento,*" I said when she finally emerged. "Take your herbs with you. He won't have them… or your soup."

I must have looked menacing—her eyes grew big, she blinked a few times, and when her mouth opened, nothing came out. She grabbed her purse and left without saying goodbye to him. If only she'd offered an inch of resistance—I wanted a reason to go for her throat.

I went back to my father and asked him, "Who *is* she?

LAS AMANTES

"*Es una ingeniera química que era colega mía hace mucho tiempo.*"

There was no way she was a chemical engineer. She seemed like a different *professional* type of woman to me. I thought my father was lying. But then he showed me her business card, complete with her name, contact information, and job title: *Ingeniero Químico*. I thought anybody could print a phony business card. She was a good con artist, and my father was gullible.

"*Sabes? Se llevó dinero de mi caja de seguridad,*" he said casually.

"What? She stole $10,000 from your home safe while you were in the hospital? American dollars? Why did you have that much money in your safe?"

"*Si, estoy seguro,*" he said.

He was 100% sure he had it, and that she'd stolen it.

"Do you want to press charges?"

"*No quiero,*" he said. "*Yo se los voy a pedir cuando venga.*"

And that was the end of the story. No charges. He'd just ask for the money next time she came to his house.

"Are you sure she'll come back?" I asked. But he fell asleep without answering me.

Of course, Beatriz never came back to see him again. She never called either. She had his money, along with my mother's fancy concert dresses and car.

A few days later, Jonatán and I decided to drive to the address on her business card. We made it out to the Mexico City airport, and scoured a number of poorer neighborhoods. There was no such address. Later on, as we organized my father's affairs, we discovered that he'd given her nearly $200,000 in American money that no one knew existed.

We consulted an attorney to see if we could recover at least some of it, but since our father had given it to Beatriz voluntarily, there was nothing we could do. It was hard to prove that he had dementia, or that she'd taken advantage of him. Our hands were

CHAPTER TEN

tied. We couldn't do anything but let go of this bloodsucker in the red dress.

Max was still talking. I forced myself back to reality.

"*Los Siete Samurais Judíos nos dicen que perdonar es el camino espiritual que todos tenemos enfrente y también el camino hacia el amor y la abundancia.*"

The Seven Jewish Samurai said forgiveness was a spiritual path in front of all of us. Not just that, but it was the most direct path toward love and abundance. Still, I was having a hard time forgiving Beatriz. How could I? She'd taken complete advantage of a sick, frail man.

"*También nos dicen que un asunto importante a considerar aquí es el principio Kabalístico sagrado de dar y recibir, como el Arbol de la Vida,*" Max said, speaking for the Samurai. The key issue here was the sacred Kabbalistic principle of giving and receiving—like the Tree of Life.

What did my father give? What did he receive?

"*La muerte de un ser querido nos da la oportunidad de crecer personalmente y de ayudar a otros a crecer hacia niveles mas elevados de existencia en el mundo material,*" Max continued.

I wasn't feeiling spiritual, and couldn't take his words into my heart. How could I reconcile that the death of a loved one could bring me the opportunity to grow personally, and to help others grow towards higher levels of existence? Max might have made it all sound so poetic, but I couldn't relate. Not now.

Either undeterred, or oblivious to what I was feeling—or both, for that matter—Max continued.

"*El señor Salomón quería dar con todo su corazón pero su luz estaba atrapada muy dentro de sí mismo y para poder dar a otros lo que está dentro de nosotros, tenemos que abrir nuestros corazones."*

So, my father had wanted to give with all of his heart, but his light was trapped inside him. To give what's inside of us, we need to open up. Was I capable of opening up to a thief like Beatriz, or to my father, who'd given so much over to her instead of giving to his children?

"Ustedes, como hijos de su padre son la luz dentro del Buddha de oro, y los únicos capaces de literalmente derritir el barro que cubre el Buddha si abren sus corazones para amar a su padre," Max said. Now he was scaring me. As he put it, *we*, the children, were the light inside of our golden Buddha father. And only *we* could melt the mud that covered him. But first, we had to open our hearts completely to him, and learn to love him unconditionally.

If this was true, then my father's soul wasn't going anywhere tonight. I was pretty closed down.

"Solamente tienen que preguntar al Creador cuál exactamente es su camino hacia servir a otros y seremos guiados hacia él porque tenemos todo lo que necesitamos adentro de nosotros mismos para tener éxito en nuestro camino," Max said. I could feel his words getting scrambled in my mind. We were supposed to do what? Ask God to show us a path toward service? How would that guide us toward what we needed to be successful in our lives? And how was the answer already inside of me if *I* couldn't see it?

I was stuck with my limitations. I would have to leave things up to the Seven Jewish Samurai to help me out. Would they be there for me when my time came? After all, if they had my father's back, I could at least hope they'd do the same for me.

CHAPTER TEN

Max and Dina sent us downstairs. They needed to continue their dialogue with my father and the Samurai in private.

After a little while, they called me back up for a private conversation with my father. I was ready to fail.

Dina said, "*Aquí esta tu papá, parado atrás de tí y esta sonriendo.*"

"Ah, that's nice," I said. "I can't see him, but I'm glad he's standing by my side, smiling."

What could my father be smiling about?

"*Puedes sentir su presencia?*" Dina asked.

"No," I said. "Quite frankly, I can't feel his presence?" What I *really* wanted to say was that I wanted to feel his presence most of my life, and that now that he was dead, I could care less. To hell with my father's ghost…and to Dina and Max for that matter!

As if she could read my mind, Dina went on.

"*Ahora tu papá esta muy nervioso, y está subiendo y bajando las escaleras. Está muy preocupado por tí, por la situación emocional de Yosef y también esta preocupado porque Jonatán no se ha casado.*"

The idea that my father was worried about us now was ridiculous. Why hadn't he cared when he was alive?

"Well, there is nothing he can do now," I answered. "Even if he's anxiously going up and down the staircase, worried about me, or about Yosef's emotional situation, or about Jonatán not being married, what is *he* going to do about it?"

Dina didn't answer my question. Instead she giggled. What was she giggling about?

"*Tu papá me anuncia que Jonatán se va a casar pronto,*" she said.

"And why is it funny that he says that Jonatán is going to get married soon? I don't get it."

"*Porque es un poquito tramposo y los espíritus no deben darle noticias a las personas de esa manera.*"

"Oh well," I said. "Tell my father not to cheat, I guess. Is he trying to ingratiate himself to his children now by giving out news he's not supposed to share?"

My father's ghost was annoying the hell out of me.

"What *exactly* does he want from me?" I asked before Dina could speak again.

I was just about finished with these psychics. By now, I was convinced they were just testing my openness and ability to forgive and forget.

Max decided to cut in.

"*Tienes que encontrar el perdón hacia tu padre en tu corazón. Es imperativo que lo hagas,*" he said.

"I'll try my best to forgive him," I said, "but it's going to be really difficult. There are many things I need to understand. And besides, you are not giving me details. Forgiveness in the whole sense of the word is very challenging. I think my father needs to work this out with the Seven Jewish Samurai, not with me. And I'll ask you again, what exactly does he want me to forgive him for? Tell him I'm not going to give him a blank check for my forgiveness."

I was done trying to hide how irritated I was. Once again, we were talking about forgiveness. We hadn't gotten anywhere since the first time Abraham brought it up, and it had been more than a few long days and nights by now.

Max and Dina were visibly frustrated with my responses. They dismissed me and called my aunt Reyna next.

I joined my brothers on the low sofa and crossed my arms. It was getting late, and I wanted to rest and be left alone. I was biting my nails now as another rumination assaulted me.

CHAPTER TEN

Soon after Beatriz left, another woman showed up at my father's door. Yolanda was younger, soft spoken and sweet looking. Luz María had told me that Yolanda frequented my father's home soon after my mother passed. She found out that my father had a stroke and came to visit him.

I invited her into the living room for coffee while my father was finishing his physical therapy. She was animated, happy to meet me, and appreciative or my welcoming.

"*Hola. Me da tanto gusto conocerte. Tu papá me ha hablado tanto de ustedes.*"

"Nice to meet you too," I said. "You say that my father talked to you about us? What did he say?"

"*Bueno, sé que vives en California y tienes una hijita. Y sé también que tu hermano Yosef tiene dos hijos y tu hermano Jonatán vive en México, pero no lo he conocido.*"

"Ah," I nodded as she shared the biographical bits and pieces that my father had shared with her—that I lived California, that Yosef had two children, and that Jonatán was unmarried.

"And…how did you meet my father?" I asked.

"*En el banco. Yo trabajaba en el banco adonde tu papá iba.*"

Of course! Where else would my father meet her but at the bank?

"*Sabes? Yo le estoy muy agradecida con tu papá. Yo lo quiero mucho y lo acompañé después de que tu mamá murió. Pero nunca quize faltarle al respeto a tu mamá porque era una dama.*"

I looked down into my coffee cup to conceal my tears. She said that she loved my father dearly, and had been keeping him company since my mother died. She meant no disrespect towards her or our family. She knew that my mother was *a lady*.

Her words sank heavy into my heart.

LAS AMANTES

"*Tu papá ha sido como un padre para mí. Siempre ha sido muy dulce conmigo.*"

"That's nice," I said. I could barely believe that my father had been like a father to her, always nice and sweet. He even helped her buy a new car and pay her rent!

"*Sí,*" she went on. "*También ha sido muy bueno con mis hijos y los adora. Ha sido como un padre para ellos. A veces me acompañaba a llevar a los niños al parque y les compraba algodones de azúcar y los columpiaba o jugaba pelota con ellos.*"

My veins turned icy as I pictured my father spending time and pouring love to her children. Playing with them in the park? Buying them cotton candy? I just couldn't believe it. My father barely knew his own grandchildren, yet here he was having a good time with a stranger's children.

Were we talking about the same person?

"*Tu papá ha sido la persona mas maravillosa y generosa que he conocido.*"

My father...the most wonderful and generous man she had ever met? That was the last straw for me. I wanted to scream!

My hand shook as I lifted the cup to my lips. I felt the fluid going down, burning as if I'd swallowed acid. Yet I just kept smiling at Yolanda like a zombie.

"I'm pretty sure his therapy is over," I managed to say. "Why don't we go upstairs to see if you can visit with him?"

"*Claro,*" she chirped. "*Gracias.*"

We went upstairs together. I wanted to make sure there would be no more stealing by another woman.

Resting in bed after his therapy, my father looked harmless. Yolanda walked in quietly. He turned his head and lit up when he saw her. When was the last time he'd looked so happy?

I left them alone, went downstairs, and sank deep into the sofa. The anger was almost asphyxiating. After a while, I went back to

CHAPTER TEN

my father's room to see what was happening. Yolanda was clipping his toenails with remarkable delicacy. I thought of Mary Magdalene washing Christ's sore feet with grace and tenderness. Yolanda looked so sweet and holy…and I felt like vomiting.

When it was time for her to leave, I thanked her for coming.

"I understand he has been very kind and generous to you," I said, "but now circumstances are different. He won't be able to give you any more money."

"*No te preocupes. Yo entiendo y eso no es importante para mí. Voy a venir a visitarlo y le voy a traer algunos DVD's y su pizza favorita.*"

She assured me that the money was not important to her, and promised that she would come back to visit, and even bring some DVDs for him to watch, along with his favorite pizza.

After she left I cried so bitterly, my insides felt raw. Such emotional intensity scared me. Yolanda was the daughter he'd always wanted—not me. She received the love he could not show his own children or grandchildren.

I was done with all of it! There would be no more crying. It was time for me to grow up. If my father didn't have it in him to love his family, but would rather shower strangers with the love he never gave us, then I had nothing more for him. Yolanda's visit had pushed me over the cliff I'd been teetering on for some time. Now I needed to learn how to fly. The realization wasn't scary—it was liberating.

Of course, no one ever saw or heard from Yolanda again. Ultimately, my brothers and I took care of my father in his final years…not the strangers he'd chosen over us.

Aunt Reyna didn't spend much time with the psychics. She came downstairs and shared what my father said to her through Max.

"*Tu papá me pidió perdón porque dijo que fue negligente conmigo y no se comportó como un hermano que se interesaba sinceramente en mí.*"

"Hmm…I'm sorry Auntie," I said. "Sounds like you also received his neglect during his lifetime. We all did. I'm sorry he didn't act like a caring brother."

"*Sabes? La verdad te confieso que he estado enojada con el por muchos años porque a pesar de adorar a tu papá como mi hermano mayor el nunca reciprocó mis sentimientos.*"

Another confession spilled out of her: she was only now coming to terms with the anger she'd felt toward him for many years. Yes, she'd adored her older brother, but she was very disappointed that he never reciprocated the sentiment, or even acknowledged her feelings. Via the psychics, my father finally acknowledged his indifference, and owned up to how much he had hurt my aunt.

My uncle Rafael was the last one to have a private audience with Max and Dina. It didn't take long either. When he came downstairs, he seemed stern. My father had asked his forgiveness for the role he played in boycotting his desire to become a doctor. Even though Rafael had gone on to become a successful accountant, he still felt cheated out of the career he'd truly wanted.

Clearly, my father carried lots of weight over many lives. Unfortunately, instead of offering support to people who looked up to him, he made decisions *for* them, and withheld love and encouragement. I could relate to these stories. I felt sad for my aunt and uncle. The whole thing also made me curious about something though: Why was my father asking them to forgive him for specific actions, yet hadn't asked anything specific of me? Was it because there were too many things for which he wanted my forgiveness, and didn't know where to start?

Just when I thought the evening was over, Max called on my brothers and me again. He seemed even more agitated now.

CHAPTER TEN

"*Su padre esta llorando y me ruega que lo ayude. Su alma esta apesadumbrada con remordimientos y se encuentra en un estado grave de arrepentimiento.*"

I grew sad for my father. Per Max, he was crying and begging for help. His soul was suffering under the tremendous weight of deep remorse, and stuck in a grave state of repentance.

"*Su perdón le ayudará a suavizar el dolor de su alma.*"

Our forgiveness, Max said, could help ease his soul's pain. A fragment of Pablo Neruda came to mind:

Las lágrimas que no se lloran esperan en pequeños lagos o serán ríos invisibles que corren hacia la tristeza?—Do tears not yet spilled wait in small lakes or are they invisible rivers that run towards sadness?

Why did my father wait to cry until he died? Why couldn't he say *I love you* when he was still alive? Why did he wait until he was gone to seek forgiveness?

"*Su papá esta triste porque el quería abrazarlos antes de morir pero no pudo hacerlo,*" Max said somberly. "*Lloró despues de morir, lágrimas que salieron de sus ojos después que falleció.*"

The deep sadness overwhelmed me too. My father, Max said, had wanted to hug us all before he died, but wasn't able to do so. Now his soul was crying lonely tears. It was too much to handle. Abraham had been the first to mentioned the crying; now Max confirmed it. I *had* to believe this was true.

The thought of crying after I died wasn't appealing. In fact, it would probably be a good idea to start making a list of people I had hurt and ask their forgiveness *now*, rather than from inside my casket!

I was slipping into a strange state—a delicate, philosophical alertness collided with confusion. I felt terribly sorry for my father.

LAS AMANTES

I wanted to forgive him, but was not ready to do it. Why was he covered in mud? Why was his heart a rock when we were young? What had happened to the promising man he was? Where had his sweetness gone? What rare illness had infected his spirit?

Could I really set my father free from his suffering, simply by saying *I forgive you,* and truly meaning it? How? Could I not end up in this same state of terrible remorse after I died? Maybe my own heart was covered in mud. After all, if I was incapable of forgiving my father, where else was I failing? It can be so easy to point the finger at others, but not at ourselves.

Finally, one soothing thought broke through my dark mental chatter: Perhaps my father and I will once again, on a timeless day, roast chestnuts together in heaven, or dance the rumba at a celestial revelry. Maybe the Seven Jewish Samurai will join in as well. That was the only solution I could think of.

CHAPTER ELEVEN
One Last Tear

"What color is the scent of the blue weeping of violets?
De qué color es el olor del llanto azul de las violetas?"

–Pablo Neruda

Sensing our deep exhaustion, Max said that was enough for another evening of talks with my father. He and Dina finally left, along with the rest of my relatives.

I crashed hard on my bed, and wasn't asleep long before seven bearded men showed up in my dream.

Japanese swords, Samurai head gear, Jewish prayer shawls…so *these* were the fabled Jewish Samurai!

"What are you doing in my dream?" I asked. Instead of answering, they flew high up through layers of clouds.

"Come back," I desperately called. "I need you!" But they continued to move away, floating in the ether above my head. A shiny object caught my eye. I looked down. One of them left his sword behind! I went to pick it up, but as I grabbed it, it disintegrated.

A cloud of white dust surrounded me.

"Hey!" I yelled. "Where do you go when you die?"

Silence. More dust. Nothing.

I woke up agitated. I didn't want them to leave without answers. They needed to come back. Max had said their mission was

CHAPTER ELEVEN

to help my father—I was beginning to believe it. Why else would they show up in my dream? My father had created so much havoc and confusion in his life that he surely needed these Jewish Samurai to get him out of the hole he'd dug.

I dragged myself out of bed, still disappointed that the Samurai disappeared before they could answer my questions. It was going to be another long day. There were just a couple of days left of the shiva, but I was ready to leave. I wanted my comforts: organic veggies from Whole Foods; shower under a steady stream of hot water; soak in a hot tub if I pleased. And no one would be around to scrutinize my every move, or say a single word about spirits! I was done with the memories that flooded my brain. I was through with my parents' ghosts.

I asked Luz María to just make me oatmeal for breakfast for a change. I was even tired with *huevos rancheros,* and rich, spicy foods. My brothers and I ate, then made it to yet another morning of prayers at the synagogue. After that, we took our positions on the low sofa. By midday our relatives arrived with more food. I admired their amazing capacity to concoct large meals with a snap of their fingers. It seemed like they were preparing for another *fiesta,* all happy and lively.

Then my cousin Ariela showed up with her little kids. Her youngest son, six-year-old Ben, had a mischievous look as he stood against the wall in the living room. He was hiding something behind his back. All of a sudden, I heard a little crack, then saw a gooey yellowish substance sliding down the wallpaper behind him. He'd cracked an egg behind his back. What the heck? By the time his mom spotted him, the egg was running down to the floor. My cousin laughed loudly—so did the rest of the family. It was like their private joke: *el coyotito flaco,* thin little coyote stealing eggs. He was allergic, they explained. He couldn't eat them, so this was his revenge.

ONE LAST TEAR

I didn't join in their amusement. I felt a cold shower drip down my spine. My stomach tightened. I was definitely cut from another fabric than they were. I could only find thin threads that connected them with me. I wanted to slap that little bastard hard.

Why would a stupid broken egg bring up so much pent-up emotion in me?

In the middle of their laughter, I asked poor Luz María to clean it up, and told her to put the eggs away so the kid couldn't find them. The stink, and the hideous smear on the wall, were more reminders that the house was falling apart. It was no laughing matter.

I excused myself from the table and went upstairs. I needed respite again. What was I supposed to say? "Ah, aren't you a sweet little kid? *Ay que mono el niño, no?*" I hid in my old bedroom. Over the years, it had become my father's room, even before my mother died. He had said that he left their bedroom because he snored and didn't want to wake my mother up. Still, I didn't like the idea of my father sleeping in my old bed, or taking over my room with its little cubbies where I once kept miniature collections and other cute girl souvenirs. He messed it all up with his *Selecciones Reader's Digest* magazines and other dumb artifacts—rusted bottle openers, receipts, worn-out rubber bands, paper clips, empty wallets, fossilized business documents, even yellowed bank statements from accounts he'd closed long ago.

Why did he have to distort my memories and poison my sweet little bedroom with these obsolete objects, and spray DDT on top of it all? It used to be my safe haven!

I sadly remembered how beautiful it had been during my childhood: light blue carpet, large mirror behind the door with its special light, and the elegant white lacquered furniture with golden edge inlays. My bed was cozy, and I had many drawers for all of my things. Finding my father's crap was an intrusion. I sat

CHAPTER ELEVEN

on my bed and remembered how, once upon a time, the room was so big, I swore the sun could fit inside of it.

That was back when I thought God lived in my closet, which wasn't as uplifting a thought as having the sun sit in the middle of my room. In fact, I was afraid of the idea of God lurking among my toys and clothes. Every night, I carefully closed the closet doors so God couldn't find me. At times the magic thinking worked—I'd fall asleep right away. Other times I stayed vigilant. Unable to close my eyes, I'd stare at the closet doors and imagine God's grim face poking out.

Sometimes I would hear a sound downstairs, and convince myself there was a burglar in the house! Paralyzed in suffocating fear under the covers, I wouldn't move a toe. That way, he wouldn't know I was here.

Whenever this agonizing idea appeared, I would have some quite reasonable arguments with the imaginary kidnaper.

"The police will catch you," I'd tell him as soon as he entered my room. "You'll go to jail."

If my argument didn't convince him, I would offer him irresistible Mexican food with *smaltz* from our abundant refrigerator.

"Did you know that Luz María made the best *chiles rellenos* in the world?" I would ask. "I can heat you some leftovers, as long as you let me go. Or, you can just take her with you, instead of me!"

And if *this* argument didn't work, I would offer my savings, my little perfume bottles, and my priceless miniatures collection. I memorized the argument in my head.

"*Mira señor ladrón, déjame ir. Te puedes llevar la comida del refrigerador que quieras. Luz María hace los chiles rellenos más ricos del mundo. Te doy todos mis ahorritos, mi colección de perfumes y mi colección de miniaturas.*"

I always won my freedom with such outstanding bargaining. In the process, I would help the poor kidnapper turn his actions around

ONE LAST TEAR

from wrong to good. I was indeed the heroine of my own salvation, not to mention his soul's deliverance—*mi salvación y la salvación de su alma*. I was the queen of good deeds. What a *mitzvah!*

If only I could bargain like this with my father.

My raw fear of earthquakes was even more challenging than those nocturnal ruminations. Poor Mexico City—*la pobrecita ciudad de México*. Built on the shaky soil of a former lake, we would have at least one strong earthquake per year. In a constant state of alert, and always dreading the next one, I often imagined my bedroom ceiling falling down and flattening me. My little dancing feet were ready to jump into a pair of shoes at any given moment during the night. I compulsively left my shoes in one particular spot next to my bed where I could find them in the dark.

When I was nine, during a particularly strong earthquake that seemed to last forever, I decided that I wasn't going to just stay paralyzed with fear in my bed all alone. *No señorita, ya no me iba a quedar en mi cama yo sola paralizada de miedo*. Armed with courage, I ran to Jonatán's room. My calm, sleepy brother invited me into his bed, and put his arm around me.

"*No te preocupes hermanita, sólo piensa que estás en un barquito y que se está moviendo entre las olas del mar*," he said.

"How do you do it?" I asked. "How can you just think that you are in a small boat, bobbing up and down in ocean waves?"

"*Sí, piénsalo. No es difícil. Concéntrate bien*," he affirmed.

"Easy for you to say…but I'll try to concentrate on it."

I tried to imagine being in a boat while everything around us moved wildly. There were crackling noises everywhere. I began singing a song I learned in first grade, when Miss Carmelita taught us Spanish vowels—

CHAPTER ELEVEN

"*La mar estaba serena, serena estaba la mar*—the sea was serene, serene was the sea. *Con 'a'...la mar astaba sarana, sarana astaba la mar. Con 'e'...le mer estebe serene, serene estebe le mer. Con 'i'...li mir estibi sirini, sirini istibi li mir. Con 'o'...lo mor ostobo sorono, sorono ostobo lo mor. Con 'u...lu mur ustubu suruno, surunu ustubu lu mur.*"

My brother and I laughed along with my silly song until the earthquake stopped. Then I went back to my room.

Why hadn't my parents come out of their room to check on us? Why hadn't they *ever* done anything like that during an earthquake?

In the morning, my father inspected new cracks in the walls, but never asked if we'd felt anything the night before—or if we'd been scared. Zero parental instincts. The door to their bedroom was always locked, and the room off limits, earthquake or not.

I was thankful that there were no earthquakes during the shiva. If an egg crushed against a wall could provoke me, then clearly my internal earthquakes were enough.

My old bedroom was no longer soothing. I couldn't find my reflection in the midst of cluttered memories. There was nowhere to hide in this house! Outrageous recollections of the past haunted me everywhere I went. I could feel my soul crawling under my skin, trying to claw its way out.

I waited upstairs until my relatives left, then went to get some fresh air and solitude. I sat on the shabby yellow chair in the backyard and felt the warm sun on my face. For a moment, I thought of nothing, just contemplated time's passing. I daydreamed that I was a woman in one of Marc Chagall's paintings, traveling from rooftop to rooftop, playing violin, flying through

ONE LAST TEAR

thin air, dancing to the rhythms of the sky. In the midst of the reverie, my mind landed on an old picture. There I was as a kid: black leotard and pink tights, my hair in a ponytail—I'm doing a ballet arabesque. But the image doesn't last long before my brothers join the picture frame. Now we're dressed in costumes for Purim, the Jewish festival that commemorates the deliverance of the Jewish people from Haman's annihilation plot. The story was from the *Book of Esther*, but Purim felt like our private Jewish Halloween—no witches, but plenty of princesses and queens.

I'm dressed like a woman from the state of Veracruz: a white regional costume with a black embroidered apron, a red clover pinned to my hair. Jonatán is dressed as Peter Pan, and Yosef as a boy scout. Or is it the other way around? The picture in my mind keeps reversing them. That's fine—I'm enjoying the trance. These were the handiest costumes we had at home. In the picture we seemed stern. Why were we not happy? There would be a costume contest, right? Oh, that's right, we knew we'd never win—not dressed like *that*.

One year for Purim, my mother got a sudden artistic inspiration and worked hard to create a pencil costume for one of my brothers. It was actually really inventive. She fashioned a cardboard cylinder with holes for the eyes and arms, and a cone on top. Then she covered it in bright yellow and brown paper. Off went my brother in his unique pencil outfit. Even though the poor thing couldn't sit or move around very well, he loved it! He may have even won a prize that year.

I snapped out of my memories and looked around the yard. Everything was wildly overgrown and unkempt. Baby tears—*lágrima de niño*—grew everywhere. How perfect, the baby tears were taking over. What remained of my mother's rose bushes seemed skimpy and sad. There were no roses in bloom. Across the way, the peach tree didn't bear any fruit. Dry vines covered the walls,

CHAPTER ELEVEN

suspended like parchment paper. How long had the yard been this way? Years? A decade? It was as depressing and disheartening as the inside of the house.

My eyes scanned around and eventually settled on an unexpected visitor: a giant lizard. It stood on a decorative volcanic rock just inches away, then started to crawl *toward* me, rather than scurry away as lizards do. It drew closer and tilted its head, adjusted its tiny eyes like it was trying to focus on me. Then it stared straight into my eyes with an intensity that was almost scary.

Was it trying to hypnotize me? *La lagartija me estaba tratando de hipnotizar!* It seemed like it wanted to tell me something. Could lizards *talk*? Was I caught in a Carlos Castaneda story?

I moved my foot, hoping to scare it away. Nothing. It stayed still and watched me. I made a shadow with my hands. Again, nothing. This little guy wouldn't leave!

"*Orale lagartija, apoco eres mi papá?*" I asked him out loud— "are you my father by any chance?"

The lizard gave a little blink, then took off with a colossal leap, finally disappearing in the dried vines. Was that my father? Can the dead shapeshift into animals as they please? I remembered the hawk from the cemetery. Now a lizard! But of course, when I actually *wanted* an explanation, there were no shamans around.

The boys in our neighborhood used to cut the tails off of lizards. Then they'd explain to us how it was okay because the lizards would grow new ones. I never believed them, and thought they were just being mean. But one time, I worked up the courage to ask my father if it was true.

He was sunbathing in the backyard, reading his Sunday newspaper.

"Hey Dad, can lizards grow their tails again if they get cut off?"

"*Sí, por supuesto que sí,*" he said adamantly.

"Really? But how do they do it?"

ONE LAST TEAR

"*Así nomás*," he answered.

"What do you mean just like that?" I asked.

"*Sí.*"

No further explanation, but since he was so *smart* about things like that, I believed him.

That was the day I decided that it was safe to venture into the backyard to ask him things. It was better to catch him outside than anywhere else—even if he looked funny wearing his old-fashioned faded bathing suit that made his belly stick out.

Most Sundays, after watching sports on TV, he went to the backyard to sunbathe. He loved to recline on his raggedy lounge chair and read one of the papers—*El Excelsior* or *El Universal*. He would be in good spirits, especially if his favorite soccer team had won. My mother would have played piano during the game, and by the time my father ventured outside, she'd be preparing our Sunday meal. I preferred to join him in the yard—even though my mother was a fabulous pianist and great cook, she never gave practical answers to my questions.

I loved these moments. My father was never in a rush to get rid of me, and I wasn't in a hurry to get back into the house. Somehow, I felt we connected out here.

After sunbathing for a while, he would pull out the hose from behind the peach tree and water his little green corner, tending to the garden with great love and care.

Sometimes, if I was angry, or in an argument with my mother or one of my brothers, he would act as a peacemaker, and let me vent.

"*No es bueno enojarte con tu mamá o con tus hermanos*," he'd say. "*Debes de hablarles. No me gusta que en esta casa no se hablen.*"

"I know you think it isn't good that I won't talk to Mom or my brothers," I'd reply, "but it's their fault. They were mean! Even if you don't like it when we don't talk, I don't feel like talking."

"*Debes hacer un esfuerzo y hablarles.*"

CHAPTER ELEVEN

"Okay, I'll make an effort and go talk to them."

And off I'd go to make amends. As neurotic as my father was, he didn't like discord among us. He was the only one entitled to be angry. Yet, I felt compelled to break the ice with anyone who'd aggravated me—just to please him.

Luz María caught sight of me sitting pensively in the backyard, and came to ask if I needed anything. I knew she was worried after she saw me so upset at the family meal. She leaned forward and patted me on the back.

"*Quiere algo de tomar o necesita algo?*"

"Nope, but thanks Luz," I said. "I'm okay. I was just remembering some things." Then I started laughing uncontrollably. Luz María looked perplexed and worried.

"Do you remember when Dalia and I flooded the bathroom in the building behind the yard?" I asked her, still laughing.

"*Sí que me acuerdo*," she said. "*Su papá estaba muy enojado.*"

"Yes, my dad got really angry with me. But we were just kids playing. We didn't know better. Well, maybe Dalia and I were not *that* innocent. How old were we?"

"*No sé, creo que tenían como doce años,*" she answered.

"Yup. I think you're right, probably 11 or 12. Let me tell you, it was so funny to us. We saw that the neighbors left one of their windows wide open. We just decided to *water* their bathroom. I think we held the hose up for about 20 minutes. We didn't think anything bad would come of it."

"*Si, me acuerdo y luego los vecinos vinieron enojadísimo a hablar con su papá,*" she said.

ONE LAST TEAR

"Yeah. I guess they knew the water came from our yard. They came here extremely angry to talk to my father. I guess we totally damaged their bathroom. My dad was furious, remember?"

"*Sí, pensé que la iba a castigar.*"

"I also thought he was going to seriously punish me. But he just reprimanded me. Of course, Dalia didn't get any reprimands from her father. She just did as she pleased and got away with it. We were incorrigible together. I was glad my father didn't have his icepick then. Maybe my mother hid it."

"*Su amiga Dalia no era muy buena amiga,*" she said.

"Yeah, I know. Dalia wasn't such a good friend. I felt bad about flooding the bathroom, but she didn't feel any remorse whatsoever. You know, she was much more malicious than I was. As we grew up, I just went along with her pranks without thinking. She actually mocked people. She had a callous attitude about things. She didn't really care what people thought, or if they liked it or not."

Luz María tried to soften the memory.

"*Pues así son los niños.*"

"You are right. Sometimes, children are like that. But Dalia had no conscience, and I didn't have a better role model. After all, she was my best friend. We even had a special language to communicate with each other and exclude everyone else at the same time. Remember when she got sick with Hepatitis B, and was quarantined for a few weeks? Well, I sat on the sidewalk, and she sat by her window. We got markers and large pieces of paper, and wrote to each other with big letters, but it was pretty inefficient. So we learned to read the other's lips! We actually became experts at understanding each other without having to talk. Lip reading became our new adventure."

"*De verdad?*" she asked. "*Yo no sabía eso.*"

"Yes, for real," I said. "Nobody knew we could talk like that. We kept it a secret. When she got well, we were in the habit of

CHAPTER ELEVEN

reading each other's lips instead of talking. Then we perfected our language and became even more inseparable."

I continued telling more stories to Luz María. She was a great listener.

"Dalia and I pushed it even further by checking every test in middle school and high school with our lip reading technique. We got away with everything that way. It was our well-rehearsed ruse. No teacher could catch us. Somehow, it didn't feel like cheating because we knew all the answers. It was more like trying to push the envelope to see if we could get away with it."

It was getting cold. Luz María suggested I go inside.

"*Ay señora, ya no esté pensando tanto, venga adentro que ya está haciendo frío,*" she said.

"Okay," I said. "I'll stop thinking so much. You're right, it's getting cold."

She made me a delicious coffee, and set a slice of chocolate cake in front of me. It felt like an hour had passed, but it had only been about 20 minutes since I went outside. The myriad of memories that could pop through my mind in such a short amount of time astounded me. They were like data files of a lifetime. My memory card was pretty full.

I smiled faintly at my brothers, who were sitting low on the living room sofa. We were all alone, weren't we? No more parents. It was just us.

Strangely, I felt responsible for their well-being, almost protective of them. *Oy!* I was already stepping into my mother's shoes. Were they going through the same tumultuous state as I was, with waves of raw, unfettered grief? I dared not ask. There was a crack in my heart that wouldn't settle. This grief made me feel brittle and restless, as if wasps had crafted a nest inside me, and were creating a nonstop ruckus.

ONE LAST TEAR

I didn't want to be without a mother and father. It made me feel too exposed. I lacked a compass to navigate this loss. Who could understand or help me? I didn't know where to turn, or how to move forward.

Despite the warm coffee from Luz María, the memories continued to fly through my brain. Even the sweet chocolate cake started to taste bitter as I remembered burying my mother years earlier. I couldn't leave the graveyard after the burial, despite the rabbi's insistence that we had to get home to start her shiva.

"Shiva *shmiva*," I muttered. I couldn't stand up. I wanted to be buried with her right on the same spot.

My daughter, who was seven at the time, insisted on being at her grandma's burial. When she saw that I wasn't responding to the rabbi's commands, and couldn't leave my mother's gravesite, she touched my shoulder softly with her little hand, and in the wisest moment of her childhood, began to sing a Sephardic love song that I had taught her. She alone, with the voice of an angel that touched people's hearts, shared this insightful moment with me. Her voice saved me from the most obliterating grief. Her melody began to pull me away from my mother's grave. It gave me the strength to stand and walk. She had an intuitive sense of the delicate balance between sanity and insanity—she must have known that I was on the verge of losing my mind. I walked away from my mother and toward my daughter, for once being able to leave the dead behind.

When we returned home to begin my mother's shiva, the thing that hurt the most was that my father never shed one tear over her death. What was wrong with him? Why was he not crying, or putting his arm around me as any father would do with an inconsolable daughter? Was he mentally ill? Shut down? Crazy?

Or was he just plain mean—*era simplemente malo?*

Max's words popped in my mind—*my father was a Buddha covered in mud.* I began repeating them like a mantra to see if they

CHAPTER ELEVEN

could calm me down. But then, another little voice cut into my thoughts:

Screw the Buddha.

He was my father, and I loved him. But why was he covered in mud? Who put mud all around him? Mud or no mud, I loved him for a long time, until my love for him started to hurt too much. Then I *truly stopped* loving him. That was it for me. I made up my mind: I wasn't going to keep loving him for free! *No lo iba a querer de a gratis.*

Maybe he was just a very simple and silly man. Indecipherable. Incomprehensible. Indifferent. Limited. Greedy. Half of a man, really, and not necessarily even a father—at least not the father I wanted.

I wanted the father I felt I deserved. Had I simply been born into the wrong family? Why did I get the muddy Buddha, and not the shiny golden Buddha?

I wanted the shiva for my father to end already. I was ready to catch a plane home to the U.S. and never look back.

Instead, I was stuck in his home with relentless memories that bit like crocodiles.

I remembered his body in the hospital bed. Had it only been a few days ago? Limp and sickly, I saw for the first time that he was *really* dying. The man who had ignored me most of my life would be gone soon. In that moment, I felt nothing—as absent of feelings as he'd been toward us for so long. Was this a contagious disease, the notion of feeling nothing…of being touched by nothing? The distance between us—a dying man and his daughter—was astronomical.

A cosmic dust engulfed me. It was suffocating.

ONE LAST TEAR

During my father's comatose week in the hospital's intensive care unit, I walked around like a zombie, my feet barely touching the antiseptic floor. My brothers and I debated for days whether or not to remove his life support—it was clear to me that his body was shutting down. My brothers didn't see it that way. Neither did my uncle.

He was suffering unnecessarily, and in the depths of my once loving heart, I didn't want that ending for him. We argued as only a family could, until his doctor called us to join him in the conference room. He explained in simple terms what was happening.

"*Todos los órganos de su papá están comprometidos,*" he said. "*Su cerebro está inflamado, tiene pulmonía, sus riñones estan fallando, su corazón y sus pulmones también estan fallando. Sus niveles de azúcar son estratosféricos. En realidad su papá tiene una posibilidad en un millón de recuperarse.*"

His words were categorical. Our father's organs were compromised. His brain was swollen. He had pneumonia. His kidneys were failing. And his heart and lungs were collapsing. Plus, his sugar levels were stratospheric. The doctor said he had a one-in-a-million chance of getting through this. He didn't use the word *dying*, but he didn't have to.

The picture was instantly clear in my mind—I started crying on the spot. I had to let go of him and our unfinished business. My aunt Reyna, sitting next to me, reached out to embrace me. The surprising gesture felt warm and reassuring.

The doctor left us in the conference room to discuss whether or not to remove the life support. My brothers and uncle weren't ready to let go. They kept citing the one-in-a-million possibility, wishfully thinking that my father could recover. My aunt and I were all for ending his suffering, and giving him a dignified finale.

CHAPTER ELEVEN

It was reasonable to us, but not to the guys. They were expecting a miracle, or some kind of medical fix. Us *girls* understood the inevitable, but the *boys* said that they wanted to leave him be as long as there was a thread of hope.

At that point, I stopped pushing. I was afraid they'd misunderstand my intent, or would judge me for it later. In wrestling with his life and death, I couldn't be the only person responsible for the final decision.

I left them to debate in the conference room, and went to the small cubicle where my father lay. He was breathing with great difficulty through an oxygen mask and a tube down his throat. He seemed reasonably at peace, yet so distant. I came close to him and held his hand; a tender moment I gave to myself. His hand was warm, soft, and puffy like in the old days.

Suddenly, a ghastly looking nurse came to draw my father's blood and interrupted me. *Buitre cabrona*! Damn vulture! She was heartless. She took my father's arm harshly and poked him with a needle. My father didn't move. The pit of my stomach tightened—I wanted to punch her.

"*Para qué carajos quieres mas sangre de mi papá?*" I gasped. "Why the fuck do you need more blood from my father?"

"*Ordenes del doctor*," she said.

"And *which* doctor ordered it?" I shot back. "That is so stupid. Can't you see? He is dying! The doctor already told us. Are you guys selling my father's blood?"

She didn't even look at me, but continued with her task. Then she left the room, carrying a tube of my father's bright blood like a trophy.

Trembling with rage, I touched my father's hand again. It calmed me down. How was it possible for his hand to be so limp? He didn't move an inch or respond to my touch, just kept breathing with the help of the mask, lost in another world.

ONE LAST TEAR

"Dad...Dad...can you hear me?" He didn't respond.

I moved to the foot of his bed and began to pray. I prayed for him, but also for help to make the right decision. I prayed for the guidance and strength I needed to pass through this moment. And I prayed for the higher good of everyone involved.

I truly wanted to end his suffering. But, was he suffering? Perhaps he was just distant. Would he come back?

I looked up to the ceiling, just above his head. I felt...or saw...or sensed a committee of people hovering there, arguing among themselves.

What a bizarre vision. Was I hallucinating? I mustered my courage and asked them if we needed to remove the life support.

"This is none of your business," said a voice, "*Tú no tienes nada que ver con este asunto.*"

Whoever these spiritual beings were, they were brusque, and seemed very busy. I decided not to ask any other questions.

A Jewish prayer began to sing its way from my lips:

"*Shemaaaa Israeeeel Adonaaaaai Eloheeeeinu Adonaaaai Ejaaaad.* Listen Israel, God is one."

Then, I calmly asked for God's will to be done. I imagined a Star of David at the head of my father's bed—big enough so his soul could move swiftly through the center of it.

That was the best I could do for him: a little bit of Jewish shamanism.

With heavy steps but a lighter heart, I left the room and vowed to stop worrying about things that didn't belong to me. I would let everyone else decide—my brothers, my father's siblings, even the spirits above my father's bed. I wasn't going to take on that role anymore.

Soon after, my brothers and I decided to call and summon the rabbi to the hospital. We could all use some spiritual consultation. The emissary from the Sephardic community came the

CHAPTER ELEVEN

next day, a nice Argentine rabbi with a different Spanish accent. When he arrived, we all huddled together in the hallway, right next to my father's spot in the ICU. He was supposed to have only one visitor at a time, but no one was going to dare ask us to leave. There must have been a strong energy field around us—even the nasty nurses left us alone.

As doctors and nurses came and went, we embarked on a spiritual discussion. We were enthralled by the rabbi's explanation of the Jewish perspective about illness, death, and dying.

"*En la religión judía, hacemos todo lo posible médicamente para extender la vida de una persona enferma, independientemente de sus sufrimientos,*" he said, explaining how in the Jewish tradition, one must do everything medically possible to extend their life, no matter how ill they are.

"*Una persona enferma tiene al ángel Rafael a su lado,*" he went on. Angel Raphael is the one who comes to the side of the sick and tries to help. Was he one of the spirits I saw above my father's bed?

"*El ángel se encuentra muy ocupado tratando de ayudarlo. Sin embargo, si el ángel sabe que se trata de un caso de una persona que esta a punto de morir, entonces se irá a ayudar a otra persona cercana al enfermo que pueda necesitarlo.*" If the angel realizes that the sick person is ready to go, he will look around to see if anyone else nearby needs his help. If so, he will leave the dying person's side, and go help someone else who is not yet ready.

It was as if Raphael was a busy *angel-bee,* buzzing around among the sick, trying to assist my father and other patients at once.

The rabbi launched into a story about a baby boy. The boy's grandfather was very ill, and couldn't attend the baby's bris—the Jewish circumcision ritual. The family wanted desperately for the grandfather to get better so he could be there. The rabbi urged the family to follow the biblical tradition and proceed with the bris eight days after the boy's birth, as was custom.

ONE LAST TEAR

With great trepidation, the parents agreed and went ahead with this covenant. After the ceremony, as the baby healed, Raphael came to assist with his healing. Since the angel was already in the house, he stopped in to check on the grandfather.

The next day, the grandfather had a miraculous recovery.

Something about this story was deeply comforting. I started to back off from the idea that my father was suffering, and that we needed to give him a merciful death. After all, the committee of spirits above his bed had been pretty direct when they said this was none of my business. I'd have to trust my father's fate to Raphael.

It was already Friday afternoon, and I got the sense that the doctor wanted to spare us from witnessing my father's transition into whatever the next phase was. He was quite hesitant when we floated the idea of taking him home. He seemed to know what was coming. Even though he didn't say it directly, the sense was that my father was not going to survive the weekend.

The rabbi suggested that leaving my father at the hospital was the right thing. He wanted us to go to Shabbat services at the temple. It sounded like a good idea to my brothers and me. After all, we were about to be fatherless. Prayer was probably the best thing for us.

After the services, we joined a rowdy crowd, including the rabbi and his wife for Shabbat dinner. I sat next to the rabbi's wife, and as she was talking to me I went into a dissociated state. I ate and swallowed almost mechanically, while my head floated through the air. It was loud, the food was greasy, and my mind was spinning so badly I needed to excuse myself.

I went upstairs to the main sanctuary. I wanted to sit alone and pray for my father.

The door to the main temple was open, so I continued to walk forward towards the front, until I found a chair that looked cozier than the rest.

CHAPTER ELEVEN

I sat and stared at the marble lion sculptures that stood stoically on either side of the arch where the sacred scrolls were housed. Above me, a group of enormous chandeliers that had survived every single earthquake hung motionless. I was at peace for a brief moment, until a river began rumbling inside me.

My tears were almost quiet at first. But soon, an uncontainable sobbing poured out of. It wouldn't stop. I stood up and tried to walk, but my feet were filled with lead. With blurry vision, I dragged myself outside the main sanctuary. I had to sit again, and fell into a corner chair.

My sobbing continued. It was as if all the tears of my life were expressed in this one great flood. The tears of losing my parents. Tears of a lifetime of grief. Tears of being away from home. Tears of no longer belonging to this community. Tears of alienation, of growing older, of the end of all innocence. Tears of no more Sunday meals. Of diaspora and nostalgia. Tears for what was, and for what never was.

My brothers must have felt that something was wrong. They came running upstairs with pure alarm on their faces when they spotted me. They swept me into their arms and held me as I cried. No one said a word. Quietly, I thanked God for them. My blood. My bros. *Los hombres.*

Slowly, and with great care and tenderness, they guided my steps outside to our car. They had never seen me in such a state, and were so brave to be there for me. I began to calm down as the car moved us along.

Back at the house, the phone rang as soon as we walked inside. It was Silvia, our private nurse. She stayed at the hospital to care for our father every night. She was crying.

Our father passed away while we were at the synagogue.

Between broken words and sobs, Silvia said that a single tear had rolled down his cheek right before he passed.

ONE LAST TEAR

Did my tears mingle with his in that very last moment of his life? Maybe that was the best he and I could do as father and daughter this time around: join together with our farewell tears.

CHAPTER TWELVE
Twisted Lies

*"There are no secrets better kept
than the secrets that everybody guesses."*

–George Bernard Shaw

We braced ourselves for another afternoon of visitors. Sure enough, the bell rang, and Luz María buzzed someone in. To my surprise, it was Dalia and her youngest sister.

Dalia wore a serious expression that I'd never seen on her face before. Black leggings, heavy makeup, and blonde highlights in her hair, she seemed old, despite her sassy look.

"I was just coming from the gym where I teach spinning classes," she said with an air of self-importance. "I drove straight here. I didn't have time to change. Sorry."

What a snob! Couldn't she change before she came to a shiva? Really? She walked in and started bragging about how many spin classes she teaches. Then, as if she remembered why she was here, she stopped herself.

"I'm sorry about your dad," she said casually. After a brief moment of silence, her chatting storm ramped up again.

I had an uneasy feeling in the pit of my stomach, but I didn't know why. There was something phony about her. I wanted to keep my distance. I hadn't seen her in years, and didn't know much

CHAPTER TWELVE

about her life, or the person she'd become. I didn't know how to interact with her after so long. And, I didn't feel like being scrutinized, especially by her—*Miss Perfect*. Here we were, checking each other out—it felt more like a high school reunion than a shiva.

Dalia couldn't help but rehash our past, and her quiet scrutiny began to feel like a corrosive acid. There was an air of pretense or superiority—she looked at me like I was a specimen frozen in time. Twenty-five years had gone by. Had it really been that long since we last spoke?

She and her younger sister sat on my mother's piano bench. I forced back a faint smile.

"I'm *so* happy to see you," she said, clearly forgetting the circumstances again, or simply oblivious. "I know this is a difficult time, but I'd *love* to catch up with you. I can't wait to hear what you've been up to all these years. What's going on in your life?"

I wasn't in the mood to deal with this. I knew she liked to gossip—she'd done it during our entire childhood. This time, I was the one feeding her a story she'd tell to the rest of the world.

I stayed quiet, not giving her too much information. Undeterred, she began a long ride down memory lane.

"Remember when we used to make strawberry jam sandwiches and bring a bunch of blankets and play camping in your backyard?" she asked. "Or that day when you dropped the ladder on my back and I couldn't breathe? Or how we tossed an apple from the third floor of school and it landed on Esther's head? Oh, how about the time we made invitations to a fake party with that nice folding toilet paper from the sports center? Gosh, and how we used to watch Eduardo for hours from your bedroom window, just *waiting* for him to drop his shirt and luckily his pants too?"

She took a quick breath. She was either nervous, detached, or completely out of her mind.

"Oh! How about when we flooded your neighbor's bathroom with the hose? And the loquat wars from the roof? Remember when we tricked the classroom into believing it was both of our birthdays and they all sang happy birthday to us? And the time we made, well, we didn't quite make the *penacho,* but instead we tossed all the feathers out in the street, and your dad made you sweep them? That was crazy."

I could feel myself fading away, like a cartoon character flattened by a steamroller. Had she been waiting all of these years for a golden opportunity to see if I remembered these things? Had she never heard of a telephone?

Yes, I remembered everything *vividly.* And much more, for that matter. Like when she left me to sweep the feathers in the rain by myself. Or when she laughed at our prank with the neighbor's bathroom while I caught hell for it. I remember her dirty feet behind the seat of the private chauffer that drove us to school, and how she complained to him, "*ándale Fernando, ya es hora de que limpies tu coche…*come on *Fernando*, it's time for you to clean up your car!"

"No," I said. I didn't mind lying. "I don't remember those things."

"You're lying! You have to remember *some* of these things. The memories are crystal clear to me. In fact, I'm seriously considering writing a book about our childhood friendship."

"Really?" I held my breath. My heart felt dangerously balanced on the pages of the book in her head—full of lies and surrealistic pranks.

"Yes!" she exclaimed. I froze like a pillar of salt. The last thing I wanted was to be a protagonist in *her* book.

At that moment, I wanted to be free from every memory. I wanted to completely erase myself from the pictures as if I'd never existed. Nothing she shared made me feel proud. I had no desire to be associated with those moments, or with Dalia for that matter.

CHAPTER TWELVE

What would happen if I simply turned and walked out right now? Just left her sitting with her sister, talking to the space where my body had been? And what if I left everything else too—the house, the street with *jacaranda* and rubber trees where we grew up, the neighborhood…even the country?

"*Pues, buena suerte con tu libro manita*," I said, smiling faintly. "Good luck with your book. *Mándame una copia cuando lo publiques no*? Send me a copy when you publish it, okay?"

I moved to the table, and begrudgingly invited the two of them to sit with me. I was pissed, but couldn't help being a good host. Besides, the endless job during shiva seemed to be feeding and entertaining people.

I offered them coffee and cake. Dalia nodded.

"Can I go upstairs?" she blurted suddenly. "I'd *love* to just look around one more time before you sell the house."

When we were kids, she loved to snoop around other people's houses and mess things up for fun. The idea of her doing something like that now sat liked a vulture in my mind. What a horrible child she'd been, always mocking other people, saying mean things behind kids' backs if their uniforms were dirty, or if their lunches smelled funny to her. Had I been that way too? Was I like her?

A caustic taste crawled up from my stomach and settled at the back of my throat.

"No way," I said adamantly. I couldn't believe her impetuousness. Was my family going to be the next victim of her critical feast?

"*Come on!*" she cried. "I bet everything looks the same."

"Everything *is* the same way that it's always been," I spat out. I wasn't kidding. There was a major contrast between our families. Here we were in the house where I grew up, with its chipping paint and creaky floors and dilapidated garden outside. Meanwhile, Dalia's family had moved to an upscale Jewish neighborhood after she finished high school. Her father, an architect, built them a lavish home, while we stayed in the old neighborhood. I bet my family's home seemed like a museum to her.

She began to get edgy. She was desperate to tour around, but I didn't need her scorn, or to be the subject of her gossip.

"Sorry," I said, "but this isn't the time to go poking around my parents' house. It's a shiva, remember?"

"Okay, you are right," she relented.

For a bit, she seemed resigned to drink her coffee and munch on a sliver of chocolate cake. Then, after a few moments, she said she wasn't feeling well, and asked to use the restroom. I believed her, of course—who would make something like that up at a shiva? Besides, she actually looked pale all of the sudden. I offered her a *Sal de uvas Picot*—a Mexican version of Alka-Seltzer—but she declined and asked again to use the bathroom. She stood up and left, but instead of using the downstairs powder room, she darted upstairs to the most run-down bathroom in the house, the one close to my old bedroom.

She stayed in there for a long time. I thought maybe the sink had fallen on her foot, or that she sprained her ankle on the broken floor tile. Oh God! Was she going to sue us? Maybe I could send the Seven Samurai up to check on her. The thought made me chuckle. Then I realized what was going on—she was snooping!

I rushed upstairs like a mad woman and caught her in the hallway. She was coming out of my old bedroom.

"What are you up to?" I demanded.

"*Nada te lo juro*," she yelped. "Nothing, I swear. I just wanted to look around."

"You haven't change, have you? You just don't take *no* for an answer."

"I'm sorry," she muttered. But I knew she wasn't. And, she still looked sick.

CHAPTER TWELVE

"Are you okay?" I asked. "Maybe you need to lie down." I offered my old bed. What the hell was I thinking? Here I was again, taking care of a *visitor*, even inviting her to my old bedroom where we used to concoct all of our pranks.

"No thanks," she said. "I threw up in your bathroom. I feel better now. I think I'll be okay."

I pointed the way downstairs. She was disappointed that I spoiled her little escapade. I'm sure she was *dying* to keep snooping. I even started to think the whole *feeling sick* thing was a ruse. But how could she be so pale if she was making it up?

We went downstairs. Dalia sat at the large dining room table. Luz María brought her fizzy water—*agua mineral de Tehuacán*.

"I'm sorry," Dalia said. "I don't know what happened to me, but I feel fine now." She took a sip of the water, then started chatting again about past memories. She was a broken record!

"Do you remember how our older brothers tied up your younger brother? Was it once? How many times did they do that? And then they pushed him down the laundry chute."

I had never heard about this prank. Were these the types of things that the boys did when the adults weren't around? I couldn't imagine my little bro trying to fight those two bullies off, only to be pushed down the dark laundry chute and into a bin of dirty clothes.

My eyes turned into fire.

"Shut the fuck up already, Dalia! How dare you laugh about *that* at my father's shiva? Are you crazy? Have you lost your goddamn mind?"

Dalia turned pale again, and grew completely silent. She tried to stand up.

"I'm so sorry," she muttered. "I didn't mean to insult you."

"Well, you did. It's time for you to leave."

TWISTED LIES

She grabbed her purse and hurried toward the door. Her sister trailed her like a mouse. I didn't need the Seven Samurai to get rid of her. I was my own warrior.

Deep sadness settled again in my heart after she left. I wanted to find Jonatán and hold him in my arms. I wanted to wash the memories away. But hell, I didn't dare ask if they were true. In my heart I knew they were. Dalia's laughing was the perfect reflection of how mean she was as a child, and what a callous woman she'd become. How many more shocks could my system take?

This shiva needed to end!

I poured some cold mineral water down my throat. I was trying to gain my composure, but the doorbell rang again. I jumped from my chair. I was at the brink, and didn't know how much longer I could tolerate this parade of people. Most of them couldn't keep quiet for a split second, or show their respect with just their presence. I kept hearing laughter in my head. Was this how a shiva was supposed to go—drive the daughter crazy? It seemed more like a circus than a shiva to me.

I looked up and saw Dina walking through the door.

"Not *again!*" I whispered, then sank lower into the sofa. There was no escape from this zoo, and the monkeys just kept pouring in.

She came straight toward me and sat on the Egyptian chair that my mother had loved.

"*Cómo estás hoy?*" she asked.

"I've been better. You?" I wasn't about to share anything about my outburst with Dalia, or the dreadful laundry chute story.

"*Quisiera hablar contigo sobre algo importante,*" she said. Naturally, she wanted to talk to me about something *important*.

"What is it *this* time?" I asked.

"*Quería solamente explicarte que tu papá murió fácilmente,*" she said. "*Su alma salió a travéz de la axila y ésta es la forma mas fácil en que el alma deja al cuerpo.*"

CHAPTER TWELVE

Dina was talking about how easily my father died because his soul left through the armpit—the simplest way for a soul to leave a body. I thought she was joking. What the hell was she talking about? She went on.

"*La mayoría de las almas abandonan el cuerpo a travéz de la boca pero la axila es una forma mas simple de despojarse del cuerpo.*"

"Well, that's nice." I said, which was about all I could muster. Apparently, most souls leave the body through the mouth, according to Dina.

"*Tu papá resistió un poco para abandonar su cuerpo pero al final todo salió bien.*"

Apparently, my father had struggled at first, but it worked out in the end. And, he'd been so attached to his body, and to material things as well, that he's still having a hard time leaving for good.

I forced a nod. I felt like a disjointed puppet. Did I need to know these spooky details?

"*Por cierto que tu papá todavía se siente muy agitado dejando su casa y continúa viniendo del cementerio hasta aquí varias veces al día.*"

"Is this for real?" I muttered. "Or are you kidding with me? My father is *still* agitated? He keeps leaving the graveyard and coming back *here* several times a day?"

"*No tengo porque mentirte,*" Dina said. "I have no reason to lie to you. *Le tomó varios días resignarse que iba a morir cuando estaba en coma.*"

"*Really*? Why did it take him several days to come to terms with his death when he was in the coma?"

"*Estaba discutiendo con un consejo de varios espíritus que estaban arriba de su cama en el hospital.*"

"He was *arguing* with a counsel of *spirits* that hovered over his hospital bed?" This I found interesting. Actually, I was stunned. After all, I'd *seen* them up there.

"*Sí, exactamente! Los espíritus estaban tratando de convencerlo de que era su tiempo de morir pero ya sabes que tu papá era un poquito necio así que no quería dejar su cuerpo.*"

I could picture the whole thing: the spirits trying to convince my father that it was his time to die, while he argued and told them it wasn't. That's *exactly* what he'd do.

"*Los espíritus estaban un poco irritados con él pero son compasivos y le permitieron ir y venir de su cuerpo para comprobar que sus órganos se estaban extinguiendo.*"

I was intrigued thinking about the spirits getting annoyed with my father as he moved in and out of his body. Even as he witnessed his own organs shutting down, he refused to leave. And then, when he finally agreed, he just bolted through his armpit, like running for the quickest, nearest door. Crazy!

"Wow," I said. "All of that was happening while he was in a coma?"

I leaned closer to her. I didn't want anyone else to hear what I had to say next.

"I kind of *sensed* a group of people hovering over his bed, just talking. I thought I was imagining things."

"*Sí que los escuchaste. Se estaban tratando de comunicar telepáticamente contigo para que pudieras entender lo que estaba sucediendo.*"

She explained that they were trying to communicate with me telepathically so I could understand what was happening.

Even if my head was spinning with Dina's story, I promised myself I would never again doubt what I sensed. Instead, I would call it my very own psychic ability. Sweet!

Dina pointed toward the spot where my father's spirit was standing in the room.

"*Tu papá está aquí parado junto a tí y te está sonriendo de nuevo.*"

CHAPTER TWELVE

I turned my head and smiled at my father's ghost—even if I couldn't see him. She said that he was smiling at me. I kept trying to catch his shadow—his ghost's reflection—in the corner of my eye. No luck. Maybe I wasn't as clairvoyant as I thought.

"*Está muy triste que no puede estar con la gente en su propia casa y desea de todo corazón poder participar de la risa y la buena comida.*"

"I'm sorry about that," I said. According to Dina, my father was sad that he couldn't be with the crowd in his own house. He wished with all his heart that he could join in with the laughter and good food.

What a strange guy. When we had family meals, he looked so remote and distant. Now that he was dead, he wanted a slice of cake and a nice conversation.

My father was smiling at my brothers too, Dina explained. He just wanted all of us to forgive him.

"What does he want forgiveness for?" I asked yet again. "What is he so obsessed about? How can we forgive him if we don't know what he did wrong?"

Dina lowered her eyes. She didn't say another word about it. She excused herself and left for a glass of water. I sat alone on the low sofa. Where was his ghost? I wanted to bear witness to his open heart, and watch the hardened mud melt away from his golden self.

When was the last time I actually saw him genuinely smile at me? I had to trace back to an old photo I remembered. I was two or three years old, and held a long stick between my hands. We were in the woods of Xochimilco, with its floating gardens and many flowers. The look on my face was intense, like I'd just discovered the essence of a tree. My father, kneeling next to me, smiled. His left hand delicately held my right wrist, almost in a worshipful gesture. He didn't want to interrupt the magic of the moment.

My mind stayed in Xochimilco. I was always captivated by the *chinampas*—crafted boats with colorful flower arrangements on their bows that spelled women's names: *Lupita, Esperanza, María, Conchita,* and *Josefina.* Each boat was ready to take visitors around the canals.

We chose *Lupita* and boarded the *chinampa*, and sat in a row of colorful wooden chairs around a long table. A Mexican gondolier took us to different parts of the canals. He used a long stick to move the boat slowly along the murky waters. Vendors approached in smaller boats with quesadillas, tacos, grilled corn on the cob *elotes*, grilled fish, and drinks. Native women offered colorful flowers. Mariachi bands played songs for a few pesos—they would tie their boats to ours and play as many songs as we paid for.

Xochimilco was an ancient place that existed since the time of the Aztecs. It was where they harvested the land, and the canals created natural irrigation. The place was charming with its myriad of flowers and vegetables growing in rich, moist soil, and ancient willow and eucalyptus trees.

How could I rescue these parts of my childhood? So many places and things remained timeless, forever carved into my Mexican soul. The land and its beauty, its vibrant colors and contradictions. Xochimilco's vividly decorated vessels. The sugar skulls on the *Dia de los Muertos*. The balloons in the park. The most artistic murals. Mexico was all color, unparalleled traditions, and rich cultures all around.

Would my connection to this land vanish now that my parents were dead? What would hold me in place? I longed for a weeping willow from the canals of Xochimilco to ground me. Perhaps I'd brought this on myself. After all, I'd left years before to *el país del Norte* to chase the illusion of love. The trees in the woods of Xochimilco have stood for centuries; I have been uprooted too of-

CHAPTER TWELVE

ten. Now I hung suspended between multiple worlds: my beloved Mexico; the places of my childhood; Jewish culture with its ancient traditions; and my adopted country where things moved quickly, in straight, monochromatic lines.

An icy chill ran through my body. I knew it was impossible to hold on to my past like a thing I could carry in the palm of my hand. But still I wanted to.

Dina returned with a glass of water.

"*Sabes*?" she asked. "*Mi trabajo no es fácil y a veces quisiera tener otra profesión.*"

"Why is your job not easy?" I asked. "What profession would you rather have?"

"*Cuando la gente se muere viene a buscarme para pedirme que les avise a sus familiares y les diga que les pasó.*"

"Oh, I get it! I couldn't imagine people coming to me when they die and begging me to talk to their relatives," I said. "That must be awful for you."

And here I was thinking that being a psychic might be fun.

"*A veces se mueren en un accidente o los matan y nadie sabe adonde está el cuerpo y ya estoy cansada de dar malas noticias.*"

"I guess it must be even more terrible when someone dies in an accident, or is murdered!" She explained she was tired of giving people bad news, or trying to help them locate bodies.

"*A veces los espíritus malignos se esconden en las coladeras, y se juntan en grupo para planear maldades.*"

Now the conversation was getting spooky. Dina's eyes began to tear up.

"*Son verdaderamente unos seres horribles que se alimentan del espíritu de otros.*"

Another chill ran down my spine. Evil spirits that hid under city sewers? Ghosts hovering together to plot evil acts and feed on other spirits? I could see why she was ready to quit her job.

"*Algunos días quisiera esconderme abajo de mi cama de tan exhausta y aterrorizada que estoy por lo que veo todos los días.*"

My heart went out to Dina as she recounted her life. She was exhausted and terrified. She wanted to hide under her bed to get away from the things she witnessed every day.

Now I saw that part of Dina's urging me to forgive my father was for her own good. She wanted to be unburdened. She had a task to complete. The longer I held out, the longer it would go on for her.

Would my father haunt her forever? I wished I could have snapped my fingers and appeased them both, but I still wasn't ready. She would have to endure the stubbornness of *my* spirit a bit longer.

She left again, this time to use the restroom. I looked under the low sofa to see if there were any evil spirits hovering near the floor. I was pretty sure I was losing my mind, because the idea made complete sense to me.

No spirits! Great. I stood up to stretch my legs. I made my way around the house, saying hello to visitors, and allowing myself the distraction.

As I meandered, I began to feel like a ghost, just floating in space, eavesdropping on the nonsensical chatter around me. Why did people feel the need to fill the space with so many words?

Was I the dead one?

The day before my father died, my brothers and I left the hospital to get a bite across the street. It was the first time we debated whether or not to remove him from life support.

In the midst of our agitated discussion, a nicely dressed woman in her early 50s approached us. I thought she was going to ask us to quiet down. That wasn't the case.

CHAPTER TWELVE

"*Siento interrumpirlos pero después de escuchar su conversación me gustaría ayudarlos. Yo soy la dueña del café y les puedo hacer sus cartas numerológicas para que puedan decidir que hacer con su papá.*"

We looked at each other and nodded in unison. Her name was Ana. She owned the café. After overhearing our conversation, she offered to do our numerology charts. She said it would help us make the right decision for our father. I was ready for some divine intervention, and Ana was eager to help.

Quickly, she wrote down our birthdays on a napkin. Then she combined the birth numbers we gave her, and did her calculations. According to the numbers, Jonatán and I shared an interest in a more spiritual path. However, I was the one whose ultimate mission in life was to find *forgiveness* towards my father, and to bring closure to our relationship. At the time, I thought it was interesting, but didn't dwell on it. Little did I know that forgiveness and closure would follow me around all through the shiva.

I continued to meander around the living room. My energy was waning. I floated listlessly along until I circled all the way back to the low couch.

I asked my brothers if they remembered Ana from the café.

"The woman who did our numerology?" I clarified. They nodded. Jonatán reached out and held my hand.

"*Ya no pienses tanto hermanita.*"

"You're right, I should stop thinking so much."

But I couldn't stop. My brain kept slipping between cruise control and overdrive. One minute, I was hyper-focused on the smallest detail. The next, I was drifting through the *la la land* of memory.

I began drifting again.

On the day of my father's death, we returned to the hospital late, after Shabbat services. A young janitor who knew Jonatán looked up from his work when he saw us.

"*Que pasó que ya regresaron?*" he asked.

"Yes, we had to come back. Our father died a short while ago."

The janitor got a funny twinkle in his eye.

"*Bueno, pues ya ni pedo!*" he said. "Not even a fart to do about it!"

We didn't know whether to cry or laugh. We just looked at each other and tried to keep straight faces. Honestly, it was the funniest thing we'd heard in days, cloaked in the cynical Mexican vision of life and death. Why even sweat it? We're all going to die anyway. Finally, in unison, the three of us began laughing so hard, rolling our way to the elevator toward the ICU.

Our father's body was on the bed, wrapped in a thick transparent plastic bag. A zipper ran from head to toe. My idea of a person's end had always involved a body covered in a sheet. Why was he in a plastic bag? Was death contagious? I almost choked.

Later, my father's daytime nurse, Angélica, joined us at his bed. When she saw him wrapped like that, she became frantic. She stalked around his bed like a madwoman, chanting over and over, "*Esto no debe ser así, así no puede ser, el señor no debe estar en esta bolsa de plástico. Yo no entiendo porqué*—it's not supposed to be this way, he's not supposed to be in a plastic bag. I don't get it."

Crying inconsolably, she lunged and began clawing at the zipper, trying to open it up. She thought my father was suffocating, and couldn't accept that he was already dead. It was like some tragic Mexican melodrama straight out of a *telenovela*. I was completely paralyzed watching it, eyes stuck open, unable to move or speak. Had one of the awful nurses put him inside the bag to spite us? Or was it basic hospital protocol? The plastic bag definitely seemed inhumane. I grew agitated. Angélica was right: this was *not* the

CHAPTER TWELVE

right ending for our father. He deserved better than this. *Anyone* deserved better. A plain sheet would have been more appropriate.

Sylvia, our father's night nurse, was also in a state of shock. She'd been with him when his soul slipped away. Now his children needed to calm his helpers down. Angélica kept grabbing at the zipper. Sylvia was in hysterics. She kept insisting through her sobs that *they* had put him in this bag and she couldn't stop them—and that she saw tears in my father's eyes when he died.

Beneath the plastic, my father's face was cloudy and distorted. I snapped out of my catatonic state and tried to help with the zipper. We managed to unzip it far enough to uncover his face. Angélica, in a strange rapture, cupped his face in her hands and tried to kiss him, as if *she* was his daughter!

"*No señor, no se puede morir*—you cannot die!" she repeated.

It was bizarre. Why would *she* want to kiss him? Shouldn't I have had the same urge? Isn't that what a daughter should do in the presence of her dead father? Instead, I felt nothing. What was happening? Was something wrong with me?

My brothers were momentarily stunned at the sight of these nurses trying to extricate our father from the plastic bag. Then Jonatán snapped out of it, left the room, and called the synagogue to ask for guidance with the customary procedures. They said we had to go home and return the next day to retrieve my father's body. They'd meet us at the hospital. We struggled to convince the nurses that we needed to leave, but eventually we did.

The next morning, after very little sleep, there was a boatload of bureaucracy to deal with at the hospital—procedures, paperwork, and more protocol—before we could take our father's body home.

Jonatán went down to the morgue to identify the body. He was definitely the bravest of us. Yosef and I just stood outside and waited.

From there, the synagogue's personnel transported my father's body to his home in a simple pine box covered with a dark blue fabric, the Star of David embroidered in the middle. They set the casket in the living room, framed by two big candles.

Was he still inside the plastic bag? I couldn't help but wonder, but wouldn't dare open the lid to find out.

It felt strange that a person with such incredible potential came to the end like this: bound up inside a box. What would become of his past? His accomplishments and failures? His mannerisms and quirks? His passions and grievances?

Death was so confusing.

There was a time in my father's life when he was a well-respected chemical engineer, a man I truly admired. Now I was standing in front of what was left of him.

I shivered, and my mind flashed back to being 12, when I would go with him to his factory on Friday afternoons.

His car was always impeccably clean. We'd drive for 40 minutes or so, and he'd park in his special spot, the one with his name on the wall. We'd always march hand-in-hand together and greet the secretaries. There'd be a Coke waiting for him, and they'd rush to get me one as well.

"*Buenas tardes, Ingeniero, que bueno que trajo a su hija*—good afternoon, Engineer, it's nice that you brought your daughter." My father would smile proudly, crack a joke or two, then offer a compliment in return.

In his office, he'd hang his sports coat behind the door, then change into his white lab coat. His name was embroidered on the right pocket. He seemed so important.

His comfortable black leather sofa always called to me. I'd sit with my Coke and watch my father behind his large desk. He even had a private bathroom—a reflection of his special status.

Eventually, he'd look up from his papers.

CHAPTER TWELVE

"*Lista?*" he'd ask.

"Yup, I'm ready." I'd jump off of the sofa.

Then we'd head down the hallway, and enter the manufacturing plant through the last door. A series of steps took us up to the scaffolds, where we'd walk and catch an eagle's view of the large warehouse.

Heading back down, my father would test the consistency of various substances that bubbled in large barrels. They all looked like glue to me. His workers stood around and watched him, while the loud machines whirled along. I was enthralled by it all. I didn't even mind the smells, or how badly my eyes teared up from the chemicals.

I would ask him about various substances.

"What is this for, Dad?"

"*Es para crear una consistencia suave para las telas,*" he'd say if I pointed toward fabric softener, or "*todo lo que vez aquí es para la industria textil,*" which meant that everything I was looking at was for the textile industry.

"What about the shampoo you used to bring me?"

"*Eso fue algo que hicimos hace tiempo. Ahora solamente hacemos productos para la industria textil.*"

"I'm sorry that you don't make that shampoo any longer. I liked it! How come you only manufacture products for the textile industry now?"

"*Así es ahora,*" he said. "*Así es como hacemos dinero...* that's how we make money now."

Then we'd move on to another barrel, or to consult with a manager. All along, my father focused on smelling and testing the consistency of everything, approving *this*, making suggestions for *that*, encouraging the workers to keep going until the products met his expectations. I loved watching how he commanded these situations. He had everyone's respect, and his employees spoke to him in polite, deferential tones.

"*Gracias, Ingeniero,*" they'd say. "*Buenas tardes, Ingeniero, como está?*" They'd wish him a good day, and ask him how he was. "*Es su hija? Qué linda, Ingeniero.*"

"*Sí,*" he'd say, and pat me on the back—his daughter was indeed here with him, and she *was* cute!

"*Todo bien Ingeniero?*" they'd ask, "*Le parece bien Ingeniero?*" And he'd reassure them that everything they were doing was okay. Then they'd thank him.

"*Hasta luego Ingeniero. Gracias Ingeniero.*"

Sometimes I fantasized about becoming a chemical engineer, especially if I was going to be treated *that* well all the time.

Occasionally, his partners would bring their daughters too—my friends Sofia and Mariana. We were all the same age, and enjoyed wandering around together like the Three Musketeers.

Once, while my father was busy doing paperwork, our little group went off to explore the area where they manufactured plastics. There were stationary covers, binders, portfolios…all sorts of products. We played with the leftovers they discarded, and lost ourselves in a little adventure until Sofia started complaining about feeling dizzy from the smell. We left and went off toward the lab.

First, I went straight to say hello to Valeria, the chief chemist. She was my favorite gal in the whole place. She was also in charge of us when we were there. With her thick black-frame glasses and long ponytail, she was very sweet, and always willing to teach us something interesting.

"Hi Valeria," I said. "What are you up to today?"

"*Lo mismo linda, tratando de crear las substancias químicas que van a fijar el pigmento de color a la tela,*" she said. "*Tu papá esta trabajando conmigo en esto.*"

CHAPTER TWELVE

"Wow, I didn't know you and *my dad* were working on that," I said. They were making chemical substances that could fix a color pigment into fabric.

"How do you do it?"

"*Tu papá tiene muy buenas ideas para lograrlo,*" she said. I was impressed that she thought my father had great ideas to accomplish such a task. My hero!

"*Quieren hacer algo divertido?*" She invited us to do something fun.

"Sure," we said excitedly.

Valeria gave us large pipettes and tubes. She instructed us to mix several substances one at a time to see how they changed colors. Then she walked us over to another table so we could practice our experiments. I was more interested in the artistic aspect of our work than the scientific one—I loved how the colors changed, and didn't really care what chemicals I mixed. For all I knew, it could have been a Molotov cocktail in those tubes! Valeria said everything was safe to play with, and we trusted her. When she stepped out to use the bathroom, we agreed to only work with the test tubes she'd pointed to. Of course, as soon as she left, I couldn't help myself. I decided to test one of the tubes that was off limits.

I opened a large vial and let a transparent fluid fall into my pipette. It changed colors rapidly—from light blue to deep green, then to red, and then to dark yellow. Suddenly, it began smoking heavily, and gave off a strong stench. I was fascinated by this emerging rainbow, and didn't pay much attention to what was actually happening. That is, until it began to boil…and then… explode!

A greenish-yellow substance landed all over my hand, dress, shoes…even my tights. Tiny holes started to form where the drops fell. First they were just specks, but soon expanded to about the size of pennies.

Sofia and Mariana came running to see what happened. They were scared, but I found the whole thing exhilarating. I didn't even care that I'd ruined my tights. I washed my hands, found a rag, and cleaned off my dress and shoes.

Before Valeria came back, we ran downstairs to our fathers. It was time to leave. We said goodbye, and promised each other we'd guard our secret.

When I got home, I hung the dress up in my closet, and threw my tights in the trash. No one ever found out what happened.

How was it that my father was always in good spirits at work, but was so moody and grumpy at home? He constantly complained about money, which I didn't understand, since both Sofia and Mariana said their parents were wealthy. In fact, they had second homes in Cuernavaca.

Standing near his coffin, I wanted to knock on the lid and ask him what happened to *his* money. But I knew I'd only hear silence.

Soon after his last major stroke, he got a call from his office secretary. He was in no shape to talk, so Jonatán answered for him.

The secretary told him that Don Manolo, the caretaker from the condominium on Colima Street, was desperately trying to contact my father. He needed to let him know that the kitchen in his condominium had burned down!

"Condo?" was all I could say when Jonatán mentioned it to me. "Did *you* know he had a condo in *la Colonia Condesa*?"

"Nope," my brother answered.

"What the heck is going on?"

"*No sé*—I don't know."

"What fucking mystery do we have to solve now?"

"I have no idea what this is about."

CHAPTER TWELVE

"Let's see if we can track down *Señor* Manolo."

Of course, there was no trace of Manolo's phone number anywhere. My father's secretary *conveniently* didn't have it, and no one knew how to get in touch with this guy.

We searched public records to see if we could track down the title, but nothing came up under my father's name. He'd probably hidden it under a pseudonym, or some other person's name.

When he recovered well enough to regain some of his mental faculties, we shared Manolo's message. He feigned that he didn't understand what the hell we were talking about, and even swore that he knew nothing about a Colima condo.

In his checkbook, we found the initials "P.E." Whoever owned those initials had been receiving a fat monthly check from our father *for years.*

"Who is P.E.?" we asked him. And again, he played clueless. Was this another woman in his life? How many people were there in his life? What was he hiding? Was there a second family?

Tired of our badgering, he finally snapped.

"*Y ya déjenme de fastidiar y déjenme en paz.*"

But his request that we leave him alone only agitated us, especially Jonatán. He wanted the truth at any cost, and kept at it. Still, his efforts were futile. Our father wasn't going to confess anything. In his mind, we had no right to confront him. If he had another family—including other children—did we have any weight in his life decisions?

I pulled Jonatán to the side.

"Let's leave him alone," I said. "There's no point. We're not getting anywhere with this situation, and we'll never get to the bottom of it. He'll never tell us anything."

"You're right," he agreed. "But this is fucked up."

"I agree."

"I have to leave," he said. "I don't want to see his face anymore."

Jonatán slammed the door on his way out. That was the end of our investigation.

A deep resentment settled in my heart. That was the moment I expelled my father from the core of my being. I wasn't going to abandon a sick man, but my heart took a hike far away from his… and from him.

The man who had held my hand so tenderly as I discovered the life force through a tree branch was not the man who argued about initials in his checkbook. Nor was he the man in the pine box, filled with lies and hidden agendas, his soul in disarray.

My father died crying—*died crying* for God's sake—and took his secrets with him.

Who was my father, really? And how could I forgive him if I didn't know the answer?

CHAPTER THIRTEEN
Raven's Dream

"In the end, everyone is aware of this:
nobody keeps any of what he has,
and life is only a borrowing of bones."
–Pablo Neruda

By the last day of the shiva, I felt like a character in a bad play. I was ready for a final applause, mostly for my own emotional endurance. *Brava!* I deserved it! I wanted to take my final bow and go home to the joy of my own thoughts, free of interruptions from psychics, relatives, and silly people looking for small talk. I was done with prayers, and sitting on the hard surface of the naked sofa. I needed to burn my dark shiva clothes, a stinky uniform I'd been wearing for a week.

Dina and Max didn't show up on the last day. Was their job done? I assumed it was. I was relieved. I couldn't endure any more lectures and revelations. I wanted to run through the house and uncover the mirrors, apply makeup, pluck my eyebrows, and get as far away from my parents' pale ghosts as possible.

I cheated with the mirror a few times. I admit it. I removed the covers and peeked to see if *I* was still there. I was worried I'd become some horror movie freak. Did I still exist? I even snuck

CHAPTER THIRTEEN

a tiny bit of blush and lipstick to make sure. And besides, how better to prove to my father that I'd forgiven him than to apply a little lipstick and smile at his ghost?

Oh vanity of all vanities! I'd truly gone crazy.

I welcomed the last evening services, and embraced the final prayer wholeheartedly. It was my last chance to proclaim what a *good* Jewish woman I was. I had done my best to go along with the plan. I might as well finish what I started.

I'd tried my best also with the forgiveness business, even reassured myself that forgiveness may come in the form of a timed-released pill, a little elixir that dissolved slowly inside me over a long time. My soul had forgiven my father; eventually, my stubborn heart would catch up.

After the final prayers, the rabbi wished us *kids* long, happy lives. Then, before he headed off to his next religious obligation, he said we needed to perform one last ritual.

"What more?" I muttered to myself.

"*Todos los familiares del señor Salomón tienen que salir de la casa y caminar alrededor de la cuadra.*"

"Do we have to do anything else besides walking around the block together?" Yosef asked.

"*No. Eso es todo. Con esto se concluye la shiva.*"

Great! All we needed to do to wrap up the shiva was to take a stroll. Of course, nothing had been *that* simple all week—why should this? The rabbi wasn't done talking.

"*Este ritual refleja que ahora ya están preparados para regresar al mundo de los vivos y a sus deberes cotidianos.*"

As he said, this walking ritual symbolized our readiness to join the world of the living, and return to our daily affairs. Too bad I wasn't feeling all that prepared to face the world yet. In truth, I was completely unsettled, but I sure was ready to leave.

RAVEN'S DREAM

It was a beautiful afternoon—breezy, sunny, and warm. I welcomed the fresh air after being stuck indoors for most of the week…and in my own thoughts. The gardeners were putting their tools away, and people were reading or chatting on benches. Children laughed and ran in the playground. Mexico City seemed full of magic and love.

Walking around the park, and slowly returning to the world of the living, I realized how much I missed this city. It was like the way you long for a kiss from the first lover you left behind. This was a city of unparalleled friendships, and magical corners and encounters—filled in every direction with the luxury of romance, openness, and creativity. But now, with both my parents gone, I was not a child of this city anymore. It felt like I'd abandoned her, and she had gone on without me. I no longer truly spoke her language. My foreign accent betrayed me; I was not a *Chilanga*—someone who lived here—but a hybrid citizen. I was of everywhere and nowhere at once: Jewish, Mexican, Gypsy, American, *gringa*, and European all wrapped into one fair-skinned, curly-headed package. I'd left for the sake of adventure. I'd grown roots elsewhere. I was *outside* of this place…an orphan. I had no city to call my own.

These cloudy thoughts comingled with the laughter and chatter of my brothers and relatives. I felt like a dark butterfly spreading my wings toward inner reflections, while at the same time chatting with everyone else. *Qué buena actriz*—what a good actress I was! I even surprised myself as I bounced between roles and navigated simultaneous realities. Perhaps it was a quality I'd inherited from my father: going along and smiling with others, while my gloomy interior ran amok.

CHAPTER THIRTEEN

After a long walk, we returned home. Jonatán sat at my mother's concert piano, carefully opened the lid and, for the first time in many years, began to play. Exquisite sounds filled the house. The power of his music brought us all together one last time.

I hid my tears from everyone.

Once our relatives left, a thick silence shrouded my brothers and me. We dragged ourselves to the dining room table to sit and face our new reality. A sticky muteness permeated the scene. Would we laugh hysterically again from the pure anxiety of it all? No. We stayed solemn. If our father was still in the house, we didn't want to disturb the peace.

Luz María offered us something to eat.

"*Como están niños,*" she asked. "How are you *kids*?"

"*Estamos bien,*" Yosef said. "We're fine."

"*Quieren algo de comer?*"

"No thank you, Luz, we're good. We don't want anything to eat." We encouraged her to take a well-deserved break. She smiled. As she left the room, she stopped and looked back to us.

"*Ya no estén tristes niños,*" she said. "Don't be sad any longer, kids."

It was as if our mother was talking through her.

It was getting dark. The door towards the back patio was cracked open about three inches. Our conversation had shifted to worldly matters—finances, the sale of our parents' estate, paying the help, and other issues to figure out.

That's when a giant moth, about eight inches long with unusually dark wings, fluttered into the living room through the crack in the door. *Una mariposa de alas negras enormes se metió a la sala por la pequeña apertura de la puerta del jardín.*

It came to rest on the ceiling right above our heads. For a moment we were speechless. Then, looking at each other again with eyes wide open, we said, "*Hola pa!*" in unison.

That triggered our wild laughter, complete with tears of relief, mischief, camaraderie, and all of the other emotions we'd repressed for days. Our bellies began to hurt, we were laughing so hard.

Was our father *ever* going to leave us alone?

Once we regained our composure, we resigned ourselves to the fact that our *moth-father* was going to be a silent witness to our decisions, and all of the *adult* business we were discussing.

"*Oye, te juro que nos esta viendo la mariposa*," Jonatán said, nodding toward the moth. "I swear it's looking at us."

"Yeah, you're right," I said. "It is *just staring at us.*"

For the next couple of hours, the black-winged moth watched while we discussed our affairs. Was our father disapproving of our decision to sell his house? If so, what were we supposed to do? Keep it for eternity? Or, was he giving us his blessing? It was impossible to know.

Finally, nervous about our father's disapproval, we decided the moth had to go. We opened the glass door, and tried to wave the moth outside with kitchen rags. It took a while, but it—or *he*—finally left.

Facing the sale of my parents' estate was a monumental task. The house harbored more than four decades of stuff. Yosef and Jonatán calculated how much we had to pay the staff. Thank goodness for their math abilities!

When we were done, we called the help to say our final farewell, and to thank them with all of our hearts. We gave them each a big check for compensation—and as gratitude for taking care of our father for so many years.

CHAPTER THIRTEEN

When we were finally done, I went upstairs and started to pack. But then I froze. The moth was in my room, stuck to the ochre color curtains. How could it have gotten in here from outside?

Ay Dios mío, me estoy volviendo loca—my God, was I going crazy?

I saw that the window was cracked open, but only slightly. Quite the persistent moth, to say the least. The contrast between its black wings and the ochre curtains was striking. It had landed on the perfect spot where it would be impossible for me to miss it.

As I walked closer to examine this unrelenting specimen, it sprang from the curtain, flew across and around the room, then continued wildly through the house.

I screamed and raced after it. When I caught up with it, it looked as big as a crow!

"*Ay hermanita, ya déjala!*" yelled Yosef. "Just let it be."

"I'm going to have nightmares," I said. I was literally shaking.

I gave up, went back to my room, and slammed the door shut.

"Screw the moth!" I muttered.

It was a restless night. A series of unsettling dreams darted through my mind. In one, I was flying high at midnight in a deep blue dark. A full moon illuminated the tree tops, and their shadows reflected in a clearing. I could see, but not through my own eyes. I had grown new yellow eyes with slanted pupils—they moved around in strange ways. I remember thinking, and somehow *knowing* that my eyes were different, but not knowing why, or how it was possible that I could focus so clearly on the space below me.

The *whoosh* of an unfamiliar, fast-fluttering sound floated past me. I turned my head to see what was happening. It was the sound of my own wings, spread wide in the vast sky.

RAVEN'S DREAM

I'd become a splendid raven with iridescent feathers and talons instead of hands, mesmerized by my own swift flying.

My raven eyes pierced through the treetops, and I wisely navigated the night under the moon. Somehow, I possessed a deep knowledge of the geography below. At some point, I decided to land. As I touched down, I left a trail of dust behind me.

I was completely alone on a prairie, a magnificent raven under the full moon. Everything was silence. There was nothing else.

I woke up startled. My heart beat like a drum. I scanned my arms and hands. No more iridescent feathers or talons. I shook my head.

Was my father trying to tell me something through this dream?

I walked for a glass of water, feeling much heavier and clumsier than I'd felt as a raven. Slow to take in the darkness, I missed my sharp slanted eyes and the whoosh of wings. My feet dragged across the carpet—the reality of human weight was disappointing.

Even after so many mysteries during the shiva, shapeshifting into this raven was truly puzzling. I wanted to discover all I could about the raven's magic…to fly above the world…to *be* the raven and leave everything behind.

At the airport, I dragged my luggage to the check-in. My suitcase was full of memories and memorabilia, dust from my past, family photos, my mother's miniature piano collection, and even some of her cooking books. I was also carrying things that no one else could see—the invisible weight of pent-up emotions the shiva had produced; my own history; the tears I held back when I wished my brothers goodbye.

I was still thinking about the raven, and started researching its meaning as I waited for my flight. In dreams, it symbolizes

CHAPTER THIRTEEN

death and rebirth, mysticism and magic. A raven in a dream can be a messenger of a great spiritual realm—a place where human and animal spirits intermingle and become one. Ravens teach humans how to stir the magic of life without fear, and how we can use the creative life force to work the magic of spiritual laws upon the physical realm.

I was *so* ready for some magic in my life, and was beyond grateful that a raven had visited and brought me its message.

I kept thinking about my wings when something clicked—the raven and the moth from the last night at my parents' home shared the same deep black color. Was there a deeper meaning to this connection? I kept on searching. Moths and ravens are powerful cultural symbols of the soul and transformation. Black symbolizes the positive qualities of protection, birth, and magic. Yet, it also possesses the negative qualities of secretiveness and sacrifice.

If the moth had truly been my father—and by now I was sure that it had been—what was *his* message? Was it one of protection? Or, was it a symbol of his secretiveness? Considering my father's inscrutable behavior, it could have been either.

I boarded my plane, found my seat, buckled in, and let out a deep sigh. My thoughts continued to flow incessantly, until they settled on something Max mentioned days ago.

"*La muerte de un ser querido nos da la oportunidad de crecer espiritualmente.*"

Okay, if the death of a loved one gives us a chance to grow spiritually, why was I feeling so lost?

"*Es necesario abrirnos a esta espiritualidad que nos va a llevar ultimadamente hacia el amor.*"

In Max's view, if I opened myself up spiritually, it would ultimately lead me towards love. Well...I wasn't feeling much love right now. Maybe I wasn't all that spiritual, despite my raven dream.

Max also said that forgiving my father could lead me to a spiritual path that waited in front of me, one that could bring abundance and love—if only I allowed my heart to touch the light that existed in my father's heart. The same went for my brothers. If we could forgive, then we could receive our birthright of abundance as *our father's children*.

But how could I touch the light that existed in my father's heart? I failed drastically during the shiva. I simply couldn't find his light.

"*Ustedes son la luz, como el Buddah de Oro*," Max had said. We *were the light*, just like the Golden Buddha.

How great it would be to find some light within.

"*La clave para su transformación y la posibilidad de abundancia existe en su capacidad de amar desde el fondo de sus corazones hasta que alcanzen el perdón hacia su padre.*"

Could I ever achieve what Max invited us to do? Was there really a *key* to my transformation? What did abundance look like? Did it even exist? Was it right there for us, waiting in the threshold of our capacity to love from the depths of our hearts until we could forgive our father?

More spiritual declarations. The frantic moth. The raven dream…so much jostled around in my brain the entire flight home. Was I really invited to embrace a spiritual transformation? Or, was it all just a sham? Or worse—stories I was concocting in my own head?

A stunning sunset took place just over the plane's wing. I traced the pink clouds with my finger. I felt depleted and lonely, and wished to bring the light back into my life, or have someone or *something* install it inside my being.

"But you did see the light," a voice said. It was like God whispering to me.

"What do you mean, *I did*?" I whispered back.

"You saw the light when you gave birth to your daughter."

CHAPTER THIRTEEN

"Ah. Yeah. *That…*"

My daughter was born on a hot August night in San Francisco. After three days of labor, she decided perhaps it was a good idea to see the light of the world. It was a rough journey, filled with hours of irregular contractions as my diaphragm opened and shut back down. The home birth I envisioned became an emergency trip to the hospital.

As soon as I got there, my doctor, a tough Chicano woman, came into my room. She seemed angry, convinced that my midwives had mishandled the birth.

"Okay dear, I am going to prepare you for a C-section," she said.

"No way, *José*," I shot back. "You are not going to do that. After three days of labor, there surely must be *something else* you can do for me besides a C-section."

"Okay," she said. "I'm wearing my power earrings tonight." She stroked the bright little hummingbirds in her ears. "I will give that baby exactly one hour to turn around and get out of there. After that, I will come in and get her myself."

"Deal," I responded, drained of all energy.

In that hour of grace, an angelic nurse who would eventually help me deliver my daughter got busy with procedures that actually allowed the baby to turn. An hour later I was ready to push.

"Push now!" my angel said.

"*No puedo!*" It felt like all power had left me. I couldn't push.

"*Sí puedes!*" someone shouted. "Yes, you can!" By then, I was so exhausted that I didn't know who was talking to me. Was it the nurse? The doctor? An actual angel?

I pushed, and pushed, and pushed…until my baby girl came out. And when she entered the world, a void inside me felt like it had transformed into white light. I was floating, levitating, moving across some new dimension. I had become one of them: *una libélula*, a lightning bug!

RAVEN'S DREAM

A split second later, everything changed. I came back to reality. Like a tender lioness, I snatched my baby up and brought her close to me. No one dared interfere with my instincts. The light in the room grew brighter and brighter, illuminated with unusually soft, yellow tones. The essence of every object in the room changed too. Everything floated with my baby and me. It was like we were made of soft, porous matter that hung suspended in the divine light.

A sweet river of laughter flooded the room. At first, it was just me laughing. Then others joined in, until our voices flowed into the hallway. Even people walking by the room seemed to be sucked into an invisible force that invited them to partake in this miracle.

My baby was wet and slippery in my arms. Her all-knowing eyes stared back at me without blinking. Her calm, peaceful presence said, "Hi there, Mom. Sorry it took a little while."

I felt like we knew each other—I recognized her as soon as I saw her from some other time, but couldn't say from when exactly. I could actually feel my heart glowing. It was about to explode into a thousand small pieces. At the same time, it was expanding and reaching into a presence that was not my own—the literal heart of the world, the heart of God.

In that moment, I understood the pure essence of the divine.

The miracle continued as I saw my daughter's entire life emerging in front of my eyes, as if a molecule was traveling through infinite time and space. I was mesmerized. Was I dreaming, or was it real?

My daughter's eyes were glued to mine. Her calm breaths seemed to come from some very distant place. I knew for sure that she and I had been together before, in a forever time.

"Who are you, little being?" I asked her. "And who has brought me such a gift?"

She just kept looking at me.

CHAPTER THIRTEEN

No one dared break our moment. No one spoke or even came close to us. I held my daughter with a tenderness I'd never known as she found my breasts full of milk, then drifted into her own state of bliss.

I could have lived in that moment forever. But like everything, it came to an end. Unfortunately, instead of ending like the way we wake from sweet dreams, it came to a sudden halt. Something was wrong with my uterus. Blood began to pour out of me. In a flash, someone else was holding my baby. The doctor, who looked quite worried, massaged my pelvis. Finally, with a last gasp of contractions, the placenta came out.

It was shaped like a heart.

The bleeding stopped miraculously.

A strong jolt from the plane brought me back to reality. I swallowed hard.

"Maybe *this is it* for me too!" I heard myself say. Were we going to crash? What if we did? Why did I think I was invincible? So what if I had seen some light in my belly? Maybe my father was in such a hurry to speak with me *in the spirit world* that he decided to take the plane down.

That would get my attention, right?

Luckily, the plane found smooth air again, and a little ginger ale was enough to settle my fears.

I closed my eyes and fell into another dream. This time, I was at my parents' home, sitting on the old sofa in the family room. I was waiting for some important spiritual entities to arrive. They were scheduled to come at dusk. The house was dim, and I couldn't see well. As I prepared for them, my husband and a woman I didn't recognize called me to help carry a sofa bed downstairs.

RAVEN'S DREAM

Halfway down the staircase, a powerful surge of energy came from my hands. I was actually able to *guide* this large piece of furniture to the living room without even touching it. It was weightless, and my power astounded me.

A peculiar fog floated toward the dining room. As I went to examine it, I began to levitate. Instinctively, I looked for Max. I knew he would help me understand what was happening. There he was! He pointed at my right hand, which held a roll of money.

"Let go," he said. "Let *everything* go." He nodded at the money. I'd been holding it so tightly that it actually hurt. Was I afraid to let it go? Was that why it hurt?

As soon as I dropped the money, my levitation stopped.

Max walked toward me.

"I have a special message for you," he said. We walked to the sliding door and looked at the tree in the backyard. Its leaves had become tiny lights, and it had grown so big that parts of it were *inside* the house.

It was a sacred tree. A gift from Max.

As I admired it, a white dove entered the house through a crack in the glass door. It was small, no bigger than my hand. It rested on my leg and allowed me to stroke its feathers. Then it stepped onto my palm and stared at me.

Another jolt! I lifted my head. Phew—the plane was still in the air. What was I to do with these messages? Every time I closed my eyes, a new one came. Now a dove! Did it reflect some sort of purity? Was it an invitation to mourn? Or was it a bird of prophecy? Was it the embodiment of the divine? Was I being guided by hidden messages in my dreams?

My daughter's birth was not the first time I gained a glimpse into a divine presence surrounding me. Many years earlier, my family and I were visiting and old hacienda in the state of Hidalgo, Mexico. *La Hacienda de Hueyapan* was a wonderful place where we

CHAPTER THIRTEEN

could roam free when we were kids. I was just nine, and had fallen in love with the old buildings in the many wings on the hacienda. I marveled at the musky scents I found everywhere, and couldn't get enough of the cool terracotta *Saltillo* tiles under the soles of my feet. Enormous weeping willows shaded nearly everything!

Each room had a special name. I meandered from room to room, passing beneath the words Thunder, Rain, Forest, Waterfall, and Redwood carved into wooden signs. I decided my room should have a name too. I called it *Nube*, which meant Cloud.

The hacienda was one of the most lucrative silver mines during the Spaniard occupation of Mexico. My brothers and I spent hours exploring the old ruins, playing in the barn on tall mounds of hay, and watching workers milk cows and goats. We ran around the lakes and ponds, and tried to spot as much wildlife as possible. The towering waterfall was unlike anything I'd ever seen. Where did the water come from? How could anything be that beautiful? My father said there were *prismas basálticos*—rock formations—under the waterfall. I loved the way the Spanish words played in my mouth, and I kept repeating them under my breath.

French glass doors in the vast dining room opened onto a glorious terrace. Giant terracotta pots full of exquisitely colored flowers framed a view of the mountains beyond. Birds sang all day long. At night there were lightning bugs that fascinated me. I wondered how their light mechanism worked.

For the first time in my short life, as a child of nature, I truly felt at home. When waiters in white uniforms came by, I sat tall like a Spanish queen and offered them thanks.

One day, our father rented horses and wagons to go on an excursion to the canyon. Riding on a wagon with my mother added to my sense of being a Spanish queen.

Our driver rode fast, making the horses canter as we jumped up and down in the wagon. A few other mothers and daughters rode with us, and everyone in the wagon got frazzled, except me. I was thrilled.

Tumbleweeds rolled by as we crossed the terrain. Red soil and desert plants kicked up and around us. Everything was new, and I was completely enthralled and curious.

The driver stopped the wagon and said we'd arrived. At first, I didn't see anything special. Then, he pointed in the direction where we needed to walk, advising us to be careful.

As I came to the edge, I saw that the land literally fell off. Ah, so this was what *canyon* meant. My mouth dropped as I came closer. My mother yelled for me to be careful. I ignored her, and breathlessly took in the most magnificently vast and profound open space I could ever imagine.

I stood still and listened to the silence around me. In that moment, I felt a broader dimensions of space open up. With the earth under my feet, and the great depth of the precipice in front of my eyes, I decided that I would never be afraid of life. Instead, I would embrace everything one way or another. I'd learn to fly off any cliff with my wings spread open. All I needed to do was to say *yes*.

Could I fly with my raven into the abyss? Would I be afraid if I did? With my parents gone, I had to remember the promise I'd made to myself all those years ago. I needed to be brave and embrace life alone.

What other option did I have?

My parents' home remained vacant and active on the real estate market for a couple of years. Was my father's ghost still wandering the halls, scaring away potential buyers? Thankfully, Luz María agreed to come a couple of times a month to water the plants, and keep the place clean.

CHAPTER THIRTEEN

When the house finally sold, I returned to Mexico City to help liquidate everything. It was a sad moment, and I was glad to have avoided visiting while the house was on the market.

Upon my arrival, Luz María was eager to tend to me one last time. Jonatán was there too. With the gas turned on, the kitchen began one last parade of *salsas, beans, rice, chiles rellenos, paellas, enchiladas,* and *quesadillas*. We were all so grateful for our eternal angel and her tireless commitment to us. She protected us like a mother bear as we went about the grueling experience of the estate sale, making sure no one took advantage of us, or tried to make deals out of ill intent.

After our delicious meal, I went upstairs to unpack and get started with the rigmarole of cleaning, emptying closets, and setting things up for sale—none of which I was looking forward to.

As I set my suitcase on the bed, something caught the corner of my eye. Shivers went down my spine. It was the *black moth*. It hadn't moved...in two years! It hung as if plastered on the ochre curtain.

I approached it slowly. Was it real? Was I imagining this? No—it *was* real. A sigh escaped my mouth.

Had I been cast in the sequel to some terrible horror movie?

I moved the curtain to see if it would fly away. Instead, the poor thing just fell in a thud to the carpet. It was dead.

I began yelling like mad.

"*Luuuuuuz, Luuuuuuz, sube prontoooooooooooo, te necesitoooooooooo. La mariposa negra, esta muerta.*"

Luz María shot upstairs like a lightning bolt, armed with her broom.

"The black moth is dead," I kept saying. "The black moth is dead."

When she saw what I was pointing at, her eyebrows lifted as high as I'd ever seen them go.

"*Ay Dios mío es el Señor*—my God, *it is* the Mister."

RAVEN'S DREAM

My father had inhabited his home for two more years. I couldn't help but feel sorry for him. What had he eaten? Had he starved? Was it even any of my business to wonder?

Luz María picked up the moth with the tip of her fingers and took it away.

It took about a week to sell everything. With the house emptied, we turned the key over to the new owners. Leaving the country with a few last sentimental objects, I didn't look back.

A funny feeling came over me as I thought about the new owners. They were a young couple just starting their journey. What dreams would they have in this big house? Would they feel the ghosts of my parents dancing *a rumba* in the shadows of their living room? If they did, would they be scared?

I shrugged off the thought and continued on my way. My parents were *their* problem now—*es su problema ahora*.

Two years since my father's death. Had I forgiven him? *Could* I forgive him? At that moment, I still didn't know. And, without knowing exactly what trespasses he'd committed, I didn't think I could. I was still in the dark, and forgiving *in the dark* was beyond my human limitations.

My heart still contracted when I thought of my father. He'd left us with nothing but the vaguest of clues. It wasn't fair. We'd never know what kind of secret life he might have lived. For me, the idea of forgiveness made me feel conflicted.

Perhaps when *I* die, he and I will meet up. I'll ask him point blank: "What the hell were you thinking?"

Perhaps he will tell me the whole truth this time.

CHAPTER THIRTEEN

As I drove away from the old street where I grew up, another memory began to take shape. A few days after my daughter was born, my parents came to visit me and meet their granddaughter. I was holding her in my arms like a proud *mamma*. My father, so moved by the experience of having a newborn in the family, asked to hold her.

Watching him hold my daughter, I could tell that he'd barely ever held any of us in his arms. He was awkward and tight—he held his breath like he was afraid of this new bundle of life.

"Relax," I said. "Look into her eyes. She can see you."

"*Los niños recién nacidos no pueden ver nada*," he declared, pretending to know what he was talking about.

"Of course newborns *can* see," I said. "Just look at her."

He stared into my daughter's eyes. She looked up at him with such intensity that he had to turn away. When he looked back, he was totally perplexed.

"*Oye, de verdad que sí me puede ver*," he said. "It is true! She *can* see me!"

"Told you so," I said.

Tears formed in his eyes. I had never seen tears of joy from my father.

The End

EPILOGUE

"Above all else,

guard your heart, for it is

the wellspring of life."

–King Solomon

Beginnings and endings are difficult, yet the stories in this book have now been told. It is time to let them all go.

It has been many years now since I buried my parents. Sometimes, I still feel that prickly feeling on the surface of my skin, a reminder that the departed may show up at my door at any time. And even if they don't, they continue to show up from time to time in my dreams.

There, my parents are not quite dead, but they are not so alive either. They are mostly sleeping. When I wake them, they don't look well. Their skin is an unhealthy grayish color, like they have not fully decided to die.

Maybe my psyche has not quite fully decided to bury them.

One thing I know for sure: it feels good to fulfill the old petition from my father, and light a memorial candle in his memory every year, just in case. I do the same for my mother. Perhaps they are happy looking down at their special candles as they burn for 24 straight hours: February for my mother, October for my father.

EPILOGUE

As I was finishing writing the book's last chapter, my auntie called to remind me of the precise date to light a candle in memory of my father, according to the Hebrew calendar. I had a long day at work, but I felt obliged to fulfill this ritual. I went straight a local supermarket to buy a memorial candle.

I asked a store clerk where I could find Jewish memorial candles. He didn't know what I was talking about. He asked another store clerk, who asked another, and so on. Finally, the general manager took me to the candle section, which was full of every possible scented candle I could imagine—but not one single Jewish memorial candle.

Out of his goodwill, and wanting to please a customer, he offered me Hanukkah candles instead. I laughed, but then got angry.

"You know, there are a lot of Jewish people in this small town," I said. "You should have memorial candles *and* Sabbath candles available to *us*."

Frustrated, I drove another couple of miles down the road to a Safeway, hoping they'd be more 'Jewish friendly.' I was thrilled to find a memorial candle there. Mission accomplished! I went home with my trophy, exhausted but satisfied. I lit the candle for my father, said a prayer, had a light dinner and went to sleep, feeling relieved.

The next day I went to Sabbath. There is a portion of every Sabbath's prayers where we honor the departed and their year anniversary by reciting the Kaddish.

I solemnly stood up and started my recitation, but tears blurred my vision. With a knot in my throat, I used my entire willpower to pull myself together. The old question came back full force: Did I forgive my father after all these years? Perhaps yes, perhaps no. I was still conflicted.

That night I had another vivid dream.

I was in a big room lying in a large bed with my husband. A divine presence filled the room around us. I could feel it in my

EPILOGUE

heart. I looked up, and saw a bouquet of white and red roses near the ceiling. The roses appeared to be flat and dried, as if pressed between the pages of a book. Some of the rose petals were suspended in the air around the bouquet. Someone, or *something*, had purposefully placed the roses in strategic areas of the room for our enjoyment.

Then a woman appeared suspended on the ceiling next to the rose bouquet. I recognized the Virgin Mary! My husband and I, holding hands, slowly began to levitate towards her. She turned to see us, and smiled with a heavenly expression in her face.

Then she blessed us, silently creating some kind of divine harmony around us. She softly touched my hand, transmitting a powerful and undeniable feeling of love and protection, and a deep sense of well-being that penetrated my entire body.

When I woke up, I remembered my dream vividly. A sensation of warmth and happiness lingered for a while. I felt as if the Virgin Mary forgave me for my shortcomings, and blessed me with her infinite love.

I was convinced that in this divine realm I could achieve the ultimate forgiveness, and experience the most authentic love. I hoped that when I die, I would experience this extraordinary liberation of my shortcomings and contradictory emotions, and my inability to fully embrace forgiveness.

For the time being, I am in my body, and my body and mind have their unquestionable limitations.

After my dream, the following poem came to mind:

EPILOGUE

Quizás
Solamente tal vez

Posiblemente
Sea delicioso morirse

Tenderse boca arriba
Dejarse mecer por las sombras
Lejos, adonde no existen mareas

Dejarse acariciar por un sol oscuro
Como un amante antiguo

Desbaratar la piel
Desabotonar las memorias
Desmadejar el tiempo
Desprenderse del peso terráceo

Muy despacio...

Danzar como espuma marina
Y desvanecerse al amanecer

Aparecer de nuevo a media noche
Frente a frente besando la luna

Flotar en las curvas del tiempo
Sin polvo y sin historia

Ligera y sin ninguna prisa

EPILOGUE

Perhaps
It may be absolutely delicious to die

Lying down, facing up
Letting yourself be swayed by the shadows
In a distant place
Where tides do not exist

Letting yourself
Be caressed by an obscure sun
Like an ancient lover

Undo your skin
Unbutton your memories
Unravel time
Detach from your earthly weight

Gingerly…

Dance like the ocean foam
And vanish at dawn

Reappear again at midnight
Face to face kissing the moon

Float in the curves of time
Without dust and without history

Weightlessly, and without hurry

ACKNOWLEDGMENTS

I owe the greatest debt of gratitude to Katya Williamson for making this book possible, and for believing that my story needed to be told and shared. She not only offered me her friendship, but I'm also indebted to her for her kindness, inspiration, wise advice and support.

I was fortunate to have worked with Dave Jarecki, for his superior editing skills, his fresh and open perspective of the use of Spanish and English in the manuscript, and his savvy observations. Dave was tireless in reviewing the manuscript several times and working patiently with me. His feedback was priceless, and his editing work allowed for the manuscript to finally become an articulate story.

I am also grateful to Lieve Maas for her superb artistic designs, elegant formatting, and for her guidance throughout the whole process.

To the many friends that read the manuscript and offered their feedback, suggestions and encouragement: I am particularly indebted to June Gottlieb, Belle Hezelhurst, and Denise Diamond. I am also deeply grateful to my dear friend, David Rosell, for his guidance, suggestions, and especially for holding my hand during the publishing phase of the memoir.

I am especially grateful to all the women at Katya's writing retreats who "couldn't wait to buy the book," and insisted that I keep writing. Their words of encouragement made this book possible when it was just a fleeting idea.

ACKNOWLEDGMENTS

I am indebted to my husband for reading the very first draft—and laughing out loud while he was reading! He believed in me, and had great patience during the many hours I spent at the computer and away from our adventures.

I am grateful to my daughter for her loving support, and for being a powerful source of inspiration.

www.ingramcontent.com/pod-product-compliance
Lightning Source LLC
Chambersburg PA
CBHW020402080526
44584CB00014B/1141